U0451012

名山 走进世界

An Overview of the World Famous Mountains

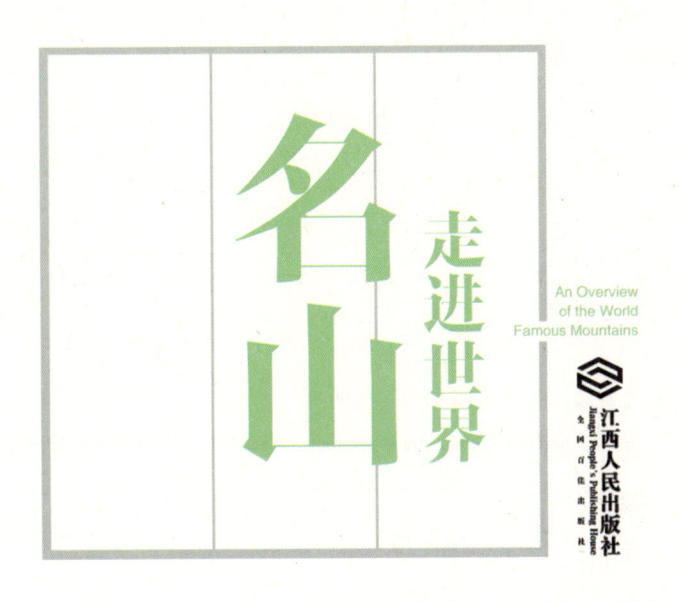

江西人民出版社
Jiangxi People's Publishing House

Compiled & Translated
by the Compiling Group for An Overview of
the World Famous Mountains

《走进世界名山》编写组 编/译

图书在版编目（CIP）数据

走进世界名山：汉英对照 /《走进世界名山》编写组编. — 南昌：江西人民出版社，2016.8
ISBN 978-7-210-08667-3

Ⅰ. ①走… Ⅱ. ①走… Ⅲ. ①山—介绍—世界—汉、英 Ⅳ. ①K918.3

中国版本图书馆CIP数据核字（2016）第186244号

走进世界名山　An Overview of the World Famous Mountains

《走进世界名山》编写组　编/译

Compiled & Translated by the Compiling Group for An Overview of the World Famous Mountains

策划编辑：章华荣
责任编辑：徐　旻　何　方
装帧设计：同异文化传媒
出　　版：江西人民出版社
发　　行：各地新华书店
地　　址：江西省南昌市三经路47号附1号（330006）
编辑部电话：0791-88629871
发行部电话：0791-86898815
网　　址：www.jxpph.com
E-mail：jxpph@tom.com　web@jxpph.com
2016年8月第1版　2016年8月第1次印刷
开　　本：787×1092毫米　1/16　印　　张：18.75
字　　数：240千字
ISBN 978-7-210-08667-3
赣版权登字—01—2016—460
版权所有　侵权必究
定　　价：108.00元
承印厂：江西金港彩印有限公司

赣人版图书凡属印刷、装订错误，请随时向承印厂调换

代序言

  名山是地球的精华，名山是游人的向往之地。千百年来，人类在发现自然、征服自然、亲近自然的过程中，与名山建立了由物质到精神、由索取到保护的复杂联系。可以说，一座名山影响和塑造了一座城市、一个地区乃至一个国家民族的历史文化和精神象征。同时，名山有不计其数的科学问题等待我们去发现、去研究、去分享。每个人心中可能都有一座世界名山，它是我们的骄傲。

  什么是我们心中的世界名山？首先，名山是地球的精华。它是大自然的作品，因为它是地平线上的高峰伟岸，是造型、色彩和线条的代表；它是生命之父，因为它是河流的发源，是植物的仓库，是动物的乐园；它是人们赞美的永恒对象，因为它是人类生存的永恒依靠。它自身也是一个生命体，厚实的积雪、丰茂的植被、不竭的飞流、沉淀的地质构造，等等，都是它生命力的外在表现。它常常由物质升华到精神，成为人类精神世界中高大、力量、刚强、坚毅、宽厚、永恒的象征。上天的公平使全球五大洲都分布有各自的世界级名山。其次，名山是游人的向往之地。它不可替代地成为千百年来人们游览、观赏的对象，成为探索自然、亲近自然、享受自然、放松自我的场所，成为观光、度假、休闲、运动甚至定居的选择地。世界名山越来越多地变成了旅游胜地，每年接待着数以亿计的游人。不同的种族、不同的语言、不同的肤色、不同的着装在各大名山会聚并和谐相处，共同欣赏、享受自然和人类祖先留下的美丽作品。再次，名山是名山管理者的事业所在。我们都是名山的管理者和保护人，受全人类的委托管理和保护着各自的名山。我们有幸为名山而工作，我们愿意为名山而奔忙，我们舍得为名山而劳累，因为它是我们的服务对象，是我们的职责所在，是我们的荣誉所系。我们为什么会走到一起来？本来大家天各一方、互不相识，却一呼即应、一拍即合，不辞辛劳、不远万里，从地球的五大洲走到一起来了。这是为什么？是什么力量在吸引我们？又是什么力量凝聚着我们？是对世界名山的共同责任感！

　　我们共同面临着许多问题：随着全球气候变暖，名山的雪际线在上升、冰雪期在缩短；随着游客数量的增多和需求的提高，垃圾在增多，景区的污染物需要更科学、更经济的处理；随着游客的外来化和多样化，人造环境在增加，服务需要多样化等。这些需要一起探讨的难题要求我们用三种眼光来看名山：一是"用科学的眼光看名山"；二是"用美学的眼光看名山"；三是"用哲学的眼光看名山"。大学作为知识生产的主力军，科学研究的前沿阵地，所具有的学科优势、人才优势和资源优势是任何社会组织和个人所无法替代的，研究世界名山是大学责无旁贷的光荣使命。

　　目前，本书名山选择的标准为：一座山，一个重要的旅游目的地，且这座山有管理机构，最为关键的是它属于世界名山协会的组成成员。这样，合计27座名山，写入《走进世界名山》一书。全书就世界名山的自然风景、人文风俗、当地文明与旅游特色做出介绍，让你足不出户就能领略山巅的雄伟和世界各地的旅游景观、民俗风情。

郑　翔

目 录

1 | 代序言

第一章　世界名山：认识世界的新视点

2　第一节　打开世界名山的瑰丽画卷
2　　　一、世界名山：文明的新理念
3　　　二、世界名山：价值的多维度
5　　　三、世界名山：遗产的重要载体
5　第二节　聚焦"世界名山研究会"
5　　　一、背景
6　　　二、诞生
7　　　三、宗旨与任务
7　　　四、章程
8　第三节　世界名山旅游的可持续发展
9　　　一、名山的旅游功能
10　　　二、名山的旅游特征
11　　　三、名山旅游可持续发展

第二章　亚洲的世界名山

14	第一节　人文圣山——中国庐山
15	一、地质景观
15	二、突出价值
17	三、推荐景点
24	第二节　五岳之尊——中国泰山
25	一、地貌景观
25	二、主要景观
30	三、旅游景区
32	第三节　灵秀佛国——中国峨眉山
32	一、地貌景观
33	二、四大奇观
35	三、旅游景点
40	第四节　中国画镜——中国黄山
41	一、地貌景观
41	二、主要景区
44	三、四绝三瀑
47	第五节　后山花园——中国香山
47	一、历史变迁
48	二、四季风光
48	三、旅游景点
52	第六节　台湾圣山——中国玉山
53	一、生态玉山
54	二、特色玉山
55	三、旅游玉山
56	第七节　东瀛圣岳——日本富士山
56	一、山岳富士
58	二、神化富士
60	三、休闲富士
62	第八节　东方仙境——韩国雪岳山
62	一、美丽景观

63		二、特色景点
66		三、旅游观光
67	第九节	东方奇山——菲律宾巧克力山
67		一、成因传说
68		二、奇异景观
68		三、怪诞动物

◀ 第三章　非洲的世界名山

70	第一节	赤道雪峰——坦桑尼亚乞力马扎罗山
71		一、自然景观
72		二、神奇传说
73		三、旅游胜地
73	第二节	海角之城——南非桌山
74		一、地质景观
75		二、景色天成
76		三、奇云传说

◀ 第四章　欧洲的世界名山

78	第一节	欧洲"脊骨"——阿尔卑斯山·埃森沃尔谨地质公园
78		一、生态景观
79		二、旅游休闲
81		三、地质公园

82	第二节　生态家园——罗马尼亚科齐亚山
82	一、优美生态
82	二、人文景观
85	三、旅游休闲
85	第三节　爱情乐园——罗马尼亚盖那山
86	一、奇异传说
86	二、相亲民俗
87	三、旅游体验
87	第四节　温泉明珠——罗马尼亚科瓦斯那山
88	一、迷人景观
89	二、独特温泉
89	三、旅游活动
90	第五节　地质奇观——德国贝尔吉施-奥登瓦尔德山
90	一、独特地层
90	二、旅游资源

第五章　北美洲的世界名山

92	第一节　北美地标——美国胡德山
92	一、火山活动
93	二、冰川景观
94	三、旅游景区
95	四、休闲活动
96	第二节　冰雪胜地——美国雷尼尔雪山
96	一、自然环境
97	二、火山构造
98	三、冰川景观
99	四、旅游休闲

100	第三节	绿野仙踪——美国沙斯塔山
100		一、自然生态
101		二、美丽湖泊
102		三、休闲活动
102	第四节	蓝岭蜥蜴——美国蓝岭山·谢南多厄国家公园
103		一、地质景观
104		二、公园形成
105		三、旅游景点

第六章 南美洲的世界名山

108	第一节	高原化石——巴西阿拉里皮山
108		一、旅游设施
110		二、特色景观
111		三、发展战略
112	第二节	生态林原——巴西瓜拉米兰伽山脉
112		一、自然特征
113		二、休闲旅游
114	第三节	滑翔天堂——巴西基沙达山
114		一、自然景观
115		二、旅游发展
116	第四节	伞降天堂——巴西伊别帕巴山脉
116		一、气候植被
116		二、旅游休闲
117	第五节	生态高地——巴西卡玛匡高地
117		一、生态旅游
117		二、旅游发展

第七章　大洋洲的世界名山

- 120　第一节　地质火山——澳大利亚甘比尔山
- 120　　　一、生态环境
- 121　　　二、地貌景观
- 122　　　三、奇异蓝湖
- 124　　　四、旅游休闲
- 124　第二节　休闲之山——新西兰南阿尔卑斯山
- 125　　　一、长白之云
- 128　　　二、探险之都
- 129　　　三、蓝宝之石
- 130　　　四、生物天堂

- 132　参考文献
- 135　与会人员名单
- 138　后　记

第一章

世界名山：认识世界的新视点

在世界各民族文化中，山因其高堪与天齐，幽可比海深，因而在人类的精神世界里，它一直作为一个神奇的物像而存在。然而，更多的时候山像一位伟大的哲人，满腹锦绣却静默无言。大山，偶尔将一粒金砂释放给溪流，却悄然传递出属于史前的信息。能读懂大山的语言，就意味着人类找到了解读地球奥秘和人类文明起源的密码。

孔子面对巍巍群山，感叹山川之厚重与"仁者"共通；李白独对庐山飞流千尺，感悟大山之磅礴气势；杜甫"一览众山小"，体味造化之神奇；苏轼"横看成岭侧成峰"，领悟自然变幻之法则。然而，在忙碌的现代都市"森林"里，人们疲于应付新的"丛林法则"，山林、荒野日益成为人类向往的心灵净土、精神家园。如此这般神奇的境遇，引得几许现代都市居民神往和缅怀。"偷得浮生半日闲"，悠游山川幽境，涤荡心胸，渐渐成为一种仪式化的生活追求。

在人类历史的长河中，遍布于世界各国的名山既是自然造化赐予人类的宝贵遗产，更是蕴藏人类文明信息的无穷宝藏。自混沌初开，大山它一直巍然屹立，无言地等待着人类的解读和发掘。

第一节　打开世界名山的瑰丽画卷

地球表面的陆地，有许多蜿蜒起伏、巍峨奇特的群山，这些群山层峦叠嶂，群居一起，形成一个山地大家族。山地表面形态奇特多样，有的彼此平行，绵延数千米；有的相互重叠，犬牙交错，山里套山，山外有山，连绵不断。山地是大陆的基本地形，分布十分广泛。尤其是亚欧大陆和南北美洲大陆分布最多。而名山是山地中一种独特的地理实体，它有一定的地理位置范围和界限，有决定其成名的丰富内涵。这种内涵在一定的历史条件下形成，具有反映时代的属性。

一、世界名山：文明的新理念

世界名山是农业文明时代的杰作，在靠天吃饭的农耕时代，人与自然有着敬畏、祈求、亲和、歌颂、寄情等复杂的情感关系。名山是从普遍物质生产功能的山地中分离出来，保护起来，作为神圣自然的代表和壮丽山

世界地形图

河的缩影，专供人们对大自然的精神文化活动需求的场所，如祭祀、宗教、游览、教育、隐读、审美和创作山水文化体验活动等，是人与自然精神联系的纽带。进入工业文明时代，在原有名山大川具有科学、美学价值的自然景观的基础上，形成国家公园或者国家风景名胜区，自然与文化融为一体，成为主要满足人对大自然精神文化活动需求的地域空间综合体，为名山所在地区创造了巨大的社会、经济和生态环境效益。当世界进入生态文明时代，"地球村"的生态安全、人类的文化遗产面临空前威胁。1992年在巴西环境与发展大会上通过的《21世纪议程》，明确阐述了山地生态系统的重要性与脆弱性，并将山地的研究和发展与气候变化、生物多样性保护、湿地保护等一起提升到全球最高级别关注的高度。基于生态文明要求，现代的名山发展需要在区域内和区域间双重循环，具有开放性和发展的规模性，更注重发展模式的可持续性、生态平衡性、产业复合性和系统性。这些名山不仅拥有奇特绚丽的自然景观，而且拥有丰富多彩的人文景观，是自然美与人文美高度和谐的统一。非全世界联合的力量难以保护人类遗产，而保护名山的核心是维护其真实性和完整性，使之世代传承，永续利用。

二、世界名山：价值的多维度

名山主要是满足人们对大自然的精神文化生活上的需要，具有独特的文化内涵和景观风貌。主要特征包括美学价值、科学价值、历史文化价值。

1. 名山的美学价值

名山是富有综合美的自然景观实体。众所周知，由山水林草等构成的自然界是美的源泉，依其内容可分为形象美、线条美、色彩美、动态美、静态美、听觉美、嗅觉美等。但是这些天然山水美都有一个共同的核心和基础，这就是形象美。形象美又可分为雄伟美、险峻美、端庄美、格局美、怪诞美等。人们按照传统的山水审美观，一般将富有美感的自然景观形象地概括为雄、奇、险、秀、幽、旷等美学特征。每座名山都由这些基本形象，按照自然的节奏和韵律（如地质演变、地貌发育、地理景观变化等）组成一个丰富多彩的美的空间综合体。而每座名山又有其总体的形象特征，如泰山天下雄、黄山天下奇、峨眉天下秀等。

2. 名山的科学价值

名山不仅有丰富多彩的自然美，而且在科学上有典型的研究价值和重要的研究意义。这种科学上的典型性，深刻地反映和渗透于研究和认识地球发展史、地质变迁、自然地理规律等学科领域中。如：澳大利亚的甘比尔山等，不仅是典型的火山地貌，而且是世界上罕见的火山景观发育形态，对研究火山地貌学有典型的科学意义；黄山等有造型优美的花岗岩山岳景观；庐山等则因山体断块隆起、地层齐全、构造典型而被称为"天然地质博物馆"，因植物种类丰富被誉为"天然植物园"。可见，名山在地质、地貌、水文、气候、土壤、植被、动物等领域中所展现的科学内涵是极其丰富的、典型的。

3. 名山的历史文化价值

世界名山几乎很少是自然形成的，除了近代名山外，绝大部分都有悠久的开发历史，丰富的文化遗产。尤其是中国的泰山、黄山等，在秦汉以前就已开发。名山的这一特点，给今日留下了丰富的文化景观和遗迹，如古建筑、宗教文物、摩崖题刻和大量历史人物活动遗存等。众多的人文景观内容，不仅反映了深邃的历史文化渊源，使之具有重要的社会历史价值，而且在艺术、建筑和工程史学方面，也有典型的学术研究价值，难怪人们把一些名山誉为"历史文化宝库"。

三、世界名山：遗产的重要载体

世界遗产源出何处？提及世界遗产，你会想到什么呢？是人类的伟大创造，还是大自然的神奇美景？是雄伟的埃及金字塔，还是古老的中国长城？都是，但不仅仅是。世界遗产是以国际法为依据、有严格批准程序的事物。1972年11月，联合国教科文组织大会通过了《保护世界文化和自然遗产公约》，简称《世界遗产公约》。此即国际法上的主要依据。那些获得世界遗产殊荣的项目，其产生都经过了一系列科学申报、认证过程，所代表的是人类及自然界的最高价值。从《世界遗产名录》可以发现，世界遗产主要代表人类及其生存环境对世界的三大贡献：

（1）人类创造：包括世界遗产类别中的世界文化遗产、人类口头与非物质文化遗产。

（2）大自然创造：即自然界的天然造化。

（3）人类与大自然的共同创造：世界遗产中的文化与自然双遗产，如黄山、泰山等；还有文化景观遗产，如庐山等。

第二节　聚焦"世界名山研究会"

一、背景

名山是全世界共同的财富，是人类共同的精神家园。在地球环境日益受损、自然资源过度开发的今天，研究和保护那些富有科学、美学和人文价值的世界名山，使其自然文化景观能世代相传、永续利用，是摆在人类面前的共同课题。

由时任庐山管理局党委书记郑翔博士倡议举办的首届中国庐山世界名山大会于2009年10月13日在庐山开幕，随后连续举办了四届。中国庐山、泰山，美国胡德山，澳大利亚甘比尔山，奥地利埃森沃尔谨（阿尔卑斯山）等10个国家12座名山的代表以及联合国教科文组织驻北京办事处官员，10个国家的驻华使领馆官员，来自世界五大洲26个国家的260多名嘉宾应邀参加大会。首届大会主题是"友谊、合作、发展"，紧紧围绕保护和发展世界名山这两大永恒话题展开讨论，共同关注在全球经济发展与环境保护中，世界名山健康发展所面临的共同机遇和挑战；促进环境保护、旅游开发、文化教育等方面的广泛合作。会上，中国庐山与美国胡德山、南非桌山等6座名山签署了友好协议书，将在环境保护、旅游开发、文化教育等方面进行广泛交流与合作。同时，在庐山世界名山大会上倡议与会的世界名山代表共同发起成立"世界名山协会"，为世界各地名山之间相互交流与合作搭建一个持久的平台，促进世界各地名山的发展、进步与世界的和谐。

　　名山是地球的精华，名山是游人的向往之地。每个人的心中可能都有一座世界名山，它是我们的骄傲。千百年来，人类在发现自然、征服自然、亲近自然的过程中，与名山建立了由物质到精神、由索取到保护的复杂联系。可以说，一座名山影响和塑造了一座城市、一个地区乃至一个国家民族的历史文化和精神象征。同时，名山有不计其数的科学问题等待我们去发现、去研究、去分享。我们需要用三种眼光来看名山：一是"用科学的眼光看名山"；二是"用美学的眼光看名山"；三是"用哲学的眼光看名山"。而大学作为知识生产的主力军，科学研究的前沿阵地，所具有的学科优势、人才优势和资源优势是任何社会组织和个人所无法替代的，研究世界名山是大学责无旁贷的光荣使命。为此，自2012年以来，由九江学院党委书记郑翔博士与世界名山协会各大洲的副秘书长积极地进行协商，筹办世界名山研究会。它是九江学院融入世界中外文化交往、理论对话和价值传播的重要平台，是中外人文交流的前沿阵地，肩负着文化传播与弘扬的任务。

　　二、诞生

　　经过多方努力，首届世界名山研究学术研讨会暨高校公共外交论坛于2013年5月13日在美丽的九江学院隆重开幕。大会的主题是"交流、沟通、共享"，会议内容主要有四项：一是成立世界名山研究会，利用各地高校学科优势为名山研究搭建学术平台；二是推动高校之间就名山的科学问题开展研究；三是加强名山所在地高校间的友好合作；四是发挥高校在公共外交中的作用。与会代表开展深入的交流与合作，达成了广泛的共识。会议期间，来自澳大利亚、美国、巴西、南非、德国、菲律宾、泰国、法国、加拿大、英国、俄罗斯、意大利、日本及中国大陆、香港和台湾高校及科研机构的60余名专家、学者，围绕大会主题，探讨了如何利用名山所在地高校学科优势为名山研究搭建学术平台，推动高校之间就名山的科学问题开展研究，加强名山所在地高校之间的交流与合作，推进公共外交研究与跨文化交流。会议上，来自五大洲的30多名代表共同签署了《世界名山研究会倡议书》，并发起成立"世界名山研究会"。研究会为非政府、非政治、非营利性、松散型、学术型的友好联谊组织（NGO）。研究会常设机构设在中国九江学院。

三、宗旨与任务

世界名山研究会的宗旨是为了世界名山永续利用的科学研究。什么是"永续利用"？九江学院党委书记郑翔博士认为：第一，只给后人提供方便，不给后人添麻烦；第二，只给后人留下完整，不给后人留下残缺；第三，只给后人增加价值，不给后人减少价值。世界名山研究会的任务主要有三项：一是研究加出版。出版什么？首先是介绍类，将众人熟知的名山集结起来；其次是已有研究成果的出版；最后是分类的专题研究出版，如保护名山的自然、水文、植被、文化、宗教、旅游等内容。二是研究加培训，成立世界名山培训咨询机构，充分利用世界名山研究会会员单位的人才优势，组织会员单位专家学者为世界名山的管理者提供培训。三是研究加咨询，为世界名山的管理与开发提供咨询。世界名山研究会的具体研究任务有"保护、旅游、促进地方经济发展"三项。

四、章程

2013年5月15日，来自澳大利亚、美国、巴西、南非、德国、菲律宾、泰国、法国、加拿大、英国、俄罗斯、意大利、日本及中国大陆、香港和台湾等16个国家和地区的高校及科研机构的60余名专家、学者，在中国九江学院召开大会，并成立"世界名山研究会"。研究会总部注册地为九江学院，以开展世界名山相关问题科学研究和学术交流与合作为工作重点。

1. 总 则

本组织的名称为"世界名山研究会"，英文名称为 World Famous Mountains Research Institute，缩写为 WFMRI。研究会总部注册地为中国九江学院，且为研究会总部永久所在地。研究会遵守本会章程和中国法律。研究会为非政府、非政治、非营利性、松散型、学术型的友好联谊组织

（NGO）。研究会的目的是为了世界名山科学价值系统展示、全球共享、世代相传、永续利用而开展科学研究工作，促进名山保护、名山旅游、地方经济发展、人与自然和谐发展。

2. 工作内容

研究会的总体工作内容是研究加出版、研究加培训、研究加咨询，整合学术力量，推动名山的科学研究；加强高校间的交流合作，促进公共外交与人文交流。为便于成员单位和研究人员交流联系，研究会建立专门的网站，并依托网站，建立世界名山研究数据库；创办世界名山研究会刊和研究专栏，刊登名山研究学术论文，交流名山研究信息。各名山所在地高校之间可根据需要建立友好合作关系，推进人才和学科建设，实行优质教育资源和研究成果共享。凡研究会成员，应发挥自身的学科、人才优势，切实担负起名山研究的义务和责任，围绕研究会列出的研究专题或自行研究方向进行研究，并积极撰写、提交学术论文。每两年开展学术研讨会，出版研究丛书。开展分类专题研究，如对名山水资源保护、名山游客行为、名山管理机构的研究等。成立世界名山培训咨询机构，充分利用世界名山研究会会员单位的人才优势，组织会员单位专家学者为世界名山的管理者提供培训。同时为部分等待开发的名山做一些旅游规划和管理工作，提供咨询服务等。研究会介绍编著有关世界名山的基本情况、基本知识的书籍，把目前对各种各样的世界名山研究中分散的研究成果集结成册，以确定在学术界的地位。让研究成果在推动世界名山保护，实现名山自然资源价值、历史文化价值和美学价值，促进名山永续利用和区域经济发展等方面发挥应有作用。

第三节　世界名山旅游的可持续发展

随着旅游者兴趣的日趋广泛，文化素质的日益提高，人们对旅游景点的欣赏要求也不断向求自然、求文化品位、求美学价值、求获得信息方面扩展和延伸。跨入新世纪，崇尚自然、回归自然更成为人们休闲度假的原则。世界名山因形成的地质条件、岩石性质、气候条件等地理因素不同，历史背景、文化建筑的不同，每座名山都有其独特的形象和魅力，吸引着成千上万的国内外游人。名山是世界的无价之宝，在旅游上更具有独特的价值，世界各国围绕名山的旅游进行开发建设，也形成了一些经验与教训。

一、名山的旅游功能

1. 满足和培育美感

由于名山具有雄险、幽秀等特点，游览时可使人们获得其他山岳得不到的综合美。游人登山，必然要经过艰辛的努力，付出相当的汗水，这种实践活动本身就蕴藏着对山岳的多种想象，雄伟、险峻、高大、幽丽、怪诞等美的感受便会在精神领地逐渐滋生、培育起来。登上名山之巅，那种居高临下、极目四野的特有感应气氛，使人有机会充分享受上述多种美感的乐趣。唐代诗人杜甫讲的"一览众山小"的感慨，就是人们体验登岳美的集中反映，而且登山次数越多，这种美的享受就越丰富、越深刻。由此可见，名山是人们领略美学艺术的集结点之一，是审美、育美的理想之地。

2. 放松身心

世界名山大都具有森林馥郁、花草丛生、气候适宜、空气清新和较多地保留着大自然原貌的特点，有助于人类健身、健心、康复精神和元气。近年来在欧美和日本兴起了一种"森林浴"，其内容包括登山观景、林中逍遥、荫下散步等。

3. 饱含丰富的文化内容

许多名闻遐迩的寺庙、宫观、古城垣、古寨堡、古战场遗址以及摩崖题刻、摩崖造像等多分布在名山之内，这些人文旅游资源，是开展历史旅游、文化旅游、科学旅游的重要条件，对了解区域历史文化，开阔眼界，增进知识有一定的作用。不少名山，如庐山、富士山、泰山等都是地貌、生物、医药、园林、建筑、绘画、美学等专业科教活动基地。

4. 避暑消夏佳地

众所周知，山岳气温一般比周围城镇低得多，特别是夏季，这种随海拔升高、气温下降的垂直递减现象十分显著。加之山岳云雾多、太阳辐射弱、空气湿度大、降水比较多等因素的影响，山岳的环境是相当凉爽和缓。在我国炎热地区，山岳的这种避暑消夏功能尤为突出。

5. 独具特色的旅游项目

名山可提供多种旅游项目，其中不少为山岳所独具。在观光旅游方面，山岳可观奇峰异石、流泉飞瀑、林木花草、虫蛇鸟兽；还可观云赏雾，观日升落。此外，还可发展登山滑雪、健身康复疗养、炎暑避热纳凉、科学考察、狩猎观鸟、冰川观光等特种旅游项目。

6. 强体健身

据高山生理研究表明，山岳气候对人体健康是非常有益的。人体为了适应高山环境，生理功能会发生一系列变化，如肺通气量和肺活量增加，周围血液循环增强，脑血流量增大，小便酸度上升，尿中乙糖胺排泄量增多，血糖下降。此外，登山对胃、甲状腺、肾上腺等也有益。至于登山在培养毅力、开阔胸怀、陶冶情操等方面的好处，人们早已普遍知晓。

二、名山的旅游特征

1. 资源特征明显，景观具有优势

名山旅游区以自然风光资源为主，具有地质地貌、动植物资源、气象气候、水资源等分布广泛、类型多样、自然特性强的自然景观，以及丰富的人文资源，具有极高的美学观赏价值、历史文化价值和科学研究价值。许多以名山为主体的旅游资源以其特有的资源特色被列为世界级和国家级的旅游景观。

2. 旅游空间有限，生态环境脆弱

虽然一般以名山为主体的旅游风景区面积较广、体积巨大，但是景区内平地少，可供游客游览的空间和地域往往比较狭小。同时，由于地处山区，与周边地区相比，经济、社会发展水平往往较低，大多是经济、文化欠发达地区，各地加快发展的愿望比较强烈，容易造成旅游活动对风景区的生态环境破坏。由于其生态系统脆弱，一旦被破坏，恢复比较困难。

3. 地跨行政区，利益调整复杂

由于面积较广、体积巨大，名山风景区涉及的行政区划普遍比较复杂，有的风景区跨越几个县，有的跨越几个乡镇，一般都跨越几个村民委员会。复杂的行政区划、众多的管理和经营单位使得以名山为主体的风景区内利益主体众多，各自权限难以清楚界定，关系非常复杂。

4. 旅游形象不突出，淡旺季差异过大

不同类型的旅游产品，具有不同的需求时间弹性。一般地，以自然资源为基础开发的旅游产品，旅游客流季节集中强度大；以人文资源为基础开发的旅游产品，客流季节集中强度较小。大多以自然资源为基础的山岳型风景区，若产品结构单一，同质性强，将会强化旅游客流月季集中强度；若产品结构复合化，互补性强，空间布局合理，将会弱化月季集中强度。

三、名山旅游可持续发展

1. 观念创新，塑造名山旅游整体竞争优势

目前，以名山为主体的山岳型风景区旅游资源的开发建设者主要是各行政区域地方政府部门、旅游主管部门及部分景区经营者等。由于旅游资源的所有权和部分经营权多掌控在各行政区域地方政府部门，所以行政部门都以自己的利益为前提，对旅游资源、旅游客源市场、旅游建设项目的竞争比较激烈。随着"大旅游，大系统"观念的逐渐深入，打破行政界限将旅游资源进行"整体综合"已经势在必行，即在满足各利益主体共性的前提下，充分考虑各利益主体自身特点，综合旅游资源优势，实行强强联合。

2. 拓展旅游产业链，塑造名山旅游品牌

名山旅游形态上由观光型旅游向休闲、度假型旅游提升；目标上由重视资源开发转向品牌塑造、市场开拓；产业由粗放型、资源型向集约型、效益型提升，将旅游观光与休闲度假、运动健身、购物娱乐、商务活动结合起来，大力发展观光、生态、文化（文物）、乡村、森林、休闲度假、运动康体等旅游，有序推进旅游度假区建设。延伸旅游产业链，形成若干个有影响、有效益、有规模的产品和品牌。重点发展旅游工艺品制造业、旅游用品制造业和旅游食品加工业，鼓励景区景点研发具有特色的旅游商品和纪念品。发展文化娱乐产业，挖掘地方民俗文化，培育和引进知名演出团体，争取承办各类大型文化体育艺术活动，筹建影视拍摄基地、文艺创作基地、水上运动基地、教科研基地等。

3. 创新旅游市场营销，整合网络资源

坚持"政府主导、市场运作、媒体引路、企业跟进"和"统一促销口径、统筹促销经营、统一促销宣传品、统一促销行动"的原则，完善政企联手、部门联合、上下联动的促销机制，旅游市场开发和产品研发的奖励机制，调动一切积极因素，整合一切资源，集中资金，重点投放，共同推广市场形象，推销旅游产品。做好旅游产品的整体促销和旅游城市形象宣传，细分客源市场。要针对旅游重点客源市场，综合利用广播、电影、电视、互联网、报刊等媒体，探索设立旅游咨询中心。通过建立中介机构、协会、信息中心等提供各类培训、咨询信息，或者有目的地组织企业家交流聚会，推动旅游企业之间的交流和协作，以及旅游企业协作联络网络的生成。通过业务衔接、资源共享、经验交流等形式降低经营成本，提高整个旅游产业的效率，产生1+1>2的经济外部效益。

4. 规范名山管理，优化旅游发展环境

引导旅游企业增强旅游品牌保护意识，积极开展旅游品牌商标注册工作。推进旅游标准化工作，指导和督促旅游企业全面推行国际标准。完善地方行业规范，分类制定旅行社、导游、景区景点、"农家乐"、旅游车船、旅游接待单位等服务规范和质量标准，严格执行市场准入和市场退出机制，实行末位公示、末位淘汰制度。综合运用年检、考核、专项检查、治理整顿等手段，加强对旅游市场主体的监管。探索发行区域旅游"一卡通"。对旅游接待房价实行最低调控价并监督执行，规范旅游景点门票价格，确定优惠控制幅度。积极开展争创文明景区景点、争做"星级导游""星级服务员"等活动，提高服务质量和服务水平。推进旅游诚信建设，建立诚信激励机制和失信惩戒机制，完善投诉处理及协调处理机制。推行旅游从业人员等级考试、技能鉴定、资格认证和持证上岗制度，抓好在岗人员的技能培训。加大依法治旅力度，抓好旅游市场监管和综合治理，严厉打击宰客骗客、强买强卖以及各种不正当竞争行为和违法犯罪活动。高度重视旅游安全，完善旅游应急体系，做好社会治安、交通安全、消防安全、设施安全、食品安全、卫生防疫、紧急救援等工作。完善景区景点游客服务中心体系和信息咨询系统、双语或多语化标识系统。畅通旅游绿色通道，严禁随意查扣外地旅游车辆。动员全社会关注、参与、支持旅游，为旅游产业加快发展营造良好的环境。

第二章

亚洲的世界名山

第一节　人文圣山——中国庐山

庐山坐落在江西省九江市境内,东临鄱阳湖,北濒长江,是一座地垒式断块山,大湖、大江、大山浑然交汇,秀丽、雄奇、险峻,刚柔相济。其以"雄、奇、险、秀"闻名于世,自古享有"匡庐奇秀甲天下"之盛誉。

1996年12月6日,庐山以"世界文化景观"列入《世界遗产名录》;2002年被评为"中华十大名山"之一,电影《庐山恋》列入世界吉尼斯纪录;2004年成为中国首批世界地质公园;2005年被评定为全球唯一的联合国CCC/UN优秀生态旅游景区,并被推荐为中国唯一提名的世界遗产保护管理奖单位;2006年1月被授予首批"全国文明风景旅游区"称号;2007年被批准成为国家5A级旅游景区;2008年获得"首批国家旅游名片"和"中国世界遗产景区十佳"殊荣;2009年相继荣获"中国十大避暑名山""中国最美十大名山"等荣誉称号。它是世界上第一个获得世界文化和自然遗产以及世界地质公园三项最高荣誉的旅游胜地。2009年成功举办了首届中国庐山世界名山大会,成为世界名山协会永久注册地。

一、地质景观

庐山雄峙于长江南岸,兀立于鄱阳湖西北,整个山体南北长29千米,东西宽约16千米,山体面积302平方千米,已命名的山峰有171座,主峰大汉阳峰海拔1474米,庐山平均海拔在1000米以上。庐山、长江、鄱阳湖三位一体的奇妙结合,特殊的地理位置,造就出具有突出价值的地质地貌景观。在地貌学上,庐山被称为"地垒式断块山"。庐山地处江南台背斜与下杨子坳隐的交接带,区内地层除三叠纪外均有系统的出露,构造明显,展现出地壳演化的主要过程。在10亿年前就开始了它的发展史,承载着地球曾发生的一次次惊心动魄的巨变。

海陆的轮番更替,地壳的缓慢沉积,气候的冷热交替,生物的生死嬗递,燕山运动的山体崛起,第四纪冰川的洗礼……西方国家的地质学家曾断言,中国无第四纪冰川。对于此说,中国地质学家李四光却加以否定,他在庐山发现了众多的第四纪冰川遗迹,并认定庐山众多奇特的地貌景观是第四纪冰川的雕琢"杰作"。独特的地质构造特征,显著的地质特色,同时兼具景观奇秀,历史文化内涵丰富的地质遗址,庐山因而被批准为首批"世界地质公园"。

二、突出价值

庐山的历史遗迹以其独特的方式,融汇在具有突出价值的自然美之中,形成了具有极高美学价值的、与中华民族精神和文化生活紧密相连的文化景观。庐山具有突出的地质构造,丰富的动植物资源,造就了"雄、奇、险、秀"为主要特征的自然美景,并与内涵丰富的历史遗迹完美结合,形成了独特的文化景观,从历史、艺术、科学、审美等角度看,均有突出的普遍价值。庐山融文化与自然于一体,集中体现和展示了中华民族的精神和文化生活。庐山的突出价值主要体现在文化价值、美学价值、科学价值、生态价值方面。

1. 文化价值

在中国名山中,庐山最早以文化群体的杰出创造载入中国历史,是中国山水景观文化的策源地,在中华文化的发展与传承方面发挥重要作用。中国田园诗的开创者、大思想家陶渊明,于公元418年前后在庐山写就《桃花源记并诗》,是人类思想史上的瑰丽篇章。中国化佛教思想的开创者慧

远,中国道教第一部大型典籍的创始人陆修静,中国山水诗的开创者谢灵运,中国第一个山水画家顾恺之,中国第一个山水画理论家宗炳,有"书圣"之称的书法家王羲之,都在庐山进行了学术研究或艺术创作。李白、白居易、苏轼、王安石等1500多名文学家、政治家、艺术家相继登临庐山生活、游览,写下3万余首赞颂庐山的诗词歌赋,使庐山成为中国山水文化的代表。

庐山是中国书院教育的典范和中西方文化融合的焦点,并一度成为中国南方文化活动中心。庐山历史上发生的重大文化演变、政治事件影响了中国历史的发展进程。从古代至近代,庐山曾经有三个时期体现了中国历史的走向。著名学者胡适1928年指出,庐山有三处史迹代表三大趋势:慧远的东林,代表中国"佛教化"与佛教"中国化"的大趋势;白鹿洞,代表中国近世七百年的宋学大趋势;牯岭,代表西方文化侵入中国的大趋势。

2. 美学价值

大自然赋予了庐山奇异的风光及自然风貌,通过人的感知和认识,带给人美的享受。庐山美学价值最为直接的表现形式就是庐山的田园诗、山水诗、山水画,它们所体现的精神美感和情结,就是庐山美的载体。

3. 科学价值

20世纪30年代,地质学家李四光在庐山首先发现中国第四纪冰川遗迹,从而使庐山成为中国第四纪冰川学说的诞生地。典型的中国东部第四纪冰川遗迹、珍贵的变质核杂岩构造、壮观的复合地貌,具有极高的地质科考价值。此外,庐山东谷别墅区有美国、英国、德国、瑞典、俄罗斯、荷兰、中国等20个国籍业主建造的别墅600多栋,它们风格迥异,既有罗马式与哥特式的教堂、融合东西方艺术形式的拜占庭式建筑,还有日本式建筑和伊斯兰教清真寺等,堪称世界建筑的杰作,具有重要的科学研究价值。

4. 生态价值

庐山气候湿润,雨量充沛,植被繁茂,草木葱茏,景色宜人。良好适宜的自然条件,使庐山植被丰富,呈垂直地带性分布。庐山属于亚热带季风气候,年均降水量在1950～2000毫升,终年云雾缭绕。随着海拔高度的增加,地表水热状况垂直分布,由山麓到山顶分别生长着常绿阔叶林、常绿及落叶阔叶混交林。据不完全统计,庐山有210科735属1720种植物,分为温带、热带、亚热带、东亚、北美等多个类型,是一座天然的植物园。

三、推荐景点

庐山春如梦、夏如滴、秋如醉、冬如玉,四季可游。唐代诗人白居易以"匡庐奇秀甲天下"八个字道出庐山的秀美和品位，宋代诗人苏轼曾发出"不识庐山真面目，只缘身在此山中"的感慨。良好的气候条件和优美的自然环境，使庐山在19世纪末就成为世界著名的避暑胜地。

1. 锦绣谷

锦绣谷相传为晋代东方名僧慧远采撷花卉、草药之处。这里四时花开，犹如锦绣，故而得名。一路景色如锦绣画卷，令人陶醉。

"锦绣仙洞"因在庐山最美的山间栈道锦绣谷的尽头，有一隐在峭崖之中的"仙人洞"得名。毛泽东同志的诗句"天生一个仙人洞"，几乎家喻户晓。仙人洞为石壁间一个天然洞穴，高7米，深14米。仙人洞又称"佛手岩"，因为洞穴顶部前端石块参差不齐，极像伸展的五指。仙人洞现为道家圣地，相传是道家"八仙"之一吕洞宾修炼成仙的地方。现在洞内有石制殿阁——纯阳殿，殿内立着吕洞宾身背宝剑的石雕像。

位于锦绣谷中的天桥，其实有天无桥，也堪称庐山一奇。天桥之奇，尚不在桥本身。桥临绝谷，绝谷之内，多峭壁峥嵘，层层刻剥，如堆如砌，蔚为壮观。不断有云雾从谷底涌起，恰似银浪翻滚，跃上桥头。俄顷，一阵山风由北而来，吹散云雾，锦绣谷、天桥又一一显现，重放奇异风采。

2. 含鄱吐日

庐山观日处位于庐山东谷含鄱峰中段含鄱口。含鄱岭与九奇峰、汉阳

峰之间的巨大峡谷，正对着鄱阳湖，如同一只张开的巨口衔住鄱阳湖，尽情地吮吸湖水，故称"含鄱口"。

　　在含鄱岭的最高处是庐山观日出的胜地"望鄱亭"。含鄱口的奇妙就在于一个"函"字，造成"千里鄱湖一岭函"的气势。黎明前，登上含鄱岭，临亭凭栏远眺鄱阳湖，开始天空是很浅的蓝色，转眼间天边出现了一道红晕，缓慢地亮起来，当亮到耀眼时，太阳便冉冉地升上水面，湖面很快就被染上了橙黄色，带着色彩的波光，特别耀眼，特别璀璨。一会儿，太阳全部跳出湖面，一片深红色。照亮了青山，染红了碧水，朝阳、湖水、峰峦构成"红霞万朵百重衣"的壮丽图景。

3. 五老听泉

　　"五老听泉"的壮景由庐山最壮观的五座山峰——五老峰和庐山最宏伟的瀑泉——三叠泉组成。五座山峰远看恰似五位老人并肩坐在鄱阳湖旁，故俗称"五老峰"；三叠泉因水分三叠奔泻而下得名。"五老听泉"是庐山风景的精华，而三叠泉凭着"不到三叠泉，不算庐山客"之说吸引游客。

4. 白鹿洞书院

白鹿洞书院是我国古代四大书院之首。宋代时，便成为我国最早的高等学府，与当时应天、石鼓、岳麓书院合称"四大书院"，被誉为我国高等教育的"书院之源"。

白鹿洞书院的创始人可以追溯到唐朝的李渤，唐贞元年间，李渤隐居这里读书，养一白鹿自娱，人称白鹿先生。长庆年间李渤任江州（今九江）刺史，便在白鹿洞筑台榭，植花木。为了纪念白鹿，李渤就将当年读书的山洞，改名为白鹿洞。到南唐开元中，在此办起学校，称"庐山国学"。宋代理学家、教育家朱熹为南康（今星子县）郡守时，重建院宇，在此亲自讲学，确定了书院的办学条规和宗旨，并奏请赐额及御书，吸引了海内外知名学者来此地讲学。白鹿洞书院因此名声大振，成为宋末至清初几百年"讲学式"书院的楷模，是当时我国的一个文化中心。

5. 植物王国

"植物王国"庐山植物园创建于1934年，是中国第一座正规植物园，在中国和世界植物园史册中都占有重要的位置。

创办庐山植物园的是中国植物学界的泰斗、哈佛大学博士胡先骕及他的助手、著名植物学家秦仁昌和陈封怀。他们历经艰辛、呕心沥血，在这片山谷中创建了中国有史以来的第一个正规植物园。

植物园总面积 5000 余亩，分松柏区、草花区、药圃、岩石园、茶园、猕猴桃园、国际友谊杜鹃园、自然保护区及温室和苗圃等。园中汇集了中外植物 5500 余种，其中属国家保护的珍稀濒危植物 150 余种。世界松柏类植物有 600 多种，这里就拥有 250 多种，被誉为中国和世界松、柏、杉、桧的活标本园。

6. 花径觅春

"花径觅春"景区的全称是"白司马花径"。公元 815 年，唐朝著名诗人白居易被贬到九江来当司马。第二年的初夏时节，他上庐山游览，住在大林寺，看见大林寺旁的山坡上，一大片桃花刚刚盛开，十分美丽，而此时，山脚下的春花早已凋谢了，白居易又惊又喜，不由写下了著名的七言绝句《大林寺桃花》："人间四月芳菲尽，山寺桃花始盛开。长恨春归无觅处，不知转入此中来。"

白司马花径现有花卉区、岩石园、花房、桃林等，又因山凹处有美丽的如琴湖，使白司马花径成为庐山一个游人必至的著名景点。1987年，有关部门又将白居易原建于山麓的草堂移建到花径公园内。草堂内陈列着有关白居易的资料、图片及字画，并在草堂前立了白居易的塑像，更好地表达和寄托后人对这位伟大诗人的追思和怀念。

7. 美庐春秋

庐山别墅的建筑起源于1895年。庐山别墅大都属于欧洲山地别墅的建筑风格，但形态迥异，在一定程度上反映了各国的房屋建筑艺术和流派。这些仙宅灵居般的别墅熔西欧建筑艺术、文化和庐山得天独厚的自然景观于一炉，具有文化和自然完美结合的双重宝贵价值。

在庐山别墅中，最有名的是美庐。美庐位于长冲河中段，坐北朝南，主体建筑面积为996平方米，庭园面积为4928平方米。它依山就势，一道清泉弯弯曲曲流贯其中，园中既有中国名贵树木金钱松、银杏、玉兰、鹅掌楸、松柏，也有引进的外国名贵树木云杉、红枫、法国梧桐、美国凌霄，整个庭园四季常青，花枝争艳，充满勃勃生机。美庐鲜明的西式建筑风格、中西文化交融的庭园布局，体现了中西文化碰撞交融的时代特征和审美取向，也体现了以人为本的情调，以其巧妙的色彩搭配、形式对功能的服从、含蓄的旋律美、与自然环境的统一和协同，给人以强烈的美感体验，充分展现了建筑和庭园艺术的独特魅力。它不仅从建筑学上来说是庐山别墅中的佼佼者，更因为先后住过蒋介石和毛泽东，而成为中国唯一的一栋住过国、共两党最高领导人的别墅。

8. 黄龙宝树

黄龙宝树景区由黄龙寺、黄龙潭、乌龙潭及三宝树景区组成。因其幽静、古典而闻名，是庐山一处天然的氧吧。黄龙寺前有三棵参天大树，人称"三宝树"。三棵大树中两棵是柳杉，一棵是银杏。相传这三棵大树是由晋朝名僧昙诜种植，距今已有一千六百多年的历史。

9. 云中街市

在群峰环耸的山中有一座中国绝无仅有的云中山城。在云中山城的中心，一条童话般的"云中街市"真真切切地展现在游人面前，以其美妙绝伦的奇姿，令境内外游人赞叹不已。

"云中街市"是牯岭山城最繁华的地方，这条街自东向西成一弯弧形，犹如清光四射却又含羞欲放的半月。正街一边是鳞次栉比的商店、酒楼，游人可以在酒楼品尝独具特色的庐山风味小吃，可以在商店购买富有庐山特色的旅游纪念品。正街另一边是淡雅温馨的公园，是游人休憩的好地方。公园里还立有一座牯牛奋起的塑像，塑像基座上有当代著名书法家启功题写的"牯岭"两个大字。

10. 五教祈福园

作为一座宗教名山，庐山有着全国名山大川中绝无仅有的一个独特的现象，就是有五个教派在此并存。为了进一步弘扬庐山的宗教文化，2010年，在庐山管理局的推进下，庐山五教祈福园正式落成。庐山五教祈福园位于五老峰景区的青莲谷内，整个项目以祈福为主题，以"天开地应、钟鸣天下、传播福音"为表达方式，以祈福线路景观设计为中心。庐山五教祈福园中最有特色的当是那口重量达38.5吨的祈福大钟了，大钟整体高度为476厘米，代表赤道40076千米；钟体高为365厘米，代表一年365天；周长为960厘米，代表我国国土陆地面积960万平方公里。钟体有佛教、道教、天主教、伊斯兰教、基督教五教标志及祝福语，钟体采用纯铜铸造，钟响声可传播至一万米之外。

第二节　五岳之尊——中国泰山

泰山是中国五岳之首，古称"岱宗""岱山"，春秋时改称"泰山"。泰山绵亘于济南、泰安、莱芜三市之间，东西长约200千米，南北宽约50千米，贯穿山东中部，主脉、支脉、余脉涉及周边十余县，位于华北大平原的南北通道与黄河中下游的东西通道交叉枢纽之侧，这一独特的地理位置对泰山影响的扩大及其文化的弘扬，起了重要的作用。数千年来，先后有十多位皇帝来泰山封禅。孔子留下了"登泰山而小天下"的赞叹，杜甫则留下了"会当凌绝顶，一览众山小"的千古绝唱。1987年，泰山被联合国教科文组织列入世界自然文化遗产名录，它是中国首例自然文化双重遗产项目。

一、地貌景观

泰山最高峰为极顶玉皇顶（玉皇峰），海拔1545米。泰山气候垂直变化明显，为泰山形成丰富的自然山水提供了有利的条件。降水的充沛使泰山形成了众多的泉瀑和溪谷，其中溪谷130条，瀑潭64处，名泉72眼。山地多变的气候条件形成了泰山丰富的气候景观。冬季岱顶常见的雾凇和雪凇以及"黄河玉带""云海玉盘""旭日东升""碧霞宝光"等气象奇观，共同造就了泰山优美神奇的自然景观。泰山地貌分为剥蚀堆积丘陵、山前冲洪积台地、构造剥蚀低山和侵蚀构造中山四大类型，在空间形象上，由低而高，造成层峦叠嶂、凌空高耸的巍峨之势，形成多种地形群体组合的地貌景观。

泰山作为世界地质公园，拥有丰富的地质资源，自19世纪末至今一直是国内外学者研究地质地貌的热点地区。这些资源所具有的科学价值对于普及地理地质知识、帮助地质学家及旅游者了解地球变化具有重要的作用。目前，泰山主要的地质旅游资源可以通过泰山地质公园博物馆进行了解，同时也可以通过地质地貌遗迹、水文地质遗迹、岩石遗址、构造遗址以及地层遗址等加以认识，主要分布在扇子崖、天烛峰、傲徕峰、桃花峪、中天门等景点及其周边地区。

二、主要景观

泰山的风景名胜以主峰为中心，呈放射形分布。历经几千年的保护与建设，泰山拔起于齐鲁丘陵之上，主峰突兀、山势险峻、峰峦层叠，形成"一览众山小"和"群峰拱岱"的高旷气势。人文景观的布局重点从泰城西南祭地的社首山、蒿里山至告天的玉皇顶，形成"地府""人间""天堂"三重空间。岱庙是山下泰城中轴线上的主体建筑，前连通天街，后接盘道，形成山城一体。由此步步登高，渐入佳境，进而由"人间"进入"天庭仙界"。

1. 泰山石刻

泰山的石刻不仅数量多、种类全，而且以源远流长、品位高著称于世，是研究历史和书法镌刻艺术的宝贵资料，具有很高的历史文化价值、美学价值、艺术价值等。目前，泰山景区现存历代石刻1687处，主要分布在岱庙、登山盘路两侧、岱顶、后石坞及王母池、普照寺、三阳观、玉泉寺等寺观内外。其中，岱庙现存石刻273处，红门景区（自岱宗坊至壶天阁）现存石刻222处，中天门景区（自壶天阁至朝阳洞）现存石刻188处，南天门景区（自朝阳洞至后石坞）现存石刻358处，竹林景区（包括普照寺、烈士祠、五贤祠、三阳观和扇子崖）现存石刻165处。

2. 十八盘

泰山十八盘是泰山登山盘路中最险要的一段，为泰山的主要标志之一。此处两山崖壁如削，陡峭的盘路镶嵌其中，远远望去，恰似天门云梯。自开山至龙门为"慢十八"，再至升仙坊为"不紧不慢又十八"，又至南天门为"紧十八"，共计1630余级石阶。"紧十八"西崖有巨岩悬空，侧影似佛头侧枕，高鼻秃顶，慈颜微笑，名迎客佛。十八盘岩层陡立，倾角70至80度。

3. 南天门

在山东泰安市泰山十八盘之尽处，旧称三天门、天门关，海拔1460米。山于此为最危耸，飞龙岩与翔凤岭之间的低坳处，双峰夹峙，仿佛天门自

开。此门于元中统五年（1264年）由布山道士张志纯创建。门为阁楼式建筑，石砌拱形门洞，额题"南天门"。红墙点缀，黄色琉璃瓦盖顶，气势雄伟。门侧有楹联曰"门辟九霄仰步三天胜迹；阶崇万级俯临千嶂奇观"。元代杜仁杰曾篆刻《天门铭》记录其事，铭曰："泰山天门无室宇尚矣。布山张炼师为之经构，累岁乃成，可谓破天荒者也。"刻石现仍在天门西侧的石室内，保存完好。

4. 祖庭岱庙

华夏名山第一庙，东岳庙祖庭——岱庙。岱庙始建于秦汉之时，宋朝时扩修，是历代帝王的泰山行宫。历代帝王登封泰山，先要在山下岱庙内举行大典，然后登山。岱庙是帝王宫城式祠庙建筑，位于泰安市正中心，北望泰山。占地近10万平方米，是全国重点文物保护单位。馆存文物一级品数量在全国2000余座博物馆中居第60位。

天贶殿，位于仁安门北，是岱庙的主体建筑，建于宋大中祥符二年（1009年）。大殿建于长方形石台之上，三面雕栏围护，长48.7米，宽19.73米，高22.3米，重檐歇山、彩绘斗拱、画瓦盖顶，檐下8根大红明柱，规模宏大，

辉煌壮丽。天贶殿与北京故宫太和殿、曲阜孔庙大成殿，合称为"中国古代三大宫殿"。

5. 日出日落

游泰山的最佳时间为每年的5月到11月。泰山日出、云海玉盘、晚霞夕照、黄河金带是泰山的四大奇观。泰山日出是壮观而动人心弦的，是岱顶奇观之一，也是泰山的重要标志。黎明时分，游人站在岱顶举目远眺东方，便能看见一线晨曦由灰暗变成淡黄，又由淡黄变成橘红。而天空的云朵，红紫交辉，瞬息万变，漫天彩霞与地平线上的茫茫云海融为一体，犹如巨幅油画从天而降。浮光跃金的海面上，日轮掀开了云幕，撩开了霞帐，披着五彩霓裳，像一个飘荡的宫灯，冉冉升起在天际。须臾间，金光四射，群峰尽染，好一派壮观而神奇的海上日出。

当夕阳西下的时候，云峰之上均镶嵌着一层金灿灿的亮边，时而闪烁着奇异的光辉。那五颜六色的云朵，巧夺天工，奇异莫测，如果云海在此时出现，满天的霞光则全部映照在"大海"中，那壮丽的景色、大自然生动的情趣，就更加令人陶醉了。晚霞夕照与黄河金带的神奇景色，与季节和气候有很大的关系。秋季最好，因为这时风和日丽、天高云淡；其次是大雨之后，残云萦绕、天晴气朗、尘埃绝少、山清水秀，你尽可放目四野，饱览其"江山如此多娇"的秀容美貌。

三、旅游景区

泰山风景旅游区包括幽区、旷区、奥区、妙区、秀区、丽区六大风景区。

泰山幽区是指中路旅游区，是最负盛名的登山线路，自登山盘路的起始点一天门经中天门至南天门，全长5.5千米，几乎全部为盘路，共有6250级台阶。沿途风景深幽，古木怪石鳞次栉比，主要景点包括岱宗坊、关帝庙、一天门、孔子登临处、红门宫、万仙楼、斗母宫、经石峪、壶天阁、中天门、云步桥、五松亭、望人松、对松山、梦仙龛、升仙坊、十八盘等。

泰山旷区是指西溪景区，是登山的西路，自大众桥起有一条盘山公路，可以直达中天门。除此之外，还有一条登山的盘路，两旁峰峦竞秀、谷深峪长、瀑高潭深、溪流潺潺。旷区主要的景观有黄溪河、长寿桥、无极庙、元始天尊庙、扇子崖、天胜寨、黑龙潭、白龙池。

泰山妙区自泰山幽区一路拾级而上。过了十八盘，登上南天门，就进入了泰山妙区，即岱顶游览区。除了深切地感受大自然的造化和先人留下的遗迹外，此处能让人真正地体会一下一览众山小的伟大气魄。妙区的主要景观有南天门、月观峰、天街、白云洞、孔子庙、碧霞祠、唐摩崖、玉皇顶、探海石、日观峰、瞻鲁台等。

泰山奥区是以后石坞为中心的景区，其特点是峰雄岩壮、怪石嶙峋、古松竞奇、鸟语花香、雄壮奇奥、美不胜收。由妙区——泰山极顶往后山乘索道可达。奥区的主要胜景有八仙洞、奶奶庙、独足盘、天烛峰、九龙岗、黄花洞、莲花洞、尧观台等。更令人称奇的是大自然的造化：著名的鸳鸯松、卧龙松、飞龙松、姊妹松、烛焰松等如珍珠般镶嵌在多姿多彩的石岩上。

泰山丽区即泰山山麓及泰城游览区。该区是无须登山而感受泰山之美的去处。其主要景观包括双龙池、遥参亭、岱庙、岱宗坊、王母池、关帝庙、普照寺、五贤祠、汉明堂、三阳观以及不断开辟的新景观等。

泰山秀区主要包括桃花峪景区、樱桃园景区，在泰山的西麓。桃花峪深幽静丽，景色奇秀，且有一条索道直通主峰。樱桃园则离城不远，鸟语啾啾，溪水潺潺。秀区是泰安人假日休闲的好去处，游人如有足够时间一定要去。

第三节　灵秀佛国——中国峨眉山

峨眉山位于四川省乐山市境内，在四川盆地西南部，西距峨眉山市 7 千米，东距乐山市 37 千米。景区面积 154 平方千米，最高处万佛顶海拔 3099 米。峨眉山，是大峨山、二峨山、三峨山、四峨山的总称。北魏时郦道元《水经注》记载："去成都千里，然秋日澄清，望见两山相对如峨眉，故称峨眉焉。"由于峨眉山的高度及地理位置，从山脚到山顶十里不同天，一山有四季。峨眉山抚弄星辰，积蓄云雨，神秘无比。自古就有"普贤者，佛之长子；峨眉者，山之领袖"之称。峨眉山自然遗产极其丰富，素有天然"植物王国""动物乐园""地质博物馆"之美誉；文化底蕴极其深厚，是中国佛教圣地，被誉为"佛国天堂"，为普贤菩萨的道场。1982 年，峨眉山以峨眉山风景名胜区的名义，被国务院批准列入第一批国家级风景名胜区名单。1996 年 12 月 6 日，峨眉山—乐山大佛作为一项文化与自然双重遗产被联合国教科文组织列入世界遗产名录。2007 年，峨眉山景区被国家旅游局正式批准为国家 5A 级旅游风景区。

一、地貌景观

峨眉山的地质演化史，经历了"八亿年的孕育，七千万年的成长，二百万年的春风时雨和潜移默化"。在数千万年的演变过程中，峨眉山经历无数次强烈的地壳运动，形成多种类型的地质构造，在国际上划分的 13 个地质代中，除缺失中、晚奥陶纪，志留纪、泥盆纪和石炭纪外，其余各时代地层均有沉积，因此被誉为"地质博物馆"。中国地质史上中生代末期的燕山运动，奠定了峨眉山地质构造的轮廓，新构造期的喜马拉雅运动及其伴随的青藏高原的抬升，造就了峨眉山。

峨眉山由于山顶上是一大片古生代喷出的玄武岩，其下岩层受到保护而得以保持高度，又因山中内部"瀑流切割强烈"，进而形成了高2000米以上的"峡谷奇峰地形"。而山顶上坚实的玄武岩又是一番熔岩平台的景象。正是大自然的内外营力雕刻，创作出无数奇特秀丽的景观，把峨眉山打扮得绚丽多姿，使雄、秀、奇、幽、险集于一山之中。

二、四大奇观

1. 云海

晴空万里时，白云从峨眉山千山万壑中冉冉升起，光洁厚润，无边无涯。佛家把云海称作"银色世界"。峨眉云海，是由低云组成，峰高云低。云海中浮露出许多岛屿，云腾雾绕，宛若佛国仙乡；白浪滔滔，这些岛屿化若浮舟，又像是"慈航普度"。近代诗人赵朴初诗"天著霞衣迎日出，峰腾云海作舟浮"，是这一景致的绝妙写照。

2. 日出

峨眉山耸立在四川盆地的西部边缘，鸟瞰纵横千里的"天府平原"，登山观日出，视野开阔，涤荡胸襟，深悟人与自然之情。伴随着旭日东升，朝霞满天，万道金光射向大地，峨眉山宛似从头至脚逐渐披上金色的大氅，呈现出秀美身姿。北宋诗人苏东坡咏道："秋风与作云烟意，晓日令涵草木姿。"

3. 佛光

佛光，又称峨眉宝光。佛家称为普贤菩萨眉宇间放出的光芒。实际上，佛光是光的自然现象，是阳光照在云雾表面所起的衍射和漫反射作用形成的。夏天和初冬的午后，舍身岩下云层中骤然幻化出一个红、橙、黄、绿、青、蓝、紫的七色光环，中央虚明如镜。观者背向偏西的阳光，有时会发现光环中出现自己的身影，举手投足，影皆随形，奇者，即使成百上千人同时同址观看，观者也只见己影，不见旁人。谭钟岳诗云："非云非雾起层空，异彩奇辉迥不同。试向石台高处望，人人都在佛光中。"

4. 圣灯

金顶无月的黑夜，舍身岩下有时忽见一光如萤，继而数点，渐至无数，在黑暗的山谷飘忽不定。佛家称为"圣灯"，飘浮的神灯像是"万盏明灯朝普贤"。圣灯现象极为罕见,关于其产生,有人说是"野火",有人说是萤火虫发出的光。较为科学的说法是某些树木上有一种蜜环菌,当空气中的湿度达到100%时便会腐烂发光。

三、旅游景点

1. 圣积晚钟

圣积寺,古名慈福院,位于峨眉城南2.5千米处,为入山第一大寺,环境清幽。寺外有古黄桷树二株,需数人才能合抱。铜钟原悬挂于寺内宝楼上,又名圣积铜钟,铸于明代嘉靖年间,由别传禅师募化建造,此钟铜质坚固,重达12.5吨,相传为四川省最大的一口铜钟。1959年,圣积寺废,钟搁置于道旁。1978年,铜钟迁至报国寺对面的凤凰堡上,并建亭覆盖保护。凤凰堡上参天蔽日的苍杉翠柏,庄重典雅的八角攒尖钟亭,环绕四周有百余通碑刻的古碑林,与古朴凝重的巨钟浑然一体,融和了自然美与人文美,堪称一大景观。

2. 萝峰晴云

萝峰位于伏虎寺右侧,距之0.5千米,是伏虎山下的一座小山峦。萝峰草丰竹秀、涧谷环流,古楠耸翠,曲径通幽。山峦上数百株古松苍劲挺拔、千姿百态,是峨眉山上少见的松树聚生地。山风吹过,阵阵松涛回荡在山谷之间。夏季雨后初晴时,烟云从涧谷袅袅升起,或从蓝空缓缓飘过,从密簇簇的松林中望去,轻盈婀娜,变化莫测,显示出峨眉山云彩变幻的流动美。云从石上起,泉从石下落。奇妙景观,美不胜收。萝峰庵,又名萝峰禅院,是一座雅致的小庙,于1987年6月重建。此庵翠竹掩映,桢楠蔽日,幽静典雅,绝尘脱俗,其门联曰:"一尘不染三千界,万法皆空十二因。"庵后为新建的塔林,墓塔林立、庄严肃穆。峨眉山的高僧大德,都把萝峰作为圆寂后的长眠之地。

3. 灵岩叠翠

灵岩寺遗址位于高桥左侧,距报国寺西南5千米。创建于隋唐年间,明代是灵岩寺的鼎盛时期。古刹于20世纪60年代全部烧毁坍塌,而"灵岩叠翠"的自然景色却依然如故,去灵岩山,赏叠翠层,仍有"仿翠摹青情不尽"的感受。灵岩地处金顶三峰后面山麓,在灵岩寺遗址上向北眺望,近处，青峰绵延起伏，茂林修竹，点缀其间；远处，万佛顶、千佛顶、金顶宛如三座巨型翠屏横亘天际，三峰挺拔而柔和的轮廓线十分清晰，由低至高，由近至远，青青的山色，由翠绿转黛青，由灰蓝到灰白，向远方层层扩展，一直延伸到与蓝天的分界线，密林掩映、丹岩凝翠、层层叠叠，呈现出灵岩的雄伟壮观。"灵岩叠翠"为峨眉十景之胜。

4. 双桥清音

清音阁地处峨眉山上山下山的中枢，与龙门洞素称"水胜双绝"。清音阁展开的是一幅青山绿水画卷。高处，玲珑精巧的楼阁居高临下。中部，是丹檐红楼的接御、中心二亭，亭两侧各有一石桥，分跨在黑白二水之上，形如双翼，故名双飞桥。近景，则为汇合于牛心亭下的黑白二水。右侧黑水，源出九老洞下的黑龙潭，绕洪椿坪而来，水色如黛，又名黑龙江；左侧白水，源出弓背山下的三岔河，绕万年寺而来，水色泛白，又名白龙江。两江汇流，冲击着碧潭中状如牛心的巨石。任黑白二水汹涌拍击，牛心石仍岿然不动，组成独具特色的寺庙山水园林环境。伫立中心亭，观黑白二水，大有山随水动之感。园林学家称它是有声的诗，立体的画。

5. 白水秋风

"白水秋风"为峨眉山万年寺之秋景名，万年寺位于海拔1020米的狮子岭下，始建于东晋，唐时慧通禅师驻锡在此，相传峨眉山五行属火，寺庙屡建屡毁，于是改名白水寺。寺庙建在群山之中突起的一座山峰上，诸峰相映，苍翠环照，一年四季，景色宜人，特别是到了秋高气爽之时，峨眉山下夏暑尚存，金顶三峰已初飘白雪，而位于中山地区的万年古刹，正处在一年中的黄金季节。林中色彩斑斓，红叶如醉，寺内的白水池碧波荡漾，蛙声如琴，丹桂飘香，令人怡然神爽，因而称之为"白水秋风"。

6. 洪椿晓雨

以清幽静雅取胜的洪椿坪，坐落在众山群峰之中。坪上，云低雾浓，古木葱茏，涛声殷殷，山鸟长鸣。洪椿坪建于明万历年间，原名千佛禅院，以寺外有三株洪椿古树而得名。春夏雨后初晴的早晨，山野空气格外清新，微带凉意，寺宇庭院一尘不染，整洁雅致。此时，山林中，石坪上，庭院里，落起霏霏"晓雨"。这"晓雨"，似雨非雨，如雾非雾，楼阁、殿宇、山石、影壁、花木、游人，以及庭院右侧的林森小院，一切都似飘忽在迷茫的境界中，呈现出一种虚无缥缈的朦胧美。游者或倚立庭院，或漫步寺外，仿佛周身被"晓雨"润湿，但抚摸衣装，却没有被雨水浸湿的痕迹，只感觉到清凉和舒适。

7. 大坪霁雪

大坪孤峰突起，高耸于黑白二水之间。位于峨眉山中部，左与华严顶、长老坪、息心所、观心坡诸山比肩相望；右有天池、宝掌、玉女诸峰环绕呼应；中心顶鼎峙于前，九老洞屏临于后，海拔1450米。大坪山势险峻，孤峰凌空，仅东北两侧各有一陡坡上下。每年秋末，金顶开始飘雪，立冬一过，大坪已是雪花满山飞舞，挺立的常绿乔木，如琼枝玉叶，似白塔矗立。严冬时，峨眉山处处雪树冰花，全山宛如银色世界。大坪和周围的群峰，变成一片洁白的净土。晴雪初霁，伫立在高海拔的山峰上鸟瞰大坪，眼前是另一番"幽峭精绝"的冬景。

8. 九老仙府

"九老仙府"是仙峰寺与九老洞的统称。在仙峰寺右侧0.5千米的九老洞，全称九老仙人洞。相传九老洞是仙人聚会的洞府。洞位于仙峰寺右侧山腰，旁边藤萝倒置，下临绝壁深渊，洞口呈"人"字形，高约4米。洞内黝黑阴森、凹凸湿润，能直立行走的通道仅100多米，往前岔洞交错、深邃神秘，未探明前，人多不敢入内。1986年，经过四川省地质队和有关专家联合科学考察后，才初步揭开了九老洞之谜。九老洞为峨眉山著名的岩溶洞穴，在长达1500多米向下延伸的通道内，有一个全封闭型的观赏空间，首先呈现出的是形状多变的空间美。第一段为浅部，有比较宽敞的厅堂及廊道式洞穴；第二段为中部，是九老洞的主体部分，这一段开始出现岔洞，多系网状交叉形的宫型洞穴，洞中有洞，上下重叠，纵横交错，仅在洞穴交错处，有较大的洞穴或竖井；第三段为深部，主要是裂隙型洞穴，一条暗溪时而沿裂缝渗出，时而蜿蜒隐入洞底。洞壁和洞顶有丰富的岩溶造型，如石钟乳、石笋、石柱、石芽、石花，等等。

9. 象池月夜

峨眉山月，自古闻名。观月的最佳地点是报国寺、萝峰顶、万年寺、

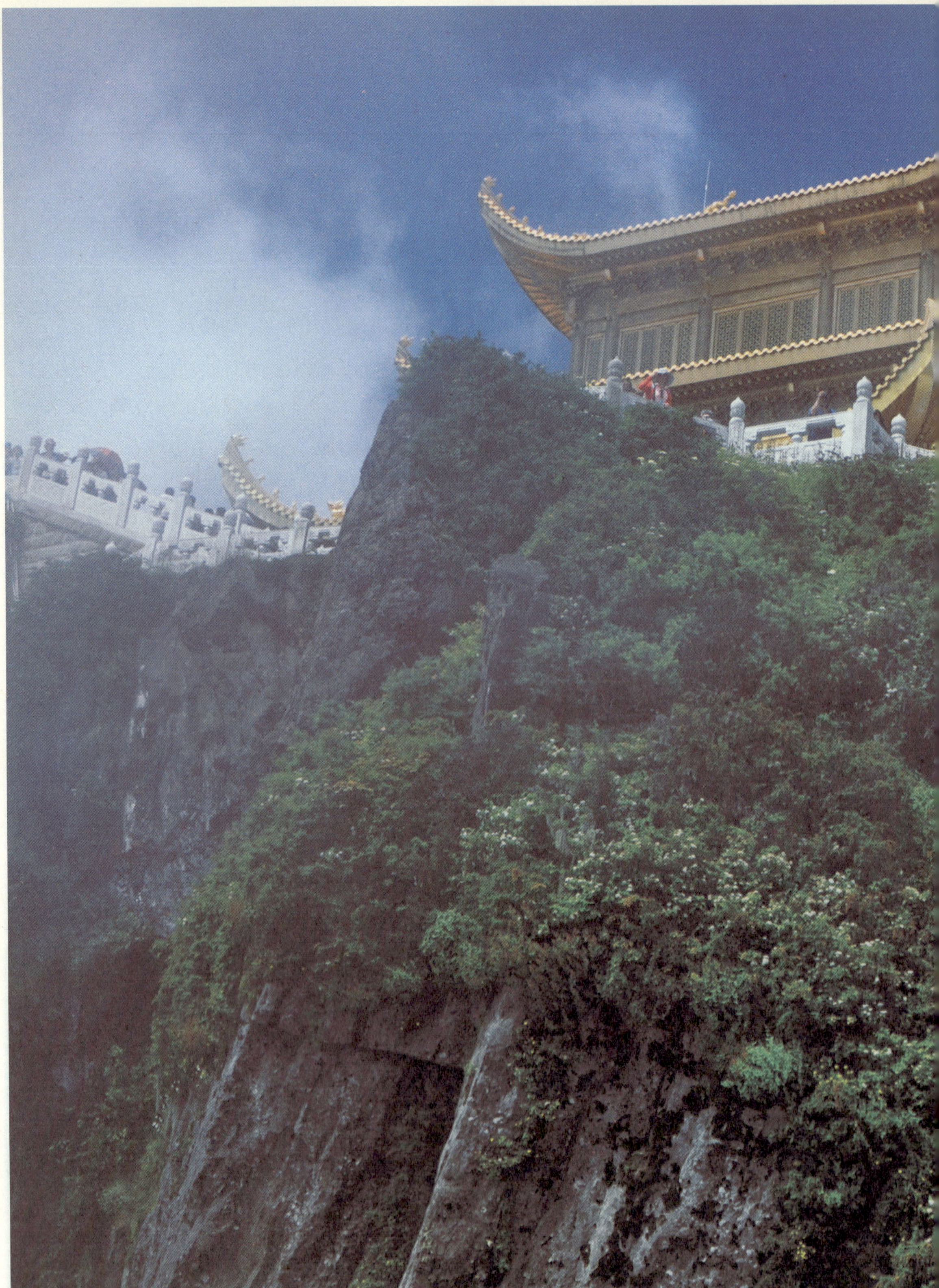

金頂

仙峰寺和洗象池等处。每当月夜，云收雾敛，苍穹湛蓝，万山沉寂，秋风送爽，一轮明镜悬挂在洁净无云的碧空，唯有英姿挺拔的冷杉树林，萧萧瑟瑟、低吟轻语。月光透过茂密墨绿的丛林，大雄殿、半月台、洗象池、初喜亭、吟月楼，沉浸在朦胧的月色里，显得庄严肃穆、淡雅恬静。月光下，古刹酷似大象头颅，蓝天映衬，剪影清晰，大殿似额头，两侧厢房似双耳，半月台下的钻天坡石阶，又好似拖长的象鼻，这应该是建筑设计师的匠心独具。皓月当空、斗转星移，六角小池内一汪清泉，恰好映现出一轮皎洁的明月，空中嫦娥、池上玉兔，遥相呼应，天上人间、浑然一体。

10. 金顶祥光

金顶是峨眉山的象征，峨眉十景之首"金顶祥光"则是峨眉山精华所在，由日出、云海、佛光、圣灯四大奇观组成。

第四节 中国画镜——中国黄山

黄山位于安徽省南部黄山市境内，南北长约40千米，东西宽约30千米，山脉总面积1200平方千米，核心景区面积约160.6平方千米。黄山原称"黟山"，因传说中华民族的始祖轩辕黄帝曾在此修炼升仙，唐天宝六年（747年）六月十六日改现名，这一天还被唐玄宗钦定为黄山的生日。黄山为"三山五岳"中三山之一，被誉为"天下第一奇山"。黄山有72峰，或崔嵬雄浑，或峻峭秀丽，布局错落有致，天然巧成，历来享有"五岳归来不看山，黄山归来不看岳"的美誉。奇松、怪石、云海、温泉素称黄山"四绝"，这些都是大自然造化中的奇迹。

黄山是我国十大风景名胜之一，1990年12月12日，黄山被联合国教科文组织列入"世界自然和文化遗产名录"。世界遗产委员会对黄山的评价是："黄山，在中国历史上文学艺术的鼎盛时期（公元16世纪中叶的'山水'风格）曾受到广泛的赞誉，以'震旦国中第一奇山'而闻名。"2002年，被授予中国国家地质公园（第二批）称号。2004年成为首批世界地质公园，从而成为世界上第一个获得世界文化和自然遗产以及世界地质公园三项最高荣誉的旅游胜地。联合国世界遗产系列邮票于2013年4月11日发行，作为世界文化和自然双遗产的黄山入选其中。

一、地貌景观

黄山经历了漫长的造山运动和地壳抬升，以及冰川和自然风化作用，才形成其特有的峰林结构。黄山群峰林立，有72峰，素有"36大峰，36小峰"之称，主峰莲花峰与平旷的光明顶、险峻的天都峰（天都峰海拔1810米，与光明顶、莲花峰并称黄山三大主峰，为36大峰之一）一起，雄踞在景区中心，周围还有几十座千米以上的山峰，群峰叠翠，有机地组合成一幅有节奏旋律、波澜壮阔、气势磅礴、令人叹为观止的立体画面。

黄山山体主要由燕山期花岗岩构成，垂直节理发育，侵蚀切割强烈，断裂和裂隙纵横交错，长期受水溶蚀，形成瑰丽多姿的花岗岩洞穴与孔道。前山岩体节理稀疏，岩石多球状风化，山体浑厚壮观；后山岩体节理密集，多是垂直状风化，山体峻峭，形成了"前山雄伟，后山秀丽"的地貌特征。再加上出露地表以后，受到大自然千百万年的天然雕琢，终于形成了今天这样气势磅礴、雄伟壮丽的自然奇观。

二、主要景区

1. 玉屏景区

黄山玉屏景区以玉屏楼为中心，莲花峰和天都峰为主体。沿途有"蓬莱三岛""百步云梯""一线天""新一线天""鳌鱼洞"等奇妙景观。玉屏楼地处天都、莲花之间，这里几乎集黄山奇景之大成，故有黄山绝佳处之称。驰名中外的迎客松挺立在玉屏楼左侧，右侧有送客松，楼前有陪客松、文殊台，楼后是玉屏峰，著名的"玉屏卧佛"就在峰顶，头左脚右，惟妙惟肖。峰石上刻有毛泽东草书"江山如此多娇"。楼东石壁上，刻有朱德元帅的"风景如画"和刘伯承元帅所做的《与皖南抗日诸老同志游黄山》："抗日之军昔北去，大旱云霓望如何。黄山自古云成海，从此云天雨也多。"

天都峰位于玉屏峰南，相距1000米，是黄山三大主峰中最为险峻之处，海拔1830米。上天都之路极为险峻，近些年来，经过建设者们的不断开拓，使登峰道路有惊无险。天都峰顶有"登峰造极"石刻，使人有"海到无边天作岸，山登绝顶我为峰"之感。

莲花峰，位于玉屏楼北，是黄山第一高峰，海拔1864.8米，峻峭高耸，气势雄伟，宛如初绽的莲花。从莲花岭至莲花峰顶约1.5千米，这段路叫莲花梗，沿途有飞龙松、倒挂松等黄山名松及黄山杜鹃。莲花峰绝顶处方圆丈余，中间有香砂井，置身峰顶，遥望四方，千峰竞秀、万壑生烟，在万里晴空时，可东望天目山，西望庐山，北望九华山。雨后，纵观八面云海，更为壮观。

从莲花峰下山，过龟蛇二石、百步云梯，穿过鳌鱼洞，便来到鳌鱼峰，此峰高1780米。下鳌鱼峰便是天海，天海位于黄山前、后、东、西海之中，为黄山之中心位置。在这1750米的高山盆地中，生长着众多国内外罕见的植物物种，黄山园林部门利用天海独特的气候条件，创建了天海高山植物园。

2. 北海景区

北海景区是黄山景区的腹地，在光明顶与始信峰、狮子峰、白鹅峰之间，东连云谷景区，南接玉屏景区，北近松谷景区，是一片海拔1600米左右的高山开阔地带，面积1316公顷。北海景区以峰为体，汇集了峰、石、矼、坞、台和松、云等奇景，天工的奇妙布局，琉璃色彩变幻，构成一幅幅伟、奇、幻、险的天然画卷，是黄山的风景窗。狮子峰、清凉台、猴子观海、仙人背宝、梦笔生花、飞来石、十八罗汉朝南海等景观令游人目不暇接。北海群峰荟萃，石门峰、贡阳山都属海拔1800米以上的高峰，形如屏障，隔开南北。海拔1690米的狮子峰头东尾西地横卧在景区之中。狮子峰上的清凉台是观赏云海和日出的最佳之处。始信峰虽不如天都、莲花峰高，也不在36大峰之列，但雄踞险壑，竖立如削，三面临壑，悬崖千丈，峰顶拳拳之地，近揽远眺，面面受奇，古有"黄山之雄甲宇内，幽秀灵齐聚后海"之句，更有"始信黄山天下奇"之誉。

3. 温泉景区

黄山温泉景区古称桃源仙境，为黄山旅游的接待中心之一。景区以揽胜桥为中心向四周辐射，桃花溪和逍遥溪贯穿其中，中心海拔高度在650米左右。主要接待宾馆包括桃源宾馆、温泉酒店、黄山宾馆等。

4. 白云景区

黄山白云景区位于黄山西部，面积1655公顷，南起云门溪上的续古桥，北至伏牛岭，东起云际、石人二峰，西至双河口畔。景区以钓桥庵为中心，钓桥庵位于石人峰下，白云、白门两溪汇合处，海拔610米。钓桥庵又名白云庵，明前为道院，清康熙间改为佛庵，后沿用地名至今。庵周围景致清幽，峰峦叠嶂，松石争奇，层竹铺翠，溪流环绕。白云景区集松、石、泉于一体，独具黄山山水之胜。白云溪水流充沛，瀑潭相接，溪畔有悬瀑10余处，潺潺流水，如同琴音；雨后水涌，急流奔腾，声震山谷；山水进泻，形成飞瀑，悬垂如练，溅珠喷玉。

5. 松谷景区

黄山素有"前山险,后山秀"之说,后山就是指黄山北大门的松谷景区。松谷景区位于黄山北坡,是狮子峰、骆驼峰、书箱峰、宝塔峰之间的山谷合称。游客抵达黄山的北大门——太平后,选择从北大门芙蓉岭进山是最佳的游览方案。由芙蓉岭徒步上山,需登爬6500余级石阶,海拔高差1100米,一路千峰竞秀,万壑争奇,巧石名潭尤为佳妙。游览松谷景区可以观赏到芙蓉峰、丹霞峰、松林峰、双笋峰等著名的山峰,仙人观海、仙人铺路、老虎驮羊、关公挡曹、卧虎石等怪石巧石,翡翠池、五龙潭等水景,芙蓉居、松谷禅林等古建筑。

6. 云谷景区

云谷景区位于黄山东部,海拔高度890米,是一处地势较低、略显开阔的谷地。宋代丞相程元凤曾在此处读书,故名丞相源。明代文士傅严漫游至此,应掷钵禅僧之求,手书"云谷"二字,此后禅院改名"云谷寺"。云谷景区主要景点有云谷山庄、古树、怪石、"九龙瀑"和"百丈泉"。

三、四绝三瀑

1. 黄山"四绝"

(1) 奇松。黄山延绵数百里,千峰万壑,比比皆松。黄山松分布于海拔800米以上高山,以石为母,顽强地扎根于巨岩裂隙。黄山松针叶粗短,

苍翠浓密，干曲枝虬，千姿百态。或倚岸挺拔，或独立峰巅，或倒悬绝壁，或冠平如盖，或尖削似剑。有的循崖度壑，绕石而过；有的穿罅穴缝，破石而出。忽悬、忽横、忽卧、忽起，"无树非松，无石不松，无松不奇"。

黄山松是由黄山独特地貌、气候而形成的中国松树的一种变体。黄山松一般生长在海拔800米以上的地方，通常是黄山北坡在1500~1700米处，南坡在1000~1600米处。黄山松的千姿百态和黄山自然环境有着很大的关系。黄山松的种子能够被风送到花岗岩的裂缝中去，以无坚不摧、有缝即入的钻劲，在那里发芽、生根、成长。著名的黄山松有迎客松、送客松、探海松、蒲团松、黑虎松、卧龙松、麒麟松、连理松、竖琴松、龙爪松——这就是黄山十大名松。每棵都独具美丽、优雅的风格。

（2）怪石。黄山"四绝"的怪石，以奇取胜，以多著称。已被命名的怪石有120多处。其形态可谓千奇百怪，令人叫绝。似人似物，似鸟似兽，情态各异，形象逼真。黄山怪石从不同的位置，在不同的天气观看情趣迥异，可谓"横看成岭侧成峰，远近高低各不同"。其分布可谓遍及峰壑巅坡，或兀立峰顶，或戏逗坡缘，或与松结伴，构成一幅幅天然山石画卷。黄山石"怪"就怪在从不同角度看，就有不同的形状。黄山峰海，无处不石、无石不松、无松不奇。奇松怪石，往往相映成趣，如位于北海的梦笔生花以及"喜鹊登梅"（仙人指路）、老僧采药、苏武牧羊、飞来石、猴子望太平（猴子观海）等。

（3）云海。自古黄山云成海，是云雾之乡，以峰为体，以云为衣，其瑰丽壮观的"云海"以美、胜、奇、幻享誉古今，一年四季皆可观，尤以冬季景最佳。依云海分布方位，全山有东海、南海、西海、北海和天海，而登莲花峰、天都峰、光明顶则可尽收诸海于眼底。

大凡高山，都可见到云海，但是黄山的云海有其特色，奇峰怪石古松隐现云海之中，更增加了美感。黄山一年之中有云雾的天气达200多天，水气升腾或雨后雾气未消，就会形成云海，波澜壮阔，一望无边。黄山大小山峰、

千沟万壑都淹没在云涛雪浪里,天都峰、光明顶也就成了浩瀚云海中的孤岛。云海日出、日落,万道霞光,绚丽缤纷。红树铺云,成片的红叶浮在云海之上,这是黄山深秋罕见的奇景。北海双剪峰,当云海经过时为两侧的山峰约束,从两峰之间流出,向下倾泻,如大河奔腾,又似白色的壶口瀑布,轻柔与静谧之中可以感受到暗流涌动和奔流不息的力量,是黄山的又一奇景。玉屏楼观南海,清凉台望北海,排云亭看西海,白鹅岭赏东海,鳌鱼峰眺天海。由于山谷地形的原因,有时西海云遮雾罩,白鹅岭上却青烟缥缈,道道金光染出层层彩叶,北海竟晴空万里,人们为云海美景而上下奔波,谓之"赶海"。

(4)温泉。黄山"四绝"之一的温泉(古称汤泉),源出海拔850米的紫云峰下,水质以含重碳酸为主,可饮可浴。传说轩辕黄帝就是在此沐浴七七四十九日得返老还童,羽化飞升的,故又被誉之为"灵泉"。

黄山温泉由紫云峰下喷涌而出,与桃花峰隔溪相望,是经游黄山大门进入黄山的第一站。温泉每天的出水量约400吨,常年不息,水温常年在42度左右,属高山温泉。黄山温泉对消化、神经、心血管、新陈代谢等系统的某些病症,尤其是皮肤病,均有一定的功效。

2. 黄山"三瀑"

"人字瀑""百丈泉"和"九龙瀑"称为黄山三大名瀑。人字瀑古名飞雨泉,在紫石、朱砂两峰之间流出,危岩百丈,石挺岩腹,清泉分左右走壁下泻,成"人"字形瀑布,最佳观赏地点在温泉区的"观瀑楼"。九龙瀑源于天都、玉屏、炼丹、

仙掌诸峰，自罗汉峰与香炉峰之间分九叠倾泻而下，每叠有一潭，称九龙潭，是黄山最为壮丽的瀑布。百丈瀑在黄山青潭、紫云峰之间，顺千尺悬崖而降，形成百丈瀑布。近有百丈台，台前建有观瀑亭。

第五节　后山花园——中国香山

香山公园位于北京西北郊小西山山脉东麓，距城20千米，占地160公顷，是一座著名的具有皇家园林特色的大型山林公园。香山海拔557米，最高峰顶有一块巨大的乳峰石，形状像香炉，晨昏之际，云雾缭绕，远远望去，犹如炉中香烟袅袅上升，故名香炉山，简称香山。香山早在1186年就出现了人文景观，香山寺曾为京西寺庙之冠。清代，乾隆皇帝曾在此大兴土木建成静宜园二十八景。1949年后陆续修复了大部分名胜，香山公园文物古迹丰富珍贵，亭台楼阁似星辰散布山林之间。香山公园于1993年至今被评为首都文明单位，2001年被国家旅游局评为AAAA景区，2002年被评为首批北京市精品公园，2004年通过ISO9001国际质量管理体系和ISO14001国际环境管理体系认证。2012年10月12日，在第24届北京香山红叶文化节开幕式上，香山被授予"世界名山"称号。

一、历史变迁

香山历史源远流长，自晋代葛洪的丹井，始有记载。金代的金世宗、章宗两朝皇帝营建香山，为其营建的寺庙赐名"大永安寺"。元代皇庆元年（1312年），仁宗帝赐钞万锭，重修香山大永安寺，并更名为"甘露寺"；文宗至顺二年（1331年），耶律楚材的后裔耶律阿勒弥创建碧云庵，形成"香山八景、碧云十景"。明代英宗正统六年（1441年），司礼太监范宏出资七十余万，"捐赀市材，命工重建，殿堂、楼阁、廊庑、像设，焕然一新，规制宏丽，蔚为巨刹。事闻，乃赐额永安禅寺"。清代乾隆帝在旧行宫的基础上进行大规模扩建，仅用九个月的时间就在香山建成大大小小的园林八十余处，其中乾隆帝钦题并赋诗二十八处，成为明噪京城的二十八景，乾隆帝赐名"静宜园"。1860年，英法联军将包括静宜园在内的三山五园内的大量珍物劫掠一空，建筑几乎全部焚毁。1925年3月12日，伟大的民主革命先行者孙中山在京逝世后，曾在香山碧云寺内停灵长达四年之久。移灵南京紫金山后，在这里设孙中山的纪念堂和衣冠冢，供人瞻仰。1956年，香山作为人民公园正式对公众开放，为首批北京市精品公园。

二、四季风光

香山公园地势高峻，峰峦叠翠，泉沛林茂。主峰香炉峰（俗称鬼见愁）海拔557米。园内各类树木26万余株，仅古树名木就达5800多株，约占北京城区的四分之一，森林覆盖率高达98%，近年被有关部门测定为北京负氧离子最高的地区之一。公园内人与自然和谐相处，鸟啼虫鸣，松鼠嬉闹于沟壑林间。这里春日繁花似锦、夏时凉爽宜人、冬来银装素裹。特别是香山红叶最是闻名。每逢霜秋，遍山黄栌，如火如荼，瑰丽无比。

春到香山，山上残雪斑驳，小草吐翠，柳絮轻扬，春信匆匆。盛夏的香山，古木荫森，泉溪流畅，芳草鲜美，踏入香山宫门，凉风扑面，暑气皆消。无论是在林荫道上，还是在任何一处景点观赏，或是在池泉旁、亭台上憩息，都会倍觉凉意侵身，清爽怡神，如入清凉世界。香山秋色，瑰奇绚丽，松柏林中点缀些枫树栾树，红绿相间，色彩斑斓。香山红叶以叶形如卵的黄栌最负盛名。遍布南山的黄栌圆叶，经霜变红，霜重色愈浓，每临秋季，层林尽染，辉映云霞。漫山红遍，如火如荼，为中外旅游者所向往。冬天，野草枯黄，松柏变暗，寒泉凝成雾霭，山风凛冽，寒冬肃杀，百景凋零，唯雪覆殿阁，金银相辉，姿态万千，又是一幅充满诗情画意的奇观。雪后玉峰耸列，琼峦凝素，瑞雪映衬寺院红墙分外妖娆，松柏傲雪，犹见劲节。

三、旅游景点

1. 香山寺

香山寺遗址即金大定二十六年（1186年）所建之大永安寺，原为金代行宫。据记载原有五层大殿，前有石坊、山门、钟鼓楼、城垣，红墙碧瓦掩映在苍松翠柏之中，为香山二十八景之一。经英法联军和八国联军两次浩劫之后，只剩下正殿前的石屏、石碑和石台阶等为数不多的几件不怕火燹的石头制品了。石屏本身有较高的艺术价值，正面中间是《金刚经》，左为《心经》，右为《观音经》，背面是燃灯、观音、普贤像。山门内有汉、满、蒙、藏四种文字的石碑，内容是乾隆书的《娑罗树歌》。山门外有几处著名古迹：（1）听法松：寺门两侧，有两株遒劲挺拔、枝叶繁茂的古松，状如听法。（2）金鸡叫：在听法松下甬路中心的方砖上跺几脚，可听到铮铮之声，犹如金鸡啼鸣。（3）知乐濠：山门前石桥下有方池，上有汉白玉雕栏，池南侧有龙头，泉水流出，名知乐濠。（4）来青轩：该轩建在依崖叠石之上，登轩四望，青翠万状，故名来青。明万历二十八年（1600年），万历皇帝祭陵归来，见此轩之匾额后，嫌小，遂书"来青轩"三个大字。寺内还有护驾松、丹井等古迹。

2. 香炉峰

香山公园最高处海拔557米，因其地势陡峭，登攀困难而俗称"鬼见愁"。香山公园先后在顶峰建起三个有特色的亭子："重阳阁"意在九九重阳登之可望京城；"踏云亭"因秋雨后、春雨前缕缕云丝穿行亭内外，犹如踏云一般而得名；"紫烟亭"因晨夕之际的薄雾淡淡如紫色云霭，时隐时现，颇有日照香炉生紫烟的味道而得名。站在白玉观景台上，远处昆明湖宛如一盆清水，各式建筑星罗棋布，使游人对北京城有全新的认识。

3. 碧云寺

西山风景区中最精美的一座古刹。这座寺院创建于元代至顺二年（1331年），距今已有600多年的历史了，当时称为碧云庵。明代正德年间（1514年），太监于经在寺后山上修建了生圹，改名为碧云寺。明天启年间，魏忠贤大加扩修碧云寺。清康熙四十年江南巡视张瑗得知碧云寺是逆臣魏忠贤之生圹而铲平。清乾隆十三年（1748年）大加扩建，在寺后建起了一座印度式的金刚宝座塔，在寺右部仿杭州净慈寺罗汉堂修建了碧云寺罗汉堂，形成轴线对称的格局，奠定了碧云寺今日规模。碧云寺依山势而建，它的建筑逐层升起，六进院落自成格局。寺院既保留了明代佛寺的禅宗特点，又吸收和发展了佛教迷宗的建筑风格。山门上有蓝地金字匾一面，上用汉、蒙、满、藏四种文字书写"碧云寺"，为乾隆手书。寺门两旁石狮峙立，雕琢精细，是明代留下的较好的石狮之一。文化大革命时期碧云寺也遭不幸，大部分雕像毁于一旦。近年来，这座古刹进行了修整油饰，碧云寺重新焕发了生机。

4. 孙中山纪念堂

孙中山纪念堂坐落在香山碧云寺内，纪念堂内正中安放着中国国民党中央委员会暨全国各地中山学校敬献的中山先生汉白玉全身塑像，左右墙壁上镶嵌着用汉白玉雕刻的孙中山先生所写的《致苏联遗书》，正厅西北隅陈列着1925年3月30日苏联人民送来的玻璃盖钢棺，堂内还陈列着孙中山先生的遗墨、遗著。

为纪念中山先生遗体暂厝之地，时"国民政府"在普明妙觉殿立"总理纪念堂"，在金刚宝座塔石券门石塔立"总理衣冠冢"。新中国成立以后，人民政府重修碧云寺后复命名为"孙中山纪念堂"（宋庆龄题写）和"孙中山先生衣冠冢"，以供后人瞻仰。

5. 香山红叶

香山红叶主要有8个科涉及14个树种，总株数达10万余株，甚为壮观。香山红叶树种很多，如五角枫、三角枫、鸡爪枫、柿树等，面积最大的红叶树种是黄栌，有近10万株。这些红叶树种叶子里含有大量的叶绿素、叶黄素、类胡萝卜素、胡萝卜素、花青素，春夏两季叶绿素进行光合作用，使叶子呈现绿色；霜秋季节，天气变冷，昼夜温差变化增大，叶绿素合成受阻，

逐渐破坏消失,而类胡萝卜素、胡萝卜素、花青素成分增多,使叶子呈现红黄、橙红等美丽色彩。其中以种植最悠久的黄栌最能代表北京香山,看万山红遍、层林尽染,五角枫叶在秋阳中红得纯粹热烈,黄色蓝色白色紫色的花海、银白色的树干、金黄色的树叶,炫目的景色,让人恍若置身于仙境之中。

从时间上,香山红叶大致分三个时段,分别有着不同的意境。第一阶段看色彩斑斓:由10月中旬到下旬,满园植物绿、黄、红色相间,远看上去仿佛一幅山林画卷,让人感受到植物景观带来的美轮美奂。第二阶段看层林尽染:由10月下旬到11月初,初霜过后,气温走低,叶色变得更加浓艳,满山红叶,层林尽染,感受金秋红叶的壮美景色,香山红叶的大气磅礴之势淋漓尽现。第三阶段看万叶飘丹:由11月初到11月中旬,随着气温持续走低,秋风吹来,红叶附着力逐渐降低,香山红叶随风飘散,落英缤纷,满地红叶,欣赏的是一种惜别的凄美。不同阶段游客看到的是不同的香山红叶之美,游客可根据自己的喜好来选择观赏。从位置上,最早变色的红叶在森玉笏和南山山坡;到中期,最理想的观赏点是索道上和北山沿线;到11月,满山红叶飘落,但静翠湖和沟谷里依然会有些元宝枫依恋着北京的深秋。从1989年至今,香山公园连续20余年举办以观红叶为主题的红叶文化节。

6. 双清别墅

香山寺东南半山坡上,有一处别致清静的庭院,即双清别墅。这是香山公园著名的红色旅游景点。其前身是静宜园二十八景之一的栖云楼。院内两道清泉,常年流水不息,一股流向知乐濠,一股流向静翠湖,此即"双清"二字之缘由。院内池旁有八角亭及参天银杏树。1917年河北省大水,督办熊希龄办香山慈幼局,在此建别墅,始称双清别墅。1949年3月25日,毛主席随党中央由河北平山县西柏坡来北平,住在此处。双清别墅是中共中央和毛泽东迁驻北平最早居住和办公的地方,是党中央指挥人民解放军向全国进军和筹建新中国的指挥部。1998年经北京市政府和北京市文物局批准,双清别墅被列入北京市博物馆行列。2009年晋升为全国爱国主义教育基地。

第六节　台湾圣山——中国玉山

中国台湾玉山，位于台湾中部，北起三貂角，南接屏东平原（台湾南部的屏东县周围），长约 300 千米。玉山主峰位于北回归线以北 2.3 千米，海拔 3952 米，不仅为台湾岛最高山峰，也为中国东部最高峰。玉山也被称为中国十大名山之一。

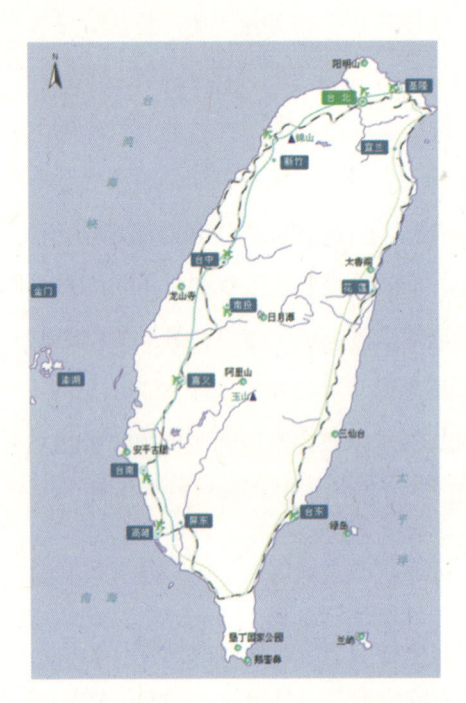

玉山国家公园为我国台湾省面积第二大的国家公园（仅次于东沙环礁国家公园），横跨南投、嘉义、花莲及高雄四县，总面积约达 105490 公顷，是典型的亚热带高山地质，其地形以高山及河谷为主。在台湾百岳中，玉山与雪山、秀姑峦山、南湖大山、北大武山合称"五岳"，为台湾最具代表性的五座高山。玉山山容气势磅礴，雄踞一方，是一座巍峨挺拔、耸入云霄的高峰，因其峰顶冬季积雪远望如玉而得名，"玉山积雪"因而成为台湾八景之一。1985 年 4 月 10 日，玉山群峰周边划入新成立的玉山国家公园。玉山是布农族与邹族共同的圣山，也是当代台湾的象征之一，被誉为"心清如玉，义重如山"。

玉山位置示意图

台湾山脉与喜马拉雅山脉一样，都是第三纪才隆起成为高山的，是中国最年轻的山脉之一。玉山位于台湾地壳上升到轴线经过的地方，山体构造相当复杂，断层很多，其东西两侧各有一条大的构造线分别与中央山脉和阿里山山脉相邻。玉山是水成岩山脉，地貌奇特，地层褶曲，使峰顶形似波涛，加上风雨侵蚀，砂岩、页岩崎岖急斜，容貌与一般山景迥然不同。突兀峥嵘，高插云天，四季积雪不化，成为四季常绿的台湾岛上的奇异景观。

围绕玉山主峰,周围还有东、西、南、北四峰,构成雄伟的玉山群峰,山峰景致孤峭绮丽,更有雪景、云海、高山彩云等壮丽景色。秀姑峦山为中央山脉最高峰,海拔3860米,与玉山主峰相对峙。山麓秀姑平原布满香清、箭竹、白枯木和高山杜鹃,此山脉上的塔芬山,山势均匀,状如金字塔,南侧有两座高山湖泊,名为塔芬池。次于玉山主峰和秀姑峦山的马博拉斯山、玉山东峰、新康山和玉山南峰,为台湾"十峻"中的四峻。所有这些山脉除了蕴含许多丰富的地理景观外,也造化了许多珍贵的生态环境。

一、生态玉山

玉山公园内蕴藏了丰富的生态资源。其原始林相和稀有野生物,随着地形、地质、气候的递变,呈现多样貌,为台湾地区最完整的生态环境。复杂的地形和气候条件,造成了繁多的植物类型。从山麓到山顶,呈现出热带、亚热带、温带、寒带等不同地带的植被景观。特别是它的高山植物,更是丰富多彩,独具特色,仅以玉山命名的高山植物就有20多种,玉山圆柏是台湾森林中生长海拔最高的一种针叶树,常形成巨木群。但在玉山风口及北峰一带,因风力强劲,使其树干无法直立生长,而形成低矮的灌木。一大片一大片地匍匐连绵数十里,蔚为高山植物之奇观。玉山杜鹃花朵硕大、

洁白,在每年的5—6月间盛开,满山满谷的杜鹃花,把高山装扮得犹如仙境。在玉山峰顶及风口一带,每年7—9月,还生长着一种名叫高山荠的十字花科植物,微小的植物体散布于岩屑地上,为玉山特有的植物,也是台湾岛上生长点最高的一种植物。

据统计,玉山有28种哺乳动物,占全台湾所有哺乳动物的二分之一。其中高山白腹鼠等8种为台湾特有种,台湾鳞鲤、台湾黑熊、梅花鹿3种为濒临绝种的动物。山椒鱼是冰河时期遗留的生物,目前只生存于高海拔山区,属于珍稀生物。

二、特色玉山

云瀑、日出、林涛是玉山的美景"三绝"。玉山峰顶常常云遮雾罩,白云弥漫山顶,或散或簇,千变万化,有时聚集成群宛如瀑布,故称之为云瀑。在玉山各个不同的位置欣赏日出,看那七彩云影、巨轮遥升、万道金光,蔽于高峰之上,也是艳丽绝伦,堪称奇观。玉山从山麓直到3600米左右的地带,分布着大片的森林,微风吹来,飒飒有声,如遇大雨,则树林哗哗,山谷隆隆,响声彻耳,令人惊叹不已。此外,玉山还有三大特点:

第一个特点是"高"。峻岭连绵是玉山公园最大的特色,公园内3000米以上、列名"台湾百岳"的山峰共有30座。居中的玉山主峰高达3952米,与南、西、北四座高峰合称为"五岳朝天"。玉山可称得上万山之王,峨眉仅及其肩,泰山只及其半,东南万山臣伏足下。

第二个特点是"雪"。玉山高耸云天,气温很低,长年有霜,其主峰曾有零下17.5摄氏度的气温记录。每年10月,山上就开始下雪,直到次年3月才止。在夏季,山顶背阴处仍有积雪,成为世间罕见的"热带雪山"奇观,而"玉山积雪"也因此列入"台湾八景"。

第三个特点是"险"。五峰之间,乱山重叠,断崖壁立,深壑纵横,枯林迷乱，若非攀登好手，绝难到达峰巅。

三、旅游玉山

玉山国家公园规划的游憩点及设立的游客中心为新中横公路的塔塔加游客中心、南横公路的梅山游客中心与东部地区的玉里、南安游客中心，此三处是一般游客了解玉山国家公园全貌的最佳去处。登山活动则集中于玉山山区，八通关古道的东埔至八通关，南安至瓦拉米的东西两出口，南横公路的关山、塔关山、关山岭山和向阳山。玉山景区分为四大区：

西北园区位于玉山园区西北侧，包括新中横公路、塔塔加、东埔、观高、八通关、玉山主峰及楠溪林道等地区。有玉山主峰、塔塔加分水岭、楠梓仙溪、金门洞断崖、父子断崖、八通关分水岭等地理地形景观；有白木林景观、冷杉、铁杉、八通关草原等原始林景观及高山寒原植物景观；有玉山西峰山神庙、北峰顶的中央气象局玉山气象站、八通关古道及台湾布农族聚落等人文景观。

南部园区位于玉山园区西南部，包括南横公路沿线、梅山—天池—中之关—垭口—南横三山及关山等地区。有南横三山及南台首岳——关山之高山地形景观及荖浓溪河谷景观；南横公路桧谷地区之桧木林景观；帝雉、

蓝腹鹇等珍贵鸟类及其他哺乳类动物景观；天池高山湖泊景观；关山越岭古道及梅山村布农部落等人文景观。

东部园区位于玉山园区东南侧，包括南安、山风、瓦拉米、大分及新康山等地区。

高山核心区位于玉山园区东北部及中央地带，包括大水窟、秀姑峦山、马博拉斯山、塔芬山、马西山等地区。

第七节　东瀛圣岳——日本富士山

一、山岳富士

富士山为日本第一高峰，海拔 3775.63 米，也是世界上最大的活火山之一。富士山横跨静冈县和山梨县，接近太平洋岸，离东京约 80 千米。这座山的名字经常在日本的传统诗歌"和歌"中出现，希世灵彦（1404—1488 年）在《题富士山》中写道："富士峰高宇宙间，崔嵬岂独冠东关；唯应白日青天好，雪里看山不识山。"富士山闻名于世，是日本人引以为傲的民族象征，被日本人民誉为"圣岳"。

富士名称源于虾夷语，现意为"永生"，原发音来自日本少数民族阿伊努族的语言，意思是"火之山"或"火神"。富士山山体呈优美的圆锥形，山体高耸入云，山巅白雪皑皑，放眼望去，好似一把悬空倒挂的扇子，日本诗人曾用"玉扇倒悬东海天""富士白雪映朝阳"等诗句赞美它，因此也有"玉扇"之称。富士山山体位于本州岛上富士断裂层的山地构造上，山顶有个很大的火山口，状如钵盂，日本人称其为"御钵"，直径约 800 米，深约 200 米；山底直径约 40 千米，是世界最大的圆锥山体，可谓"万古天风吹不断，青空一朵玉芙蓉"。山顶终年积雪，山色优美。2013 年 6 月 22 日，第 37 届世界遗产大会批准将富士山列入联合国教科文组织《世界遗产名录》。

1. 山体变迁

作为日本自然美景的最重要象征，富士山是距今约一万年前，过去曾为岛屿的伊豆半岛，由于地壳变动而与本州岛激烈互撞挤压时所隆起形成的。从形状上来说，属于标准的锥状火山，具有独特的优美轮廓。富士山

在山体形成过程中，大致可以分为四个阶段：先小御岳，小御岳，古富士，新富士。它的主体部分由熔岩流、火山灰和火山沙砾堆积形成，共有八峰，剑锋是它的最高峰，由于八峰的分布同莲花的八片花瓣相似，故有"八瓣芙蓉"之美誉。

2. 潜在威胁的火山活动

富士山是一座活火山，历史上有记载的第一次爆发是在公元800年，而最近的一次则是在1707年，当时的剧烈喷发让100多千米外的江户（即今天的东京）都笼上了一层厚厚的火山灰，时间持续长达两周，城市完全被烟土笼罩，上空火山灰厚达5厘米，喷出的岩浆曾淹没了两座较老的火山。2000年10月，山下10千米深处开始发生轻微的震颤，并持续八个月之久。根据日本地球科学和灾难预防研究所（NIED）的数据，在震动的高峰期，也就是2001年4月，一个月之内发生了100次地震，这一数字远远高于此前20年里的年平均值15次。目前，富士山不断发现山体出现异变河口湖的湖水减少，山体出现300米长的裂缝，一部分地区地下水大量涌喷，让当地人感到不安。如果出现岩浆阔展活动，会出现部分地区坍塌，富士山的文化意蕴也将随之瓦解。

3. 风景如画的生态环境

富士山的北麓有山中湖、河口湖、西湖、精进湖和本栖湖富士五湖。山中湖最大，面积为6.75平方千米，湖畔有许多运动设施，可以打网球、滑水、垂钓、露营和划船等。河口湖是五湖中开发最早的，这里交通十分便利，已成为五湖观光的中心。湖中的鹈岛是五湖中唯一的岛屿，岛上有一专门保佑孕妇安产的神社。湖上还有长达1260米的跨湖大桥。河口湖中所映的富士山倒影，被称作富士山奇景之一。

富士山的南麓是一片辽阔的高原地带，夏季绿草如茵，为牛羊成群的观光牧场。山的西南麓有著名的白系瀑布和音止瀑布。白系瀑布落差26米，从岩壁上分成十余条细流，似无数白练自空而降，形成一个宽130多米的雨帘，颇为壮观。音止瀑布则似一根巨柱从高处冲击而下，声如雷鸣，震天动地。富士山也称得上是一座天然植物园，山上的各种植物多达2000余种，垂直分布明显，海拔500米以下为亚热带常绿林，500~2000米为温带落叶阔叶林，2000~2600米为寒温带针叶林，2600米以上为高山矮曲林带。每年都可以在山体附近看到130多种野生鸟类，各种动物和昆虫也很常见，不过高原特有的动物分布变化不很明显。

二、神化富士

富士山作为日本第一高峰，被视为艺术创作灵感源泉和朝圣地，同时也拥有数不清的传说与不解之谜。主要体现在以下三个方面：和日本国土以及民族起源有关的缘起神话；和佛教有关的因缘神话；和富士山名称由来有关的不死仙山神话。

1. 富士传说

富士山作为日本民族的象征而成为文学、美术创作的题材。日本简练的和歌、俳句中，赞美富士山的佳作俯拾皆是，对其赏不够、写不完、思不尽。日本最古的和歌集《万叶集》就记载了发生在富士山的动人故事。奈良初期的宫廷歌人，号称三十六歌仙之一的山部赤人，赞美富士山"巍巍一秀峰，举目趣无穷"。江户前期诗人松尾芭蕉有诗赞美富士山"云雾萦峦时，须臾绘百景"。在日语中，"富士"与"不尽""不死""不仁"等汉字的读音相近。大概"富士山"这个名字与历史传说都有着直接的关系。

2. 徐福化鹤

在日本，有关徐福的遗迹和传说，其范围北起青森，南到九州，几乎遍及全日本。据说，当年秦始皇派徐福率童男童女各五百人到蓬莱园的不二山（即富士山，意为"唯一"的意思，日语发音和"富士"相同）寻长生之物。在灵山深处，他们发现一种依靠山雾生长的名为"浜梨"的植物（即玫瑰），它结出红色果实，具有延年益寿的作用，徐福为之大喜。可惜，此时秦始皇已经去世。于是，他自己吃了长生不老药，在环境优美的山麓定居下来，传播中国的文化。若干年以后，徐福死去，变成一只翱翔在富士山上空的鹤，到元禄年间（1688—1704年），鹤也死去，落在附近的福源寺内。当地富士山人还在寺内修建了"鹤塚"，祭祀它的神灵。至今还有人将富士山附近唤作"鹤都"，而这个故事也一直在日本人民中广泛流传。

3. 富士信仰

日本人自古崇拜富士山，把富士山尊奉为"富岳""灵峰"，认为山里居住着镇守日本的众多神明，一个民族的信仰便出现在那块离天很近的地

方。对山的崇拜在日本文化史上形成由来已久的宗教心理——"富士信仰"。中世的信仰范围遍布关东（东京都、神奈川及千叶、玉、茨城、群马、栃木县）和东海道地方（静冈、爱知、三重县及岐阜县南部）。近世初期，宗教家长谷川角行（1541—1645年）苦心孤诣，系统整理教义，且大力鼓吹之，庶民信徒从者如云，聚成一大宗教集团——"富士讲"。他们在富士山山顶建庄严神社，信徒成群结队，身穿白褂，手拄铃木杖，脚步踏清响，敬虔地夜登晨至，顶礼膜拜。富士山山顶设有富士山本宫浅间大社，用于祭祀富士山的神灵。既是宗教信徒的朝圣之地。至今，也是游人游踪常到之地，参拜行列仍为富士山夏季风情一景。

三、休闲富士

1. 登山活动

自古以来，日本人就把富士山看作"灵峰"，认为它是"镇守"日本之山，因而也就成为人们憧憬和信仰的对象。在日本广为流传"没登过富士山的人是无知者"之说。日本人登富士山始于平安时代（794—1192年）中期，日本人对富士山的信仰与儒教结合起来后，登山的人数有所增加，并扩大到许多地区。进入江户时代（1603—1867年），登富士山成了许多江户人一生当中必定要完成的一件大事。明治维新（1868—1912年）时期，攀登富士山是一项非常隆重的宗教仪式，山上气候变化无常，自然界与生物界各种神秘现象造成人们对山岳的敬仰与崇拜，人们登山热情很高，很多人以多次登顶为荣。

每年9月中旬到10月中旬富士山开始积雪，一直要到第二年6月融化，有时候7月中旬仍旧会有残雪。每年的七八月份是攀登富士山的最佳季节，其他季节封山。而8月份台风数量增多，因此，推荐7月中旬登山最为适宜。从富士山山脚到山顶，有吉田口、须走口、御殿场口和富士宫口4条登山路线，有10个停歇点。大多数人在第5个停歇点就返回，汽车可达第5个停歇点，再从这里至山顶需要4个小时。

2. 山顶观日出

登山顶观日出,这是每名攀登富士山的游人最美好的愿望。日本人将看日出叫作看"御来光"。在山腰上住宿的登山者需要凌晨4时左右起床,沿着山间蜿蜒的小径攀上顶峰,才可观看日出。日出之前,凭栏远眺,静静的群山、滚滚的白云,宛如一幅素雅的水墨画。透过浩渺的云海,脚下的城市里点点灯火在闪耀,仿佛从仙界看到了人间。随着第一道富士山晨光冉冉升起,东方渐渐出现灿若绸缎的彩霞,红日驱赶着薄薄云雾,满山遍野朝晖尽染,顿时又变得色彩斑斓、异彩纷呈,短短一刹那,富士山奇景一览无余。

3. 山中观云海

风云变幻莫测,也是富士山的一大特色。从登山到下山这短短十几个小时中,往往就会忽而碧空无云、风和日丽,忽而浓雾弥漫,甚至骤然间下起豆粒般的大雨。山上山下气温相差一二十摄氏度。这是由于富士山特殊的地理环境所造成的。当地人根据多年的经验,往往从观察富士山山顶的"笠状云"变化来预测当地的天气。笠状云是由于水蒸气和大气一起越过山顶时,突然遇到冷气变成云粒,加上风向而形成的。人们总结出"笠云环山巅,天晴;笠云向上升,天晴;笠云像鸡冠,下雨;笠云沿山下,刮风;笠云卷山头,风雨;笠云像横线,下雨;笠云像个帽,下雨"的气象规律。

4. 欣赏高山湖泊群

富士山山顶有一巨大火山湖,直径约800米,深约200米。在富士山北麓有富士五湖,从东向西分别为山中湖、河口湖、西湖、精进湖和本栖湖。在山中湖东南的忍野村,有涌池、镜池等8个池塘,总称"忍野八海",与山中湖相通。西湖岸边有富岳风穴、青木原树海、红叶台、鸣泽冰穴、足和田山等风景区。这些湖泊海拔都在820米以上,湖光山色交相辉映,是富士山著名的风景旅游区。

第八节　东方仙境——韩国雪岳山

雪岳山（又名雪狱山），位于韩国东海岸江原道东草的西南方，朝鲜半岛东部太白山脉最高峰，海拔1708米。由于雪岳山的主峰大青峰一年有5~6个月积雪，长年不化，岩石是像雪一样的白色，所以被称为雪岳。雪岳山是金刚山的延续，有"南金刚"之称，被公认为是韩国最著名的自然景观。雪岳山国立公园于1965年11月被指定为天然纪念物保护区，又在1973年12月被设为公园保护区，占地大约375平方千米，是第二大国家公园。同时，因为雪岳山保有500多种野生动物及1000多种稀有动物，1982年8月被联合国教科文组织指定为"韩国唯一的植物保存地区"，其中以枫叶最为著名。

一、美丽景观

雪岳山作为韩国代表性的山岳景观，拥有各种奇岩怪石，以恐龙脊背、巫山岩、龙牙长城等为中心形成奇观，是韩国最具岩石景观美的国立公园。溪谷景观以十二仙女汤、千佛洞、百潭为中心，众多的瀑布和大小不一的沼、潭与岩石景观相映成趣，形成美轮美奂的自然景观。从地质学角度来看，雪岳山雄伟的山峰和多样的景观主要是由于大规模花岗岩的侵入形成了壮观、广阔的景观的基本框架；因岩石和节理引起的差异风化形成了包括险峻地形在内的奇岩怪石等景观。花岗岩山峰如蔚山岩，显示出较平坦、广阔和偏圆的地形；而斑岩类却形成了崎岖不平和嶙峋突兀的景观。雪岳山山顶上有丰富的高山植物群落，这里不但是北方系植物的南限地带，同时也是南方系植物的北限地带。

自古以来，接近雪岳山都是不太容易的，因此，雪岳山的文化资源在韩国的国立公园中是比较少的，主要文化资源有新兴寺、百潭寺、凤顶庵、五岁庵等。

二、特色景点

雪岳山地跨江原道束草市、麟蹄郡、高城郡、襄阳郡等四个市郡。以最高峰大青峰为中心，东面（束草市、高城郡、襄阳郡）称外雪岳，西面（麟蹄郡）为内雪岳，外雪岳又分北、南外雪岳。进入外雪岳，可以从雪岳洞的入口物淄进入，也可经束草尺山温泉后越过牧牛斋山岭进入。千佛洞溪谷是从大青峰流下的泉水向北流入物淄时而形成，其中卧仙、飞仙台、金刚窟、文殊潭、五连瀑布、阳瀑布、阴瀑布、天堂瀑布等组成了雪岳山最具代表性的景色。从大青峰沿山脊至弥乘岭的恐龙山脊展示着极度的山岩石壁之美。土旺城溪谷附近有释迦峰、纹绣峰、普贤峰等高峰，还可观赏六潭瀑布、飞龙瀑布、仙女峰、土旺城瀑布、华彩峰等大自然创造的杰作。蔚山岩溪谷以新兴寺为起始点，一直到北面高耸的蔚山岩，内有内院庵、继祖庵等。南外雪岳位于雪岳山国立公园的南面末端。王色川流经大青峰和点凤山之间，内有铸钱谷溪谷和五色泉水、五色温泉。

雪岳山不仅随季节变换展现不同的风采，甚至根据所跨行政区域的不同，景观、气候和文化也会不同。如果说外雪岳的千佛洞溪谷两侧的奇岩绝壁给人一种男性的刚劲之美的话，那么内雪岳的百潭、伽倻洞溪谷展现

雪岳山景区功能分区图

出的则是女性柔和幽深的美。在南雪岳则可以同时领略到大青峰的雄伟和五色温泉的温婉雅致。雪岳山景点有阿尔卑斯滑雪场、神兴寺、五色药水、马登岭、大声瀑布、卧臣台、飞仙龟、权金城等。

1. 阿尔卑斯滑雪场

阿尔卑斯度假村的滑雪场位于陈富岭的高原盆地内,是积雪量最大及降雪期最长的地区。村内有韩国国内独一无二的滑雪博物馆,可一览滑雪的历史。冬天还可在此享用滑雪场、室内游泳池、保龄球馆、雪橇场等各种附属设施,夏天可参加高尔夫练习、草坪雪橇、生存游戏、漂流等。

2. 新兴寺

新兴寺,原名神兴寺,是真德女王(?—654年,新罗第28代王)七年前后由遍访全国名山的慈藏律师建造的,时称香城寺,之后多次破损后

重建。在去往新兴寺的路上有巨大的青铜坐佛像，佛像位于宽阔的花岗岩高台之上，高十多米。过了佛像右转，在溪流上有一座新建的吊桥。过了桥，在石头砌成的长墙一侧有天王门，通往寺内。入口的两旁有巨大的四天王雕像（持刀的持国天王、抱琵琶的多闻天王、托塔的广目天王、握龙的增长天王）。新兴寺的佛像是善正寺创建的时候立的，有弥勒佛、观音菩萨、势至像等义湘大师直接雕刻的佛像，寺中还留有当时建造的法堂、大雄殿、冥府殿、保济楼、七星阁等建筑，以及重点文化遗产第443号的香城遗址三层石塔。

3. 五色药水

由朝鲜时代（1392—1910年）城国寺的僧侣发现的五色温泉，坐落于襄阳以西20千米、寒溪岭东南5千米左右处，向南约30千米处有五色药水。五色温泉在海拔650米的高地喷出，从小溪岩盘三处涌出的药水含有铁和碳酸水成分，由于铁含量大，对胃肠炎、贫血、神经痛等具有很好疗效。温泉特点是温度为42℃，氯、硫黄、铁等主要成分分布均匀，接触皮肤时感觉润滑、柔软，略有一点腥味。五色温泉因为皮肤美容效果奇佳，又被称为美人温泉。1982年江原道实施地质勘查后，该地区被正式指定为五色温泉地区。

4. 赏枫宝地

韩国枫叶姹紫嫣红，有其独特的"枫"景。雪岳山可以说是韩国境内能最先看到枫叶的地方，雪岳山山顶更是欣赏红枫的最佳地点。9月末山顶上的枫叶颜色渐渐变浓，到10月中就会掀起枫叶的"红色"热潮。

游客可以坐缆车到山上的观览台，当缆车升到半空，此时远眺群山，红橙黄绿的光谱四面映照，美不胜收。千佛洞溪谷是雪岳山中的绝景，在巍峨挺拔的石峰间，形成了"V"字形峡谷，内有瀑布、深潭、红叶、溪流，延绵12千米，构成奇特的景观，可算是雪岳山最美丽的景区，也是韩国山谷景色的代表，当然也是赏枫的绝佳之处。点凤山的铸钱谷是韩国最出名的红叶名胜，灿烂而耀眼的枫叶与奇岩怪石浑然一体，形成绝景。

登雪岳山有数条路线，其中以千佛洞溪谷、五色温泉、铸钱谷、百潭溪谷等路线最适合赏枫。这里周边旅游设施众多，如洛山海水浴场、镜浦

台以及雪岳温泉乐园等，爬了一天山后在按摩温泉里泡一下，将会非常惬意。

三、旅游观光

雪岳山与东海岸相临，夏天有很多到东海岸避暑的游客探访此地；漫长的冬季到周边滑雪场和温泉的观光客也会光顾雪岳山；秋季是雪岳山旅游的旺季，奇岩怪石和溪谷与形形色色的枫叶相映，形成一道道绚丽的风景线；春天，海洋性气候和高山气候相融，形成了独特的景观，既能看到春花也能看到冬雪，这种奇观吸引着众多游客的脚步。

许多旅游者喜欢步行领略野外大自然的风光，每年大约有 500 万游客前往雪岳山，大部分的游客不爬山，只在外雪岳地区周围走走。他们待在新兴寺附近以及权金城山庄，最远也就只是到蔚山岩、飞龙瀑布、千佛洞山谷等。如果在南雪岳，游客的最终目的地一般是五色药水温泉或仙女汤瀑布，一般短程游客喜欢去海拔低的地区。

登雪岳山的路上有数家食肆，有些隐匿在枫树群中，深秋时候边赏秋边饮食，分外惬意。束草的特色小吃有鲜生鱼片、鱿鱼米肠、大叔米肠、荞麦面、咸兴冷面、豆腐等。每年 4、5 月和 10、11 月是生鱼片味道最鲜美的时候。春天的比目鱼、红鲷、乌鱼、鲈鱼最好，秋冬则属鲫鱼最好。大浦港和东明港的生鱼片店较集中。鱿鱼米肠则是在鱿鱼内装上糯米、胡萝卜、洋葱、芝麻叶等加热蒸出来的小吃，清淡可口。而大叔米肠原是朝鲜的小吃，是在明太鱼的腹内塞上绑好的泡菜、豆腐、猪肉等材料后制成的。

第九节　东方奇山——菲律宾巧克力山

巧克力山位于菲律宾保和岛（Bohol，又称薄荷岛）中部，是卡门（Carmen）附近的一处自然奇景。由1268个面积相同、几近完美的圆锥形山丘组成，高度介于40到120米之间，占地达50平方千米，居高临下鸟瞰，好像一个个堆放在地上的干草堆。每到夏季，"干草堆"都会干枯，转为褐色，犹如一排排巧克力摆放在大地上。巧克力山这个叫人垂涎欲滴的名字由此而来。

一、成因传说

在菲律宾薄荷岛人中流传着一个传说，该岛中央一座圆形的小山是一个名叫阿罗哥的巨人流的眼泪变成的，当他所爱的一个叫作阿洛亚的普通女子不能接受他的爱时，他一病不起而死去。另外，传说古时有两个巨人用石头向对方互相投掷，巨石一个一个掉在地上，便形成了数以千计、造型优美的圆锥形山头。令人奇怪的是，人们无法准确地知晓这些聚集在一个地方的山丘是如何形成的。据说200万年前，这里并没有山，而是一片汪洋大海，这些山都是海底珊瑚生活的地方，珊瑚世代代生长，形成了一个个小山一样的珊瑚礁。后来由于地壳抬升，这些珊瑚礁才露出水面，形成了现在的巧克力山。还有一种说法认为，这是一个古老活火山的自我毁灭，它喷出来的大块岩石四散，后来覆盖上了石灰石，随后从海床中涌出。它们都由石灰岩组成，可能只是数百万年雨水侵蚀的结果，但它们显得非同寻常，因为这里没有一般石灰岩地区所常见的溶洞系统或地下通道。

二、奇异景观

一般来说，山上都会长树长草。处在寒带和温带雨水比较稀少地区的山，秃山秃岭的比较多、植被较差；而处在亚热带、热带临海地区的山，雨量充沛，山上的植物都枝繁叶茂。但巧克力山有点怪，薄荷岛被称为生态岛，差不多四面都是海林。巧克力山周围其他形态的山无不如此，独独这种特大号的超级"馒头"，却是基本上只长草不长树。而且馒头山上的草还是变色草，一过夏天，就开始由绿变棕，直到整个变成巧克力色。温带寒带的树草因温热变化而随之枯荣变色是天经地义的，但热带的薄荷岛一年四季常绿之地，这种山也变色怎不是一奇呢？巧克力山奇还奇在它规模庞大，据最新的统计数据，这种巧克力山有1776个，占地达300多公顷，分布在6个镇上，这么多的馒头山，当地的地质学家却始终研究不出它的成因，只知道它们是石灰岩质的山。它们为什么全都规规整整地呈馒头圆状？为什么山都不甚高？为什么山上只长草而草到夏季就变色？且山只变成巧克力色，这些都是千古之谜。

三、怪诞动物

你听说过四不像吗？薄荷岛上的四不像是袖珍型的，学名塔西亚，俗名大眼镜猴。它在薄荷岛上独有的地位有点类似中国的熊猫、澳大利亚的考拉熊，但比熊猫和考拉更珍贵，据说全岛仅剩下2000多只。它是上帝在造物时开的一个小玩笑，创造出的一种世界上最小的灵长类动物。有多小，反正把它放在手掌上，是足够显示手掌宽裕度的。握不盈手的小动物，被称为猴儿。看脑袋它的确有点像猴，但不能把眼睛考虑进去。眼睛得和猫头鹰的眼睛去比较，圆圆的、大大的、不成比例地在面颊上努突着，既亮又有神。它的身子不好跟什么动物去比较，好几种动物都有那样的身子，毛不长、皮质厚，因小而有一种软软的、毛茸茸的感觉。在你能想到的袖珍动物中容易联想到鼠类。但说松鼠没条纹，说老鼠、田鼠又比老鼠、田鼠有毛性。若还是从猴子那考虑也就是颜色上差不多，全身除了四肢都呈棕黄色。能确切形容的只有四肢了，前腿是蜥蜴腿，后腿是青蛙腿。尾巴也属概念模糊的，像老鼠，长长的，至少长出它的两个身子，由粗而细地耷拉着。在薄荷岛几乎所有的旅游景点、度假村、教堂都有大眼镜猴的小纪念品和文化衫，它们是薄荷岛的明星。

第三章

非洲的世界名山

第一节 赤道雪峰——坦桑尼亚乞力马扎罗山

乞力马扎罗山（Kilimanjaro）位于坦桑尼亚东北部及东非大裂谷以南约160千米，赤道与南纬3度之间，是非洲最高的山脉，素有"非洲屋脊"之称，许多地理学家称它为"非洲之王"，它也是一个火山丘。山的主体沿东西向延伸将近80千米，主要由基博、马温西和希拉三个死火山构成，面积756平方千米，其中，中央火山锥乌呼鲁峰，海拔5892米，是非洲最高点。乞力马扎罗山有两个主峰，除了乌呼鲁，另一个叫马文济，两峰之间由一个十多千米长的马鞍形的山脊相连。远远望去，乞力马扎罗山是一座孤单耸立的高山，在辽阔的东非大草原上拔地而起，高耸入云、气势磅礴。乌呼鲁峰峰顶有一个直径2400米、深200米的火山口，口内四壁是晶莹无瑕的巨大冰层，底部耸立着巨大的冰柱，冰雪覆盖，宛如巨大的玉盆。在赤道附近"冒"出这一晶莹的冰雪世界，世人称奇。可是100多年前，当第一

个看到它的德国人兴奋不已地把消息上报给英国皇家地理学会时,地理学会批评德国人轻信民间传说,拒不相信赤道上有雪。直到1861年,他们派探险队亲自查证才改变了看法。1887年,现代人的足迹终于抵达山顶。在酷热的日子里,从远处望去,蓝色的山基让人赏心悦目,而白雪皑皑的山顶似乎在空中盘旋。常伸展到雪线以下缥缈的云雾,增加了这种幻觉。山麓的气温有时高达59℃,而峰顶的气温又常在零下34℃,故有"赤道雪峰"之称。乞力马扎罗山地区已经于1968年被辟为国家公园,其中生长着热、温、寒三带野生动植物。这一奇特的自然景观,是人类不可多得的珍贵自然遗产,联合国教科文组织已于1981年将其列入《世界文化与自然遗产保护名录》。

一、自然景观

乞力马扎罗山因为阻挡了印度洋上潮湿的季风,故水源充足。水流和气温条件相结合,使乞力马扎罗山从山脚至山顶,由热带雨林气候变换至冰原气候。南坡水源充足有农田和茂密的森林,北坡为半干旱灌木。其自然风景包括赤道至两极的基本植被,在海拔1000米以下为热带雨林带,

1000~2000 米间为亚热带常绿阔叶林带，2000~3000 米间为温带森林带，3000~4000 米为高山草甸带，4000~5200 米为高山寒漠带，5200 米以上为积雪冰川带。

一般在 2000 米以下的山腰部分，气候温暖、雨水充沛。在肥沃的火山灰土壤上，生长着咖啡、花生、茶叶、香蕉等经济作物。山脚部分，气候炎热，即使在树荫下，气温也常在 30℃ 以上，到处是浓墨重彩的非洲热带风光。山麓四周的莽原上，非洲象、斑马、鸵鸟、长颈鹿、犀牛等热带野生动物以及稀有的疣猴、蓝猴、阿拉伯羚、大角斑羚等在那里自由自在地生活着。这里是世界上著名的野生动物保护区，也生长着茂盛的热带作物，除甘蔗、香蕉、可可外，最多的是用来纳布制绳的剑麻，铺天盖地、一望无尽。

二、神奇传说

乞力马扎罗山是坦桑尼亚人心中的骄傲，他们把自己看作草原之帆下的子民。据传，在很久以前，天神降临到这座高耸入云的高山，以便在高山之巅俯视和赐福他的子民们。盘踞在山中的妖魔鬼怪为了赶走天神，在山腹内部点起了一把大火，滚烫的熔岩随着熊熊烈火喷涌而出。妖魔的举动激怒了天神，他呼来了雷鸣闪电瓢泼大雨把大火扑灭，又召来了飞雪冰雹把冒着烟的山口填满。这就形成了今天看到的这座赤道雪山，地球上一个独特的风景点。这个古老而美丽的故事世代在坦桑尼亚人民中传诵，使大山变得神圣而威严无比。乞力马扎罗山高高的山顶白雪皑皑，山腰云雾缭绕，充满着神奇莫测的气氛，尤其是黄昏的时候，山顶的云雾偶尔散去，银白晶莹的峰顶在金色的夕阳照耀之下，露出妖艳的容颜，五彩缤纷、绚丽灿烂。多少世纪以来，许多当地人认为乞力马扎罗山是"上帝的宝座"，对它敬若神明，很多部族每年都要在山脚下举行传统的祭祀活动，拜山神、求平安。

三、旅游胜地

乞力马扎罗山是世界著名的旅游胜地，坦桑尼亚政府充分利用这一得天独厚的自然条件，大力发展旅游事业。这里建有非洲风格的星级旅馆，可以满足来自世界各地的游客的食宿要求。乞力马扎罗国际机场有14条国际航线通往世界各地，设施齐备、通信先进，五大洲的游客可以乘飞机直接抵达乞力马扎罗山山麓。

乞力马扎罗山是世界各地的登山爱好者云集的地方，登山一般选在每年的1—3月中旬，这时候的天气非常晴朗，温度适宜；其次可选7—9月份，这时候的温度较低，空气比较干燥。乞力马扎罗山有两条登山线路，一条是"旅游登山"线路，游客在导游和挑夫的协助之下，分3天时间登上山顶，体验"一览众山小"的滋味。另一条是"登山运动员"线路，沿途悬崖峭壁，十分危险。每年都有大约15000人试图攀登乞力马扎罗山，其中有40%的人能成功地登上顶峰。当然，无论从哪一条线路登上山顶，对异国他乡之人来说，都是终生难忘的幸事。

第二节　海角之城——南非桌山

桌山（英语：Table Mountain，阿非利堪斯语：Tafelberg）意为"海角之城"。桌山是世界上最古老的山峰之一，在这个世界上静静矗立了3.6亿年。桌山为平顶山，可俯瞰开普敦市和桌湾，耸立于高而多岩石的开普半岛北端。前拥波光粼粼的大西洋海湾，背枕一座乱云飞渡、形似巨大长方形条桌的奇山。桌山对面的海湾是天然良港，并因桌山得名为桌湾。

桌山靠近大西洋一侧有两座小山，分别为狮头峰、信号山；靠近开普敦南部的一侧则有更为险峻的山峰为魔鬼峰，它们就像桌山伸出的左右两只手臂，紧紧地拥抱着山脚下的开普敦城区。因桌山较接近市区的地理位置，被开普敦市政府选为"南非之美"的宣传路标。桌山也是一座绿色的航标，因它是非洲大陆南端近海地带唯一的高山，来往于东西方的船只要到达山脚，就等于完成了航程的一半。而桌山那平坦的绿色山顶，也曾被不少欧洲航海家描绘为"旅途上难得一见的餐桌"。2011年，南非桌山与亚马孙雨林、越南下龙湾、巴西和阿根廷交界的伊瓜苏瀑布、韩国济州岛、印度尼西亚科莫多国家公园、菲律宾普林塞萨地下河国家公园同列为新出炉的世界新七大自然奇观。桌山所代表的开普敦区已经列入联合国教科文组织世界遗产的一部分。

一、地质景观

桌山的地质结构以火山岩为主，为沉积叠岩，是几千万年来大风不断侵蚀、作用的结果，形成了蔚为壮观的风蚀地貌。风蚀地貌大多见于岩性强弱相间的沉积岩（主要是砂岩、泥岩等）地区。由风蚀作用所形成的风蚀地貌在大风区域有广泛的分布，特别是正对风口的迎风地段发育更为典型。南非开普敦正好位于大西洋的巨大风口上。突兀隆起的海拔1087米的桌山正对风口的迎风地段，风蚀作用特别强烈，风蚀地貌发育典型。由于岩性、岩层形状等因素的影响，风蚀地貌多种多样，有棱角明显、表面光滑的风棱石；有圆形或不规则的椭圆形的小洞穴和凹坑；有孤立突起的岩石在经受长期的风化和风蚀作用以后，形成上部大、基部小、外形与蘑菇相似的蘑菇石；有垂直裂隙发育的岩石在经过风蚀后，形成一些高低不等、大小不同的孤立的风蚀柱；等等。这些风蚀地貌在桌山到处可见。多种多样的风蚀地貌，构成了桌山独特的地质景观。

二、景色天成

"桌山"其实是一组群山的总称，位于开普敦城区西部，狮子头、信号山、魔鬼峰等，千姿百态、气势磅礴。令人惊奇的是桌山主峰海拔1087米，山顶却平展似一个巨大的桌面，山顶平面长1500多米，宽200多米，开阔无比。由于地处两洋交汇的特殊地理位置，加上地中海的奇特气候环境，山顶终年云雾缭绕，充满神奇莫测的气氛，淡淡的白云覆盖在山顶上，头顶着蔚蓝色的天空，人在山上走，物在云中游，犹如遨游在太空。山上怪石林立，形状各异，有的像挺胸的巨人，有的像翩翩起舞的仙女，有的像戳破青天的宝剑……这些大自然的天成杰作构成了一座天然博物馆。

桌山植被十分茂密,且种类繁多,据说有2600多种。山上终年开花不断,特别是春季,可看到花海覆盖绵延无尽的奇景。桌山上最有名的花为帝王花，又称菩提花，也是南非的国花。这种花颜色多变，白色清丽淡雅，粉红色娇媚动人，紫红色富丽华贵。花期从5月到12月,一朵花能开几个星期之久。

三、奇云传说

关于桌山有一个久远而有趣的传说：一天，一个名叫范汉克斯的海盗在桌山附近和一个魔鬼相遇后，他们便在一块马鞍形的岩石旁一边吸烟斗，一边攀谈起来。那天情绪不错的魔鬼向海盗透露说，山上只剩下一个为赎回罪孽的魔鬼保留的温暖洞穴。准备改邪归正的海盗灵机一动，提出与魔鬼进行吸烟比赛，谁赢了，那个温暖的去处就属于谁。他们的竞赛一直延续至今，因此桌山上总是云雾缭绕。为什么冬天没有云了呢？那是因为魔鬼和海盗现在年事已高，在阴冷潮湿的冬日暂停比赛。

第四章

欧洲的世界名山

第一节 欧洲"脊骨"——阿尔卑斯山·埃森沃尔谨地质公园

阿尔卑斯山是欧洲中南部大山脉,覆盖了意大利北部边界、法国东南部、瑞士、列支敦士登、奥地利、德国南部及斯洛文尼亚。该山自北非阿特拉斯延伸,穿过南欧和南亚,直到喜马拉雅山脉,从亚热带地中海海岸法国的尼斯附近向北延伸至日内瓦湖,然后再向东北伸展至多瑙河上的维也纳。欧洲许多大河都发源于此,水力资源丰富,为旅游、度假、疗养胜地。

一、生态景观

阿尔卑斯山山脉主干向西南方向延伸为比利牛斯山脉,向南延伸为亚平宁山脉,向东南方向延伸为迪纳拉山脉,向东延伸为喀尔巴阡山脉。阿尔卑斯山山脉可分为三段:西段西阿尔卑斯山从地中海岸,穿过法国东南部和意大利的西北部,到瑞士边境的大圣伯纳德山口附近,为山系最窄部分,也是高峰最集中的山段,在蓝天映衬下洁白如银的勃朗("勃朗"在法语中是白的意思)峰(4810米)是整个山脉的最高点,位于法国和意大利边界。中段中阿尔卑斯山,介于大圣伯纳德山口和博登湖之间,宽度最大,有马特洪峰(4479米)和蒙特罗莎峰(4634米)。东段东阿尔卑斯山在博登湖以东,海拔低于西、中两段阿尔卑斯山。阿尔卑斯山山脊将欧洲隔离成几个区域,

是许多欧洲大河（如隆河、莱茵河和波河）和多瑙河许多支流的发源地。从阿尔卑斯山山脉流出的水最终注入北海、地中海、亚得里亚海和黑海。

　　阿尔卑斯山山脉地处温带和亚热带纬度之间，成为中欧温带大陆性湿润气候和南欧亚热带夏干气候的分界线。同时它本身具有山地垂直气候特征。阿尔卑斯山山脉的植被呈明显的垂直变化。山上植被可分为亚热带常绿硬叶林带（山脉南坡800米以下）；森林带（800～1800米），下部是混交林，上部是针叶林；森林带以上为高山草甸带；再上则多为裸露的岩石和终年积雪的山峰。阿尔卑斯山山脉的植物带，反映了其海拔和气候的差异。在谷底和低矮山坡上生长着各种落叶树木，其中有椴树、栎树、山毛榉、白杨、榆、栗、花楸、白桦、挪威枫等。海拔较高处的树林中，最多的是针叶树，主要的品种为云杉、落叶松及其他各种松树。在西阿尔卑斯山山脉的多数地方，云杉占优势的树林最高可达海拔2195米。落叶松具有较好的御寒、抗旱和抵抗大风的能力，可在海拔高至2500米处生长，在海拔较低处有云杉混杂其间。在永久雪线以下和林木线以上约914米宽的地带是冰川作用侵蚀过的地区，这里覆盖着茂盛的草地，在短暂的盛夏期间有牛羊放牧。这些与众不同的草地——被称为"alpages"（高山盛夏牧场），阿尔卑斯山山脉和植物带都是从这个词衍生出来的——都位于主要的、横向的山谷的上方。在沿海阿尔卑斯山山脉南麓和意大利阿尔卑斯山山脉南部，主要是地中海植物，有海岸松、棕榈、稀疏的林地和龙舌兰，仙人果也不少。

　　生活在阿尔卑斯山的动物对于高山环境已很适应。虽然熊已消失，但高地山羊（它同岩羚羊一样，动作异常敏捷）却被意大利皇家猎物保护区保护了起来。旱獭在地下通道中越冬。山兔和雷鸟（一种松鸡）冬季变成白色（保护色）。

　　二、旅游休闲

　　阿尔卑斯山景色十分迷人，是世界著名的风景区和旅游胜地，被世人称为"大自然的宫殿"和"真正的地貌陈列馆"。它是欧洲最大的山地冰川中心。山区覆盖着厚达1千米的冰盖。各种类型冰川地貌都发育丰富，冰蚀地貌尤为典型，并有许多冰川侵蚀作用形成的冰蚀崖、角峰、冰斗、悬谷、冰蚀湖等以及冰川堆积作用的冰碛地貌。还有1200多条现代冰川，总面积约 4000 平方千米。中阿尔卑斯山山麓瑞士西南的阿莱奇冰川最大，长约 22.5 千米，面积约 130 平方千米。山地冰川作用还形成许多湖泊。最大的湖泊莱芒湖（日内瓦湖）被雪山草甸、牧场、葡萄园包围着，湖水终年不冻，色彩深蓝，与天空融为一体。自古以来，许多名作家、大诗人都赞美、讴歌过它。亨利·詹姆斯称它是"出奇的蓝色的湖"；拜伦则把它比喻成一面晶莹的镜子，"有着沉思所需要的养料和空气"；巴尔扎克则把它说成是"爱情的同义词"。另外，还有四森林州湖、苏黎世湖、博登湖、马焦雷湖和科莫湖等。山地冰川呈现一派极地风光，是登山、滑雪、旅游胜地。

近百年来，阿尔卑斯山已成为休假和疗养的场所。夏天，这里是避暑胜地；冬季，这里是冬季运动之乡；旅馆、饭店等供旅游者享用的设施应有尽有。山中有欧洲地势最高的希尔顿饭店，坐在饭店的旋转餐厅里，人们可以观赏阿尔卑斯山的山景。这里还有欧洲海拔最高的火车站，乘火车可以直接到达少女峰看冰川奇景。许多地方有电缆车直达山巅。游人若在领略雪趣时遇险，有直升机可以提供救助，山里也有专门治疗骨折、摔伤的医院。

除了登山、滑雪，阿尔卑斯山山区中还有著名的温泉休养胜地洛伊克巴德，拥有 22 个露天、室内温泉池，每天有约 300 万升的温泉水流入私人公共的温泉浴池中。洛伊克巴德是从罗马时代开始发展起来的温泉城市，这里以大众温泉中心和现代化的阿尔卑斯温泉中心为主，并且有很多吸引人的设施。

三、地质公园

埃森沃尔谨地质公园位于奥地利施蒂利亚州，隶属阿尔卑斯山的北部，其岩体基本由灰岩和白云岩组成，沉积时段从二叠纪至现代，超过 2.5 亿年，为晚二叠世至三叠纪碳酸盐岩分布区，是三叠系安尼阶的命名地。古新世以来，阿尔卑斯运动的强烈活动塑造了这里丰富多彩的地貌景观，激流、瀑布、灰岩峡谷、洞穴等引人入胜，其中克劳斯洞是欧洲重要的石膏—石灰岩洞穴。三叠纪地层中还保存有奥地利最大的爬行类化石和大量白垩纪腹足类、双壳类化石。大冰期的冰川流动留下了重要的冰川遗迹，是阿尔卑斯维尔姆冰期的命名地。埃森沃尔谨也是奥地利古冶铁之乡，冶铁作坊随处可见。

地质公园的地质旅游分会成立于1999年。地质旅游业可以追溯到1892年，欧洲主要石膏洞穴之一的迦姆斯地区克劳斯洞穴安装了电灯对公众开放。迦姆斯地区的地质中心还特别安排了永久性陈列室展示毗邻地区的地质环境和采矿史。在提供地质旅游路线的同时，还现场呈现岩石、化石、大地构造运动、流水侵蚀以及人类活动对各种地质作用带来的干扰遗迹。这些地质遗迹中有白垩、第三纪边界事件中用肉眼就可看到的证据，这一点十分罕见。在导游带领下野外旅行采集到的化石可在指导下制作，然后，置于显微镜下观察研究；甚至在近旁溪流中物色到的卵石，经切割打磨后也可制成举世无双的纪念品。

第二节　生态家园——罗马尼亚科齐亚山

罗马尼亚科齐亚国家公园位于南喀尔巴阡山脉的中南部，沃尔恰县东北部，洛特鲁山东南部，它从一片山凹中拔地而起。奥尔特河从山脚下流过，从远处看它就像是一个由陡峭的山坡和无数的堡垒组成的岩石巨人。科齐亚国家公园占地17100公顷，于2000年3月6日设立为自然保护区。

一、优美生态

科齐亚国家公园北部是疏松地层，南部是沉积地层。该地区地势突兀，突如其来的海拔落差，造就了奥尔特河谷的壮丽。这里植被十分丰富，大约有930个物种，除了特有的植物群，还有数量可观的地衣。这里还是许多稀有动物的栖息地，如伪装蝎、蝮蛇、野猫、貂、黑山羊等，是南喀尔巴阡山脉特有的动植物的代表性山区。公园内还有许多奇观，布尔祖峰（海拔1506米）、篱笆谷、分离峰、科齐亚的斯芬克斯、石鹰、石番茄、象牙剪、特拉扬塔、提阿塔、科齐亚石门等。

二、人文景观

科齐亚国家公园既有宝贵的景观、温泉、地形、水文、动物、植物等自然资源，也有罕见的人文资源（古迹、传统和当地社区等）。

科齐亚公园是一片充满历史的广阔天地，有证据表明，这里很久以前就有人居住。这里有许多以前被 Seneslau 占据的领地，现在仍有土著居民居住着，他们沿袭着古老的生活习俗。距离科齐亚国家公园最近的社区是 Brezoi、Calimanesti 市以及一些村庄。Calimanesti 市由于温泉而成为主要的旅游城市。Brezoi 市以前是大的木制品加工中心，但是现在已经停工，因此城市经济在衰退。当地人以农业，主要是牲畜和水果为主要经济收入。国家公园内部有两个僧人社区：图尔努（Turnu）和 斯坦尼索拉（Stânisoara）修道院。

这里建了许多华丽的教堂和修道院，最著名的是科齐亚修道院。科齐亚修道院承载着罗马尼亚人 600 多年的艺术、圣恩、和平、尊严和宗教发展经历。修道院以前是个避难所，建在这个与世隔绝的地方，除了考虑优美的自然环境，还考虑到它的军事战略意义，因为从前这里是个军事要塞。关于古代米尔统治时期的首次记载是在 1388 年，修道院里还保留着他的画像，他穿着中世纪的服装，手持修道院的模型，可见他的威严。站在他旁边的是他的儿子，后来继承了他的王位。在北部教堂的许愿板和修道院创

办的福利院也有他的画像。米尔死于 1418 年初,像当时其他西方国家埋葬他们仰慕的君主那样,他被葬在一个石棺里,坟前立着一块碑。这块碑在 1916—1918 年外国入侵期间遭到了毁坏,后来通过教区的努力,这里重立了一块新碑"瓦拉几亚国王,卒于 1418 年"。修道院后来经过几次扩建和装修,现在墙壁上画有这些创始人的画像。后来的几个世纪以及 20 世纪初,在历史古迹董事会的支持下又经历过几次修缮。然而仍有一些建筑因第一次世界大战时发生在奥尔特河谷的战役以及随后的外国侵略战争而严重被毁。战后,修道院又重现原貌,而且多了七个窗户,每扇都刻有不同的古代时期的花形。另在半山腰,有罗马尼亚天主教的建筑杰作,内有大量的神秘的符号。教堂周围是美丽的花园和巨大的植物园,从图尔努修道院开始,丛林中有一段漫长的崎岖不平的路,路两旁是岩石,直接通往斯坦尼索拉修道院,勇者可以继续前行到达科齐亚山山顶。

三、旅游休闲

科齐亚国家公园是罗马尼亚人和国外游客熟知的旅游目的地。之所以受游客青睐，是因为它的地理位置。这里靠近一些修道院，最有名的要数科齐亚修道院，还有两个温泉度假地 Calimanesti 和 Caciulata。游客来到这里还可以欣赏美丽的 Cheile 瀑布和 Lotisorului 瀑布，以及大科齐亚、卡帕塔尼山、都伯-克里内什蒂和奥尔特峡谷的旖旎风光。科齐亚国家公园目前开展的主要旅游活动有徒步旅行、体育运动探险、野外露营和竞赛项目、历史古迹游览、科普教育旅游、温泉疗养等。

第三节 爱情乐园——罗马尼亚盖那山

盖那山位于罗马尼亚西部阿普塞尼山区，是阿普塞尼山的一部分，海拔高度 1468 米。阿普塞尼山上每个村庄或者定居点都有自己的历史，可追溯到罗马时期，讲述从它的形成到现今的故事。由于山顶地势平坦、视野开阔，人们选择在此建立聚会场所以便大家聚会和保持联系。每年 7 月，依照基督教传统会举行一个集会，是青年男女求婚、商业集会、乡村歌舞表演的重要集会，盖那山也因此而广为人知。

一、奇异传说

盖那山有着令人惊叹的美景和悠久的历史，亦留下了众多的神话传说。资料表明该集会首次出现是在1816年，当时的盖那山山顶天气格外晴朗，白云笼罩着山峰。开始叫作少女交易会，但是并没有人买卖妇女。举办集会曾经是为了让人们寻根问祖，散居在各处的山民聚集在盖那山进行社交和庆祝活动。

传说很久以前，有一只会下金蛋的漂亮的母鸡，她的巢穴就隐藏在山顶。以前人们经常保护她，作为报答，这只母鸡每年从她秘密的藏身之地下山一次，拍打着翅膀飞向年轻人，变成一个美丽的女神，赐给年轻夫妇一枚金蛋，保佑他们幸福长寿。人们欢呼、祈祷和感恩，女神在欢呼声中伸开双臂飞向天空，变回一只母鸡，消失在人们的视线中。那时候这座山的山顶总是被白云笼罩，代表着忠诚和爱情，所以这座山叫作盖那山，盖那是罗马尼亚语"母鸡"的意思。后来贪婪和邪恶之人决定要猎杀她，不断寻找她那值钱的金蛋。有一天，有人偷了金蛋，但却在途中丢失了金蛋，并最终坠入深深的海峡。母鸡回到她的巢穴，没有看到金蛋，非常伤心便决定永远离开这个地方，定居到另一座山。人们乞求她再回到这里，可是奇迹却没有发生。盖那山留下光秃秃的山顶，经常遭受暴风雨雪的袭击。人们经常来到这座山上，真诚地希望能够得到祝福，洗涤心中的贪念。

二、相亲民俗

现在，每年7月20日在盖那山山顶举办的节日吸引着罗马尼亚全国各地的人来参加，欣赏音乐、传统舞蹈和其他的当地节目。节日期间，成千上万的罗马尼亚人穿着传统服装聚集在盖那山，期待着遇见"那个特殊的人"。他们在此结交远道而来的异性朋友，玩耍、聚会、唱歌、跳舞、相爱，最终可能还会结婚。当地人认为夫妻只有在盖那山上完成婚礼才能得到幸福。节日其实就是一个大型的相亲活动，这一民俗节日在中欧和东欧一带非常有名。

庆祝活动一大早就开始，来自阿夫拉姆扬库的著名的女子山笛乐队通过鸣山笛来宣布庆典开始。有人带来精细的棉布和织布机，雕好的长笛和许多陶器。其他地方的人带来装饰着鲜花的衣服、皮帽子、野果子和一些药材。从阿普塞尼山来的人带来山笛、木桶、餐具和木盆。人们可以在此欣赏深受欢迎的传统民族服饰，观看特兰西瓦尼亚舞蹈霍拉舞，购买精美的手工艺品。提前一天到达的惯例仍在执行，这就是为什么星期六晚上在阿夫拉姆扬库举行的庆祝活动好像比第二天的交易会更让人印象深刻的原因。每个参与者从家带来食物，传统食物有玉米粥，里面加牛奶和猪油、熏肉、洋葱，当地人把它与 palinca（一种烈性白兰地）媲美。

三、旅游体验

在美丽的盖那山山顶集会、欣赏美景、呼吸新鲜空气，品尝美味佳肴，观赏传统舞蹈，其实不失为利用这个节日保护当地民俗传统的一剂良方。游客如需要体验活动的乐趣，驾车上山无疑是最方便和舒适的方法。当然游客也可以在维拉德乘车到达山脚下，然后再爬上山顶。开普尼离盖那山很近，也可以从那出发前往阿布德，然后再到罗西亚蒙大拿，就会豁然发现自己身处阿普塞尼山的金属城堡，一片金色的土地。从阿夫拉姆扬库社区出发上山到山顶大概9千米，中途在距离盖那山山顶5千米处有个克莱尤旅馆可供游客休息。

第四节　温泉明珠——罗马尼亚科瓦斯那山

科瓦斯那山位于罗马尼亚中部科瓦斯那县，这个名字来自斯拉夫语的"quasi"，意思是"酸"（指的是这里矿泉水的味道）。该县面积3710平方千米，人口22万人（2002年），距离首府圣格奥尔基（奥尔特河畔）31千米，西南距布拉索夫60千米，东北临巴克乌，东南接布泽乌。首府人口6万7千人，面积虽小，但却是特兰西瓦尼亚的中枢城市。这里有连绵的山脉、茂密的丛林、清澈的河流和湖泊。

一、迷人景观

科瓦斯那景色迷人，是一种原生态的美。拉黑塔山瓦黑斯谷的码头风景如画，河流两岸山石耸立，在此变成一条3千米长的狭窄河道，两岸充满野性自然的美令人陶醉。山上有大约60个洞穴，最大的一个是 Meresti 洞穴，是东喀尔巴阡山脉最长的洞穴。市中心可以找到被当地人叫作"魔鬼池"的地方，它是城市的标志，实际是一种泥浆和含碳氧化物、硫的气体的喷发现象。1881年对外开放，最初用于治疗。据资料记载，在1700年前这一自然现象发生在更北边，但是现在却神奇地移到了市中心。原来的地方就留下了一个小坑——"小魔鬼池"。地质学家认为，魔鬼池是碳的释放：矿泉水从地下喷射而出，气体在旋转和聚集。19世纪曾有过几次爆发，分别在1837年、1857年、1864年和1885年，喷射最高的一次在1837年，最后一次大的喷发发生在1984年。现在的魔鬼池已经完全没有危害了。

人文景观主要是博物馆和许多教堂。如罗马天主教教堂 Ghelita，年代久远，建于1245年，风格独特，教堂内有珍贵的壁画；还有圣格奥尔基教堂、13世纪浪漫主义风格的要塞教堂 Ghidfalau；15世纪意大利文艺复兴时期风格的 Biborteni 教堂，保留着原有的壁画碎片；还有 Olteni 教堂、Baraolt 教

堂和 Aita Mare 教堂。Ceausescu 别墅位于仙女谷一个偏僻的地方，特别美丽。

二、独特温泉

科瓦斯那县自然条件得天独厚，主要以山地结构为主，山区面积占到 60%。由于地处火山活动带，火山岩矿化后给这里带来了含碳、碳酸盐、碘、溴、铁、砷等矿物含量达 3.2~22.4 克／升的天然矿泉水、矿物泥和大量的碳酸气孔。矿物质温泉是该地的一大特色，共有大大小小 1500 多个温泉，而在海拔 564 米高的科瓦斯那山山凹中就拥有 1000 个保健温泉度假村。

温泉水终年不断，而且水流量很大，有些可达每小时 10 立方米；水的味道很特别，而且温泉水有一种特殊的治疗价值，早在古罗马帝国时期就因良好的治疗效果而远近闻名。碳酸气孔广泛分布于周围 40 公顷的土地上，可以喷射天然气体，有扩张血管、降血压、增强肌肉、增加脑供血量、提高身体远端的温度、镇痛、针灸的功效，可以治疗心脑血管疾病、中枢和外周神经系统疾病、运动系统疾病、消化道疾病、肾病、男性病、泌尿系统疾病、皮肤病、内分泌、妇科疾病和老年病……这在欧洲是绝无仅有的。

气候条件也是这里的温泉具有治疗作用的一个因素。这里属于亚高山带气候，夏天凉爽怡人，冬天寒冷干燥。年平均气温 7℃，湿度在 75%~80%。七月平均温度为 17℃，一月平均温度约为 5℃。空气中富含负氧离子，可以舒缓中枢神经系统。多种天然治疗因素结合其他医疗方法，例如温泉中心的水疗设备：碳酸气孔装置、温泉水沐浴设施、内部矿泉治疗设备、喷雾器和吸入装置、石蜡疗法等，成功治疗了各类疾病，使得科瓦斯那温泉度假地成为欧洲最有名的治病温泉之一。

三、旅游活动

在科瓦斯那，住宿很方便，有十多家酒店和数不清的小旅馆，可满足各个层次的消费者。豪华酒店有专业的医务人员提供温泉理疗服务。有些酒店靠近森林，非常安静，空气清新，健身设备齐全，是度假的好去处。

第五节　地质奇观——德国贝尔吉施-奥登瓦尔德山

德国贝尔吉施-奥登瓦尔德山世界地质公园面积2300平方千米，位于德国西南部，东西处于美因河谷和莱茵河之间，南依莱卡河谷，北靠麦塞尔化石坑。于2004年2月被联合国教科文组织列入第一批世界地质公园名录。

一、独特地层

公园内有记载欧洲中部地区大约5亿年前重大全球性历史事件的独特地层，曾有格言这样描述它："在花岗岩与砂岩之间——漂移着的大陆。"莱茵河、美因河谷和莱卡之间的地区不仅出露大量的各种岩浆岩和沉积岩，还留下了两次全球地质构造的遗迹。第一次是华力西造山运动形成的岩浆弧——大陆碰撞的先期峡谷，第二次是莱茵河地堑的形成，代表了阿尔卑斯造山运动期间的欧洲大陆分裂的最初阶段，这在欧洲中部地区是独一无二的。通过研究各个阶段形成的典型岩石地层和地貌特征，可以得到全面性了解。因此，这一地区提供了研究地球历史、了解地球动力学过程的特殊窗口，具有特殊的地质学意义。

二、旅游资源

公园基于独特的地质背景开发了以体验为导向的地质旅游网络，它包括各种设施和地质旅游产品。当地人支持可持续的理念和吸引地质旅游的活动，并认为这是贝尔吉施-奥登瓦尔德山地质公园网络建设长期共同的任务。贝尔吉施-奥登瓦尔德山地质公园信息系统跨越的范围从"花岗岩和砂岩之间"自然风光，到发育局部景观各单一剖面的发现区，每一个地质景观都代表了地质文化景观中特有的相互联系与发展。

第五章

北美洲的世界名山

第一节 北美地标——美国胡德山

　　胡德山位于美国波特兰市东南偏东 80 多千米,克拉卡玛斯县和胡德河县交界处,是俄勒冈州北部喀斯喀特火山弧地区中的一座层状火山,由美国太平洋沿岸的一个俯冲带形成并且依附于太平洋西北地区,属喀斯喀特山脉,是一座死火山,最后一次喷发约在 1865 年。胡德山海拔 3424 米,是俄勒冈州的最高山峰,也是全美著名的高山之一。1792 年为英国航海家布劳顿首次测出,以英国将领胡德勋爵之名命名,早期移民以其积雪山顶为路标,亦是旅游胜地胡德山国家森林公园的中心点。

一、火山活动

　　作为俄勒冈州的第一高峰和喀斯喀特山脉的第四高峰,胡德山被认为是俄勒冈州火山中最有可能爆发的火山,虽然从历史上看,爆炸性喷发的可能性不大,但是在未来 30 年中,存在 3%~7% 的爆发概率。因此,美国地质调查局(USGS)认为它具有"潜在的活跃性",而民间一般认为它是一座休眠火山。

受到冰川侵蚀的山峰区域主要由安山岩或英安质熔岩圆顶（熔岩穹丘）组成；更新世时期的崩塌产生了雪崩和火山泥流（快速移动泥石流），火山泥流跨过哥伦比亚河直到北方。最近的一次小规模喷发事件发生在1907年8月。在下次爆发时，靠近山顶的斜坡上的冰川可能成为一个具有潜在危险的火山泥流源。山顶附近的火山喷气孔会释放出如二氧化碳和二氧化硫的气体。

自1950年以来，每年在胡德山都会发生几次震群型地震，最显著的发生在1980年7月和2002年6月。胡德山的地震活动由位于温哥华和华盛顿的美国地质勘探局喀斯喀特火山观测站监测，并且每周更新（火山活动明显的时候每日更新）。

二、冰川景观

胡德山由欧洲探险家在1792年首次发现，由于当地的地震活动不是太剧烈，多年来保持了稳定的海拔高度，高度变化在几米范围内。1993年的一次科学考察测量其高度为3426米。由于海拔高，胡德山上形成了12个冰川和雪原，游客最集中的地方是帕尔默冰川。帕尔默冰川部分位于廷伯莱恩小屋滑雪场，是多数登山路径的必经之路。这些冰川几乎全部位于海拔1800米以上，这也是胡德山上冰川的平均海拔高度，超过80%的冰川表面地区都在海拔2100米以上。山上冰川和永久雪原面积达到13.48平方千米，容积达到0.348立方千米。艾略特冰川是最大最厚的冰川，体积为0.090立方千米，雷达测量出的厚度达到110米。表面面积最大的冰川是库拉德冰河系统，面积达到2.149平方千米。

在2100米的海拔上，冰川和雪原覆盖了大约80%的山体面积。从1907年至2004年，冰川平均减少了34%。胡德山的冰川在20世纪上半叶都在减退，而在60年代和70年代开始回升或至少降低了减退的步伐，从那以后又回到了一种减退的模式。新冰期最大的冰川程度形成在18世纪早期。在距今29000到10000年前的最后一次大型冰川运动中，冰川下降达到790到700米的高度，距离胡德山顶峰有15千米的距离。冰川退却释放了大量的冰水沉积物，其中一些填补了胡德河谷上游靠近帕克代尔的地区，使这一地区变得地势平坦,并形成了迪伊平地。

三、旅游景区

胡德山所在的胡德山国家森林公园覆盖了 4318.17 平方千米的土地,包括总面积 1271.03 平方千米的四个指定的自然保护区和超过 1900 千米的徒步路径。另有八个荒原地,覆盖了 1260 平方千米的面积。

1. 政府营地

在胡德山的南面海拔 1188 米的地方是一个小型私人社区。这里是进行众多户外冒险活动的出发地,包括滑雪、徒步、山地自行车骑行、采摘美洲越橘以及巴洛路探险。附近小道交错,冬夏都可以使用。而在此开展冬季运动的历史可以追溯到 20 世纪早期,在廷伯莱恩、萨米特和雪碗等度假胜地都可以进行滑雪和滑板滑雪运动。

2. 廷伯莱恩小屋

政府营地再往上就是廷伯莱恩小屋。廷伯莱恩小屋地处胡德山略低于帕尔默冰川的南翼,海拔 1828 米,是美国国家历史地标性酒店和滑雪度假地。小屋位于大熊湖,周围交通便利,临近机场,靠近魔术山高山滑道、大贝尔湖和雪峰滑雪场,附近还有大熊湖天文观测台。作为国家历史地标,廷伯莱恩小屋建于 20 世纪 30 年代经济大萧条时期,当时的工程由联邦工程项目管理局负责。这栋庄严的建筑由石材和大型原木建造,一直以来都受到精心维护。廷伯莱恩小屋采取的是"公有民营"的经营方式,以酒店、餐厅和滑雪胜地的形式向公众开放。每年有来自全球各地近 200 万游客在这里受到热情的接待,当地林务局解说人员还为游客提供小屋的参观服务。小屋酒店内有精致的油画、纺织品、木雕、石雕和金属制品,其陈设布局既尊重了传统又体现了创新。客房有着独特的乡村气息,家具陈设、房间装修和便利的现代化设施融为一体,体现了古朴和现代的交融。作为俄勒冈州最著名的旅游景点之一,小屋拥有全年滑雪的环境、一流的美食、宽敞的活动室以及贵宾接待服务。

3. 蒂莫西湖

蒂莫西湖是胡德山国家森林公园最受欢迎的家庭露营和垂钓目的地之一。湖的南岸有四个成熟的露营地,另外两个附近的营地可供游客练习骑术。

北岸有三个较小的不是太完善的露营地。为远足、山地自行车和马术运动所开辟的山路小径体系环绕整个蒂莫西湖。蒂莫西湖的支流地区拥有非常美丽的湿地环境，克拉克马斯湖边的橡树林刀叉草地、蒂莫西湖北臂以及小陨石坑草场都是观赏湿地野生生物的理想场所。蒂莫西湖是一个人工湖，于1958年由波特兰通用电气公司建造，用于水力发电。俄勒冈政府在1400英亩的湖水中养殖了彩虹鳟鱼，湖上也可以骑摩托艇，但速度不能超过每小时16千米。

4. 克拉克马斯河

1988年，美国国会划定克拉克马斯河的75千米作为联邦野生风景河流体系中的一员。从它的起源奥莱利湖风景区到大悬崖，优美的景色和临近波特兰的地域优势使得克拉克马斯河的这一部分成为俄勒冈州最受欢迎的休闲地区之一。河流蚀刻出一条深深的峡谷，两旁岩石峭壁，山体斜坡上植被茂盛。克拉克马斯河中包含不同的鱼类，对于渔业生产具有重要意义。此外，还有总长超过1664千米的含鱼溪流和河流流入克拉克马斯河。奇努克鲑鱼、银大马哈鱼和硬头鳟在这些水域产卵，养育后代和迁移。本土的鱼类则包括割喉鳟鱼、虹鳟鱼、溪红点鲑和濒危的硬头奇努克鲑鱼。

四、休闲活动

胡德山有6个滑雪区：廷伯莱恩地区、胡德草场、雪碗滑雪区、库珀山嘴滑雪区、雪兔滑雪区和雪峰滑雪场，总共覆盖了超过18.6平方千米的滑雪地形，其中廷伯莱恩是北美地区唯一的提供全年高山滑雪拖曳升降服务的滑雪区。

胡德山有6条主要的登山路线，包括了总共30个不同的冲顶点，攀登难度也从2级到5.9级不等；其中最受欢迎的攀登路线是南线，始于廷伯莱恩小屋，沿帕尔默冰川直上到克雷特大岩石（冰川顶上巨大的凸起）。法国圆顶是一处受欢迎的攀岩区，位于胡德山的西侧。这一安山岩岩壁提供了

14 条攀爬路线，高度从 20 多米到 50 多米不等。最受欢迎的路线是巨人楼梯，难度在 5.6 级，大部分路线都用螺栓固定。

第二节　冰雪胜地——美国雷尼尔雪山

雷尼尔雪山是一个巨大的层状火山，位于美国华盛顿州西雅图东南 87 千米，是美国本土和喀斯喀特火山弧地区地形特点最鲜明的山，最高峰海拔 4392 米，是喀斯喀特山脉的最高峰。雷尼尔雪山被认为是世界上最危险的火山之一，被 IAVCEI（国际火山学和地球内部化学研究协会）列入十年火山研究项目。由于冰川含量巨大，雷尼尔雪山具有产生大量火山泥流的可能性，对整个皮阿拉普河流域具有潜在的威胁。1890 年，美国地名委员会宣布该山被称为"雷尼尔"。1897 年，太平洋森林保护区被称为雷尼尔山森林保护区。1899 年，美国为了保护庄严肃穆、雪裹冰封的雷尼尔山自然景色，以此山为中心建立了面积约 980 平方千米的雷尼尔山国家公园。

一、自然环境

雷尼尔山地势突出，在晴朗的日子，它矗立在西雅图塔科马市区东南地平线上，以至于当地人有时就将其称为"大山"。在能见度非常高的时候，远在俄勒冈的波特兰和英属哥伦比亚的维多利亚都可以看到它。雷尼尔山有三个高峰，最高峰被称为"哥伦比亚峰"；第二高峰被称为"成功点"，海拔 4315 米，位于峰顶高原的南缘，"萨克萨斯克里夫"山脊的顶端；最低的山峰被称为"自由帽"，海拔 4301 米，在西北边缘，可俯瞰"自由山脊""日落剧场"和"威利斯墙"。山顶最高处是两个火山口，每个直径超过 305 米，东面的火山口较大，与西面的火山口部分重叠。火山产生的地热使两个火山口的边

缘区域不会产生积雪和冰冻，造就了世界最大的火山冰川洞穴网络，全长近3.2千米。在西面的火山口的最低处有一个小火山湖，长约40米，宽约10米，深约5米，湖面海拔达到4329米，是北美最高的火山湖。由于处于30多米厚的冰层下，火山湖只有通过洞穴才能进入。卡尔本河、皮阿拉普河、莫维奇河、尼斯阔利河、考利茨河都发源于雷尼尔山的同名冰川。怀特河的来源是温斯罗普冰川、埃蒙斯冰川和弗莱英潘冰川。怀特河、卡尔本河和莫维奇河汇入皮阿拉普河，皮阿拉普河在塔科马注入科曼斯门特湾；尼斯阔利河注入莱西东部的皮吉特湾；考利茨河汇入凯尔索和朗维尤之间的哥伦比亚河。

雷尼尔山现在仍有不少冒气的岩洞和温暖的矿泉水。高耸入云的雷尼尔山是美国东部前往俄勒冈地区和自太平洋进入普吉特海峡的西海岸的船舶航行的陆标。雷尼尔山常常被云霞或雾气所笼罩，只有在夏秋之际的晴朗日子里才一露雄姿。位于东坡的埃蒙斯冰川是美国最大的冰川，其余如厄斯奎利冰川、考里兹冰川和英格兰哈姆冰川等都很著名。广泛分布的冰川，在夏季里消融，形成条条湍急的溪流和飞泻的瀑布，流水之声不绝于耳，在山谷里回荡。这里是华盛顿州最有名的旅游胜地，集中了冰川、瀑布、森林、湖泊和丰富的野生动物等自然景观。

二、火山构造

雷尼尔山是喀斯喀特火山弧地区的一个层状火山，其早期的熔岩沉积物据估计有84万年的历史。这些早期沉积物形成了雷尼尔山的雏形，也被称作原始火山锥，而如今的火山锥形成于50多万年前。

主要由安山岩构成的雷尼尔山受到高度侵蚀，山体斜坡上布满冰川。它曾经的海拔高度可能在4900米左右，比现在要高。在距今大约5000年前，发生了一次大型岩屑崩落，形成了奥西奥拉泥石流，造就了雷尼尔山现在的海拔。在过去，雷尼尔山发生过多次岩屑崩落，由于大量的冰川存在也产生过巨大的火山泥石流，泥石流一路延伸到如今的塔科马和西雅图南部地区。这种大规模的岩屑和冰川崩落使雷尼尔山的高度下降了500米，降到了现在大约4300米的海拔。大约在530年至550年前，发生了埃雷克特龙泥石流，但规模远不及奥西奥拉泥石流。在大约5000年前的大崩溃后发

生了多次火山喷发，直到最近 1000 年以前，火山熔岩和火山灰才累积形成了现代的火山锥。在雷尼尔山已经发现了多达 11 个全新世火山灰层。

三、冰川景观

冰川是雷尼尔山最引人注目的动态地质特征。26 个主要冰川加上常年积雪的场所，总共覆盖了大约 93 平方千米的山体表面，冰雪体积达到约 4.2 立方千米。

冰川在重力的影响下移动，这种重力来源于冰川搬运岩石时产生的共同作用，以及冰晶体之间和自身内部的变形。靠近冰川表面和沿中轴线的地方移动速度最快。1970 年 5 月期间测出的尼斯阔利冰川的移动速度达到每天 74 厘米。由于冰川底部的融冰含量增多，夏季的流量一般比冬季大。

雷尼尔山的冰川体积在过去变化显著。如在最后一个冰河时代，从大约 25000 年到大约 15000 年前，冰川曾覆盖了现在的雷尼尔山国家公园周围的大多数地区，并且延伸至现在的普吉特湾盆地的周边。在 14 世纪和 1850 年之间，雷尼尔山的多数冰川沿山谷而下，推进到了自最后一个冰河时代以来的最远程度。这一时期，世界范围内也发生了很多类似的冰川移动。地质学家把这一时期称为"小冰河世纪"。在"小冰河世纪"，尼斯阔利冰川从"冰川桥"向下推进了 200 到 240 米，塔荷马和南塔荷马冰川在"冰川岛"底部融合，埃蒙斯冰川则推进到了怀特河营地 1.9 千米的范围内。"小冰河世纪"的冰川退却缓慢，直到大约 1920 年退却速度才加快。从"小冰河世纪"到 1950 年，雷尼尔山的冰川向下降了大约四分之一的高度。然而，从 1950 年一直到 20 世纪 80 年代初，由于受到世纪中期相对较低的气温的影响，许多大型冰川继续发育。卡尔本、考利茨、埃蒙斯和尼斯阔利冰川在 20 世纪 70 年代末和 80 年代初的发育得益于 60 年代和 70 年代期间的高降雪量。自从 20 世纪 80 年代初以来，发育进程开始减缓，许多冰川开始不断变薄和消融。

四、旅游休闲

雷尼尔山是登山者向往的地方，这里有美国阿拉斯加州南部最大的冰川，在这里登山必须越过熔岩、冰川、冰原、冰洞、深沟和塔形冰块等极为复杂的地形，攀登难度大，极具挑战性。大多数登山者需要两到三天时间才能达到顶峰。登山队必须要有冰川旅游、自救和野外旅行的经验。每年约 8000 至 13000 人尝试攀登，大约 90% 登山者会选择从东南翼缪尔营地出发，其余大部分则经过东北的舒尔曼营地攀登到埃蒙斯冰川。大约有一半的人能够成功登顶，而天气和体能则成为登顶失败的最常见原因。

雷尼尔山国家公园还是滑雪和冬游的好场所，徒步旅行、雪地健行、越野滑雪、摄影、露营等活动非常受欢迎。在乐园谷一带，1971—1972 年冬季的降雪量曾创下世界纪录，也为滑雪运动提供了绝好的条件，增添了雷尼尔山严冬的魅力。在雷尼尔山旅游，可以沿着 145 千米长的山间小路漫步，这条路有个充满诗意的名字——寻幽山径。山径两侧的风光因海拔不同而变化，低处是茂密的森林，高处是银色的冰雪世界，冰原与密林之间是高山草地，草地上野花竞放，争奇斗艳。

"天堂"及"日出"两处景点尤其受到珍视与保护。"天堂"高约 1402 米，位于雷尼尔山西南方的隆迈尔山的北面。这里地势愈来愈高，转过几个陡峭的弯，便来到被人们称之为"天堂"的景点，风景绮丽。这里也是雷尼尔山国家公园内最受欢迎的一处景点，除了有漂亮的山景之外，还有潺潺的流水、清丽的瀑布和湖泊。在"天堂"的南边和西南边分别是倒影湖和那拉达瀑布，再北边一点则是天堂河，知名的尼斯卡利冰河和天堂冰河就是从这儿进入公园的。位于雷尼尔山北边的"日出"，则是国家公园内最高的景点，也是观赏山景最佳的地点。在这里不但可以欣赏到冰河的壮丽奇景，还可以眺望公园内另一座秀丽的贝克山以及太平洋。

第三节 绿野仙踪——美国沙斯塔山

沙斯塔山，位于美国加利福尼亚州北部，喀斯喀特山脉南端，海拔4316米，圆锥形，由安山岩组成。山顶的积雪终年不化，有大小7个冰川。沙斯塔山是一座死火山，最近的一次喷发是在1786年。

沙斯塔山所在的沙斯塔国家森林由联邦政府指定，美国林务局管理，是加州最大的国家森林。森林面积894552公顷，包括五个荒野地区，数百个高山湖泊和总长10103千米的溪流和河流。1954年，沙斯塔国家森林和特里尼蒂国家森林正式合并成为沙斯塔-特里尼蒂国家森林。西部森林（原来的特里尼蒂国家森林）位于加利福尼亚海岸山脉的东部，主要位于特里尼蒂县，但也延伸到蒂黑马、沙斯塔和洪堡县的部分地区，覆盖了422361公顷的面积。东部森林（原来的沙斯塔国家森林）位于加州中央山谷和沙斯塔山谷北部之间，它覆盖了锡斯基尤、沙斯塔、特里尼蒂和莫多克县的部分地区，面积为471926公顷。

一、自然生态

沙斯塔-特里尼蒂国家森林位于克拉马斯山脉东部和南喀斯喀特的交汇处，森林内有五个国会指定的荒野保护区，包括城堡岩荒原、钱斯卢拉

荒原、沙斯塔山荒原、特里尼蒂高山荒原和尤拉波利荒原。虽然海拔不高，但是植被茂盛，有浓密的灌木丛、林地和草地。在高海拔的特里尼蒂高山、埃迪斯山和沙斯塔山等地区，森林过渡到山地丛林和亚高山林地，最终成为高山岩石和岩屑堆。

在雷丁镇北部沙斯塔湖周围的低海拔山麓丘陵地带，森林和植被主要是灰松、球锥松、西黄松、蓝栎、黑栎、槲树和花旗松。灌木多样性非常高，常见的低海拔林下灌木有白叶石兰、小叶鼠李、加州七叶树、加州咖啡豆和西部紫荆。而溪流峡谷地带气候潮湿，树木和灌木则以阔叶枫、西美蜡梅、山茱萸、白桤木和柳树为主。在中海拔地带，兰伯氏松、翠柏、白冷杉和杰弗里松取代其他树种加入到花旗松、黄松和槲树的行列。越橘、鞣皮栎、绿叶石兰、金叶锥栗成为主要的林下灌木。在沙斯塔山东部和北部的喀斯喀特地区，常见的是蔷薇科淡灰色灌木和鼠李。在中海拔的克拉马斯山脉的迂回曲折的小道上，翠柏和杰弗里松林则聚居了银穗树、栓皮栎和古生常绿灌木。再往西，延绵的南福克山脊把沙斯塔-特里尼蒂国家森林和六河国家森林一分为二，这里主要生长着鞣皮栎、花旗松、金叶锥栗。海拔更高的亚高山森林主要由山红杉、铁杉、西部白松、红松组成。海拔最高的植被主要是狐尾草和白皮松。在克拉马斯山脉的山地草甸和河边地带有丰富的加州猪笼草、西部杜鹃，偶尔还可以看到奥福德雪松。

二、美丽湖泊

沙斯塔、刘易斯顿和特里尼蒂湖是"威士忌-沙斯塔-特里尼蒂国家历史保护区"的一部分。沙斯塔湖的湖岸线全长有587千米，由许多狭长港湾和水湾组成。著名的四大狭湾是萨克拉门托湾、麦克劳德湾、斯阔克里克湾和皮特湾，它们的所在地景色旖旎，有着独特的地质风景名胜。刘易斯顿湖邻近威瓦维尔镇，正好位于特里尼蒂大坝的下游，刘易斯顿镇的北部，蓄水量稳定。铁峡谷（沙斯塔湖东北，大

弯镇附近）、刘易斯顿湖、麦克劳德（麦克劳德镇南部）、沙斯塔湖和特里尼蒂湖都是大型水库，可以钓鱼、划船和露营。在沙斯塔湖还可以租用船屋，森林里也有很多钓鱼的机会，有几个高山湖泊位于特里尼蒂保护区（沙斯塔镇西部和西南），多数湖里都有鳟鱼。这里因为可以进行鲑鱼和虹鳟垂钓而非常受欢迎。这些溪流也邻近威瓦维尔，贯穿整个"特里尼蒂高山荒野保护区"。

三、休闲活动

沙斯塔-特里尼蒂国家森林提供各种各样的休闲活动，包括徒步、背包旅行、登山、骑马、露营、划船、钓鱼、观光、高山滑雪、滑板滑雪、越野滑雪、雪地摩托车，等等。

沙斯塔-特里尼蒂国家森林拥有超过736千米的步道，包括东西两侧248千米的太平洋山脊步道。火山遗址风景小道全长800千米，可以驾车沿小道欣赏加州北部的火山。莫多克火山风景小道始于麦克劳德，沿途可以欣赏到森林东部的一些独特的火山风光，小道一直延伸到麦迪森湖、熔岩床国家纪念碑和图利湖。

霍夫曼山防火瞭望塔位于麦迪森湖火山的熔岩流地区。瞭望塔保留了原有的建筑特色，现在是一个可以提供过夜休闲娱乐的僻静场所。瞭望塔小屋海拔2228米，可以俯瞰沙斯塔山、拉森峰、麦克洛克林山和各种其他地貌。360度的瞭望塔观景点可以欣赏到部分北加州著名的风景，范围从北部的图利湖盆地到南部的福尔河河谷。此外，还有靠近沙斯塔湖的螯恣山瞭望塔和靠近森林最南端的普拉提纳镇的后溪瞭望塔。后溪瞭望塔由公共资源保护组织建于1934年，可以容纳8人住宿，从木屋后面的房间可以俯瞰整个森林，屋内生活设施一应俱全，也可供出租。

第四节　蓝岭蜥蜴——美国蓝岭山·谢南多厄国家公园

谢南多厄国家公园位于美丽的弗吉尼亚蓝岭山，占地将近800平方千米，北起弗吉尼亚弗朗特罗伊，南至特克盖普，靠近韦恩斯伯勒。公园地形狭长，西面是广阔的谢南多厄河和谢南多厄山谷，东面是弗吉尼亚皮德蒙特连绵

起伏的丘陵，谢南多厄河穿过峡谷向西流去，马萨纳滕山矗立于河的南北支流之间，这一区域的景色异常美丽。蜿蜒的柏油路两侧，树林和草地之间形成了宽广的过渡地带。谢南多厄因其形状常被比作当地产的蓝岭火蜥蜴，而路就是火蜥蜴的脊梁。除了著名的天际线大道，公园有近40%的土地面积322.04平方千米已经被指定为荒野保护区，并作为国家荒野保护系统的一部分，最高峰是海拔1235米的玳瑁山。

一、地质景观

谢南多厄国家公园坐落在弗吉尼亚州中北部的蓝岭山脉。这些山脉形成了一个独特的高地，海拔达到1200米以上。在蓝岭山脉和谢南多厄河谷之间，一些地方地势起伏超过了900多米。蓝岭山脊的西面是谢南多厄河流域盆地，东面是詹姆斯和拉帕汉诺克河流域盆地。

公园里有弗吉尼亚最古老的岩石，年龄超过10亿年。公园还因其古老的岩层而著名，主要由绿岩和花岗岩组成。该园区所处的蓝岭背斜西段，位于阿巴拉契亚褶皱冲断带东缘，区域性古生代结构特征明显。古生代晚期的阿莱干尼造山运动（325到260百万年前）使公园内的岩石发生折叠、断裂、扭曲和变质。而新生代差异侵蚀则造成了蓝岭山脉崎岖的地形，尽管一些后古生代构造活动也发生在该地区，但第四纪表层沉积物随处可见，这些沉积物覆盖了大部分基岩。

二、公园形成

谢南多厄比起其他公园有更多的人类历史产物，它位于景色美丽但有人居住的蓝岭山的一部分，这里几乎把弗吉尼亚分成了两部分。和大多数国家公园不同，谢南多厄是几代人曾经居住的地方。公园围起的这段山岭少有通道，规模庞大的山脉让早期的拓荒者不得不穿过坎伯兰山口进入宽阔的谢南多厄山谷。

在成为公园之前，这里大部分地区都是农田，几乎90%的当地居民以土地为生，许多人曾在山谷的苹果园及附近地区工作，现在还有少数地方保留了旧农场的原貌。1926年议会决定把该地区设为国家公园后，为了让这一地区适合设立国家公园，弗吉尼亚州政府买下了位于蓝岭山和谢南多厄河谷大概4000块私人拥有的土地，然后州政府把这片土地捐给了国家。没有任何一个其他公园的建立需要买下如此多的私人土地，也没有任何一个其他公园的建立需要国家公园管理局在一片已有人居住的土地上规划设立。

公园设立时大多数公园用地都是被侵蚀的山坡、不能再用的农田和稀疏的二、三代森林。从18世纪早期开始人们就从这里获取木材了，但在这片山区工作的人们不得不离开以留出空间建造公园。国家公园和天际线的创建工作开始于1930年一次严重的干旱之后，这次干旱给这一地区的农作物和果园带来了毁灭性的打击。尽管自然灾害是创建公园的部分原因，但因为建设公园而造成的流离失所却是一个不争的事实，搬迁违背了当地人的意愿，即使是少数人留了下来，他们也失去了赖以生存的社区。在公园建成开放后，数以百计的家庭离开了这一地区，有的是自愿，有的是强制离开。在受影响的8个县中，很多当地人强烈反对搬迁，他们认为搬迁让他们失去了自己的家园和社区。多数搬迁家庭来自麦迪逊县、佩吉县和拉帕汉诺克县。

许多人离开了原来的木屋和农舍，政府出资让他们在外面挨着公园的地方定居了下来。在强制搬迁的同时，也有少数人在他们的土地被征用之后得到政府允许可以留下来继续生活。虽然政策允许想留下来的老年人和残疾人享有土地终身租用权，但大多数人都理性地离开了他们的家园。消失的社区和家庭成为建设美国最美丽的国家公园和景区道路的代价。后来，森林恢复，它们遮盖了放牧、耕作和采伐原木造成的"伤疤"。原产的动物也回来了，黑熊、浣熊及负鼠这种美国仅存的有袋动物又开始和西部开发时期那样在这里漫步。

三、旅游景点

1. 科尔宾木屋

科尔宾小木屋是一场森林火灾后遗留下来的三座原木建筑之一，是这一区域传统山居木屋的原始范例。这个木屋由乔治·科尔宾和几个朋友建于1910年，那时他们在这里砍伐原木。科尔宾一家在这里居住了很多年，依靠自己种出或做出的东西为生。今天，这个小木屋由波托马克阿巴拉契亚山间小道俱乐部维护，并出租给俱乐部成员和公众。俱乐部也沿着阿巴拉契亚山间小道经营了很多乡村木屋。

2. 胡佛营地

公园是胡佛营地的所在地。胡佛营地是胡佛总统从华盛顿（哥伦比亚特区）离开外出休假的地方。胡佛一开始对自己休假地的要求非常简单：他要求休假地距首都不超过160千米，在没有蚊子的高地上，靠近有鳟鱼的河流。现在，政府官员仍然在周末到营地的木屋里居住。

3. 天际线大道

天际线大道是公园最有名的景点，全长169千米，沿山脊贯穿整个公园。这条路上有75个俯瞰点，可以驻足观赏壮观的树林、山脉和著名的谢南多厄河谷。162千米的阿巴拉契亚小径也在公园里。这些小道中最著名的景点是旧抹布山，在那里可以体验刺激的攀岩活动和欣赏弗吉尼亚州最壮丽的景色，还可以骑马、露营、骑自行车和欣赏众多的瀑布。最高的瀑布位于天际线大道35千米附近，高度达到31米。不仅如此，公园内有十几个瀑布的高度都超过了12米。天际线大道是密西西比河以东的第一条国家公园管理局管理的道路，在美国历史古迹名录中被列为国家历史地标，它也被指定为国家级风景大道，是秋季驱车旅游的理想场所。

4. 谢南多厄河谷

谢南多厄河谷是美国阿巴拉契亚大山谷的一部分，大部分在弗吉尼亚州境内，从波多马克河畔西弗吉尼亚州的哈帕斯费里附近向西南延伸，东连蓝岭，西接阿利根尼山脉。谢南多厄河流经9县：西弗吉尼亚州的柏克莱和杰弗逊以及弗吉尼亚州的弗雷德里克、克拉克、谢南多厄、华伦、罗京安、佩奇和奥古斯塔。河谷长约240千米、宽约40千米，一般认定南抵詹姆斯河，因此罗克布里奇县也在其范围内。马萨纳滕山从哈里森堡以东向东北绵延80千米，最高逾914米，将谢南多厄河分为南北两汊。史上著名穿过蓝岭山的隘口包括急流口和石鱼口，后者目前有一条州际公路经过。

知名的19世纪谷地公路（目前亦为州际公路）的通道早期曾为美洲原住民使用，后来成为西部拓荒的要道。1707年法国人米歇尔曾至河谷南部探险，1716年英国殖民总督斯波茨伍德率领远征队越过蓝岭山抵达谢南多厄河。1730年左右白人开始来此拓居。观光名胜主要有乔治·华盛顿国家森林、谢南多厄国家公园、勒星顿附近的天然桥，还有该区域的许多石灰岩山洞。东边，通过国家公园的山景公路和往南的蓝岭公路（均沿蓝岭山山脊开辟）与河谷平行。2005年开放的谢南多厄河谷博物馆主要展示该区域的艺术、文化和历史。该馆坐落于弗吉尼亚州温彻斯特的一座综合园区内，园内还有数座花园及一栋历史性建筑。

第六章

南美洲的世界名山

第一节　高原化石——巴西阿拉里皮山

　　阿拉里皮地质公园位于巴西塞阿拉州南部沉积岩地区，属于塞阿拉阿拉里皮沉积盆地的一部分，面积 5000 平方千米，地处赤道附近，濒临大西洋，是巴西离欧洲、北美的最近点。该公园是由塞阿拉州的科技和高等教育秘书处倡导成立的，并得到了卡里里地方大学的配合。2005 年 12 月被列为世界地质公园，公园主要以古化石著称。

一、旅游设施

　　阿拉里皮地质公园位于巴西塞阿拉州的南部，海拔 750 米的圣克鲁斯制高点，是一个位置极佳的俯瞰观察点，它位于桑塔纳杜卡里里城附近，可以俯视阿拉里皮盆地部分区域。

　　在蓬塔尔十字架矗立的高原上有为游客提供便利的设施，有一个饭店，一个以古生物学为主题的广场，在瞭望塔旁还有一个小教堂。这个高原被茂密的植被覆盖着，其间是土路和小路，沿着这些路，游客可以到达科学及旅游遗址。古生物尤卡博物馆坐落于桑塔纳杜卡里里市，它是项目研究的基地，其中包括本地化石找寻，它成了向来此的游客宣传古生物重要性的主要渠道。人们把科学兴趣与当地的宗教和显现当地神秘色彩的巨大的十字架结合在一起，这十字架向人们展示着刚过去的两个世纪。

　　里亚舒杜梅尤公园是观察阿拉里皮盆地丰富地貌的最佳地点。此地区有丰富的灌木丛，且有本地典型的动植物群。本地的代表景点是依然在喷涌的三眼未经污染的泉水。此地区给沿路提供了食物、瞭望塔、信息站、天然取水池。这个公园是限制性使用的，受到来自当地大中学校研究团体和参观者的监督。它的自然环境的保持状况和便利设施是令人满意的。这个公园接待参观者的基础设施建设较完善，它有一条环园路可以到达大多数重要景点，这些景点可以供人欣赏，也可以供人研究此地的动植物群和自然水资源的特点。

桑塔纳杜卡里里的农村将建 PTEROSAUS 公园，面积达 23 公顷，属于卡里里地方大学，它将成为阿拉里皮地质公园的主要部分，也将是巴西唯一的此种类型的公园。此项目的主要目的是重建沙帕达阿拉里皮地区白垩纪时期的环境。初期的目的是保护和维持这个区域的挖掘。这个区域从外表就能看到几层沉积岩，它含有重要的珍贵化石。从这一点看，此地区的挖掘需要修建一个类似于浓荫庇护平台的简单建筑，以加强保护这个地区，为保护挖掘和古生物研究提供支持。通过挖掘，研究者、学者和参观者就能研究和了解本地沉积岩层中化石的储存情况。后期，则可以通过白垩纪时期的动植物化石的摹本重塑地球生命史的环境。白垩纪时期是地球上出现花的时期。植物化石在沉积层中经常被发现，这些沉积岩被用到了像房屋地面铺设、外墙壁装饰等的市政建设中。PTEROSAURS 公园作为当地游览的又一中心，将进一步得到巩固。这个偏远的乡村尽管还没有辅助设施，每年却接待大约 18000 名参观者，包括研究人员和学者，他们都兴趣盎然地研究尤卡古生物博物馆里所搜集的 7000 块化石。

二、特色景观

历史悠久的查韦斯矿山是"查韦斯矿业和工业"矿山开采公司石膏开采工业联合公司的一部分。它勘探位于桑塔纳杜卡里里和新奥林达市的几个矿井，为水泥生产企业提供原材料，生产浇铸和冲洗矿业的植物酸及一些特殊的添加剂产品。选择这个地方作为阿拉里皮地质公园的主要一部分，目的是揭示地质的石膏层重要性和潜在启发性。另一方面，由于这是一个不再使用的矿井，所以这种矿石转化成石膏时的用处，工业使用中适宜的方式，为在挖掘过程中运用这种自然资源的适宜正确的形式纠正一些不合适的做法和保护自然环境及周围的地貌，都能得到完美的体现。当前，由于开采所形成的敞开的矿井洞口对周围的环境形成了强烈的冲击，不过这种冲击由于外面的中性覆盖物的重新排列从而得到了缓解，就像阿拉里皮塞阿拉高地区的其他地区通过当前石灰石的开采而成功实施的那样。还有，阿拉里皮地质公园及其系统的建立能对提高当地群众对保持和维护这些古生物遗产的重要性及好处的意识具有教育作用，同时它也为当地旅游开发提供多种选择，为人们带来就业机会和创造收入，为这种重要的化石储藏的无节制的开采带来另外的利用方式。

卡里里石矿位于离新奥林达镇 3000 米的地方，可经新奥林达和桑塔纳杜卡里里之间的 CE-166 高速公路到达。它由无脊椎动物、有脊椎动物和植物化石构成，它的岩石是从黄色到奶油色的水平平行的薄片石灰石。卡里里的石头挖掘活动改变了这个山坡的自然面貌，形成了新的地貌。这些矿井的呈现有利于对自然构造进行观察和分析创造环境。自 19 世纪以来，在当地的建筑中就有使用卡里里石建房的传统，这一点与这个州的其他地方有所不同，非常值得关注，其他地方都是用砖来建房的。

在 BATATEIRA 河源头处分布着一系列的小瀑布，景色非常美丽，覆盖着大量还未被人类勘探的浓密植被。BATATEIRA 河沿岸地区被划分成了不同用途的区域，如休闲、服务、供给等。在河的源头，靠近泉水的地方，有茂密的植被，还有一些小路，在路旁和一个农田中间分布着一些私人庄园和俱乐部。尽管有一个公共俱乐部，利用河水开发了人工游泳池、小瀑布等娱乐设施，还使用河水供给整个建筑，但本地区绝大部分分布的都是大农场和住宅。在克拉图市周围，一系列的泉水为本地区的小溪和河流提供了水源，在这些旅游胜地开发了一些传统的休闲活动和生态旅游。BATATEIRA 河泉是一个对公众开放的旅游胜地，游客可以通过一些小路徒步到达这个地区以游览其丰富的自然风貌。

COLINA DO HORTO 地区已完全成为北茹阿泽鲁市的市区，因此它被大量建筑物所占据，不过仍能欣赏到一些自然风貌。与旅游相关的活动，特别是宗教旅游，从朝圣事件到帕德雷西塞罗一直得到了加强，被视作全巴西最重要的宗教事件之一。在这里，每年有来自所有东北部地区和巴西其他地方上的超过 250 万人的朝圣者聚积此地。在朝圣活动期间，COLINA DO HORTO 不仅成了朝圣的中心，连续九天的祈祷之地和宗教徒的参观场所，还成了宗教手工制品的大型商场。

三、发展战略

巴西塞阿拉州政府通过城市秘书处在福塔莱萨市帕塞尔区东北海岸成功召开了"地质公园和地质旅游国际研讨会"。本次研讨会的主要目的是为了向与会代表介绍"联合国教科文组织世界地质公园计划"，强调阿拉里皮地质公园对卡里里市发展的重要性，促进巴西和美洲区新地质公园的创建。尽管阿拉里皮地质公园和塞阿拉州政府做出了大量的努力，但将阿拉里皮地质公园塑造成塞阿拉州、巴西、美洲区甚至世界地质公园网络的成功典范仍然是他们面临的一个巨大挑战。为此，阿拉里皮地质公园和塞阿拉州政府决定向成功典范——葡萄牙纳图特乔地质公园学习，制定"城市计划"战略，由城市秘书处牵头，旅游、环境、文化与科学等秘书处、卡里里区域大学和包括地方企业及文化、社会联合会在内的其他实体合作共同推动战略的发展。而且，这项战略还有可能通过大学、地方团体以及综合了地质学、生物学、人类学、历史学、考古学、博物馆学、经济学、建筑学、环境学、管理学、营销学、设计学、信息学、旅游学等多门学科的国际国内合作，让年轻人参与其中。最重要的是必须为这项战略成立一个管理机构以确保阿拉里皮地质公园在政治周期外的稳定运行。"城市计划"将来发展的一个重要成果就是使目前没有被利用的地质遗迹很好地服务于旅游业。

第二节　生态林原——巴西瓜拉米兰伽山脉

　　巴西瓜拉米兰伽山脉，占地 3822 平方千米，位于塞阿拉州的中北部，它包含了瓜拉米兰伽等 12 个自治区。瓜拉米兰伽自治区位于海拔 865 米处，它完全处于巴图尔特地带的环境保护区内。在其领土内，横躺着海拔 1115 米以上的中音海峡。以塞拉德巴图尔特著称，它是一幅多变的山水画，那里的山和山谷向人们展示了别具一格的美。

一、自然特征

　　该地区有着强烈的地质构造活动和相当崎岖的形态。它的土壤是由前寒武纪的基底岩石构成的，也有一些红黄灰化贫瘠的土地被残枝落叶滋润得具有高肥沃力。瓜拉米兰伽属于热带性气候，冬天的降雨量往往比夏天

多，它的年平均气温是 20.9℃，年平均降雨量大约是 1560 毫米。九月是最干燥的月份，降雨量只有 28 毫米。11 月是一年之中最温暖的月份，其平均温度为 21.6℃，而六月的平均温度则是 19.9℃。这是一个拥有开花植被的热带雨林，它包含许多令人印象深刻的五彩花和树，在这些植物中有一种被人们用作一个国家的名字，那就是"pau-brasil"。大部分的热带雨林位于高海拔处，亚热带雨林位于中海拔处，而在一些海拔较低的区域则是一些浓密的灌木群。由于这个地区的气候以及地理位置所造成的物理差异，导致山上的物种高密度分布，从而形成了真正的生物多样性遗传库。

二、休闲旅游

热带雨林和那里独特的、传统的村庄给游客提供了很多有关音乐、戏剧、艺术以及原生态的一些体验。用当地的话说，"瓜拉米兰"就意味着"红鸟"。18 世纪时，"Missao de Palma"代表团为了传道、扩建畜牧场以及咖啡种植

园来到这个山区。该地区曾经被许多民族所占据，特别是在19世纪开始自我巩固，一些城市集聚地后来都变成了村庄和城市。

对于那些喜爱户外运动和生态旅行的人们而言，这是一个实现速滑、登山、徒步旅行、骑脚踏车兜风、步行和鸟瞰美景的好地方。当然，你也可以体验当地的文化、音乐、戏剧以及艺术节。

瓜拉米兰伽山脉距巴西东北部塞阿拉州的首府福塔雷萨只有一个小时的车程。从山的最高点可以看到两个壮观的景象，一个是半干旱地区，也叫"林原"，另一个是葱翠群山。在这里，一个主要的节日就是爵士和蓝调音乐节。在年度盛事中，你还可以欣赏到民族和国际音乐，当然也有许多与戏剧和视觉艺术有关的活动。瓜拉米兰伽除了文化吸引人外，它美丽的自然景色、精湛的工艺和当地国际化的烹饪法也是相当吸引人的。

第三节　滑翔天堂——巴西基沙达山

巴西基沙达山坐落于地球上最古老的地区，建立于6亿年前的前寒武纪年间，这里的气候具有高效的风化作用，数千年来侵蚀了无数的斜坡和孤立的石峰。这些集中的石林不仅具有罕见的美丽风景，而且它还是一个进行岩石攀登和其他极限运动的好地方。

一、自然景观

该地区属于热带半干旱气候。冬天的降雨量往往多于夏天。基沙达山的年平均气温是27.1℃，年平均降雨量大约是765毫米。最干燥的月份是只

有 2 毫米降雨量的十月。但基沙达山地区是一个非常严重的干旱地区，植被都是一些包含仙人掌和多刺低树的茂密的卡廷加群落。在地势高一点的地方，则是一个多刺植被的森林。

二、旅游发展

在基沙达山有一个石林的天然纪念馆，它距福塔雷萨大约有 160 千米，旨在保护稀有、独特、美丽的石林。

对于那些喜爱户外运动和生态旅行的人们而言，这是一个体验徒步旅行、速滑、登山、越野、骑马、骑脚踏车、鸟瞰全景、滑翔、跳伞等活动的好地方。基沙达和伊别帕巴山脉被誉为是滑翔天堂（距离 300 千米以上）。

虽然未被充分开发，但是它具备发展旅游业的巨大潜力，特别是生态旅游和极限运动旅游。除了巨石以外，基沙达山还有一个可以体验极限运动的地方，那就是"Acude do Cedro"。它是建于一百多年前的巴西最古老的大坝。还有两个自然保护区，一个是建于 2002 年 10 月 31 日的石林天然纪念馆，另一个是建于 1998 年 11 月 5 日的私人保护区的遗产——德克萨斯蓝调庄园。

第四节　伞降天堂——巴西伊别帕巴山脉

巴西的伊别帕巴山脉绵延 110 千米至瑟奥莱东北部，有 40 多千米跨越海岸线，多处山峰超过千米，峭壁险峰主要在东北部的瑟奥莱州，而在西部则地势缓和，平均高度 750 米。

一、气候植被

伊别帕巴山脉属于热带气候，冬季降水多于夏季，年平均气温 26.1℃，年平均降水约 725 毫米，一年中最热的月份是十一月份，平均气温在 27.1℃，六月份平均气温为 25℃，在一些城市有记载的温度也有低至 13℃。伊别帕巴山脉全年气候条件适宜，降水主要集中在瑟奥莱地区，该地区偏西几千米处，降水明显减少，植被向半干旱植被过渡。自北向南，南部山区是热带草原，东北部山区绿荫蔽日，呈现出热带雨林植被，被认为是大西洋丛林。这里盛产蔬菜和花卉，出口欧洲，也盛产甘蔗。

二、旅游休闲

著名的风景名胜区伊别帕巴山脉聚居着不同种族的居民，有塔普伊奥斯人、塔巴伽奥斯人等，在葡萄牙人入侵瑟奥莱之前，这些居民都给欧洲人介绍过好些农作物。对于那些喜欢享受生态活动和生态旅游的旅游者来说，这里是他们享受生命的天堂，可以徒步、岩降、山地骑行、骑马、观鸟、滑翔、伞降……这里是伞降天堂，飞行距离可达 300 多千米，同时，在这里还可以享受多种文化、音乐、电影和艺术节。

第五节 生态高地——巴西卡玛匡高地

一、生态旅游

卡玛匡高地位于巴西南部瑞里奥格兰德州,包括巴吉、南卡萨帕瓦、皮涅罗马查多、博阿维斯塔地区的皮拉蒂尼和桑塔纳各地区,是卡玛匡河流的发源地。该地区主要植被为稀疏的树林,其间分布着草原和灌木,著名的东南山地区以家庭畜牧业为主。由于该地区社会经济和生态环境的特点及历来缺乏传统科学的应用,使得该地区始终未能开展现代化农业。经济以动物饲养为主,主要是饲养牛羊。特色食品如面包、蛋糕、奶酪、葡萄酒、蜂蜜和果酱等旅游业也在兴起,尤其值得关注的是原生态和观光业。

二、旅游发展

高卡玛匡项目提出了该区域发展的战略及行动方案,鼓励综合可持续的区域增长。该倡议始于 2006 年,最初是为了促进和鼓励家庭畜牧业,家庭畜牧业因其以当地草原及其他自然资源为基础发展,被认为是一种生态型生产方式。在过去六年多的工作中，该项目持续发展，现在已进入建立高卡玛匡集体品牌的阶段，高卡玛匡品牌被使用在一些当地出产的产品上，如羊肉、自制蛋糕糕点、手工艺品、羊毛皮革、旅游活动，等等。高卡玛匡地区一部分的工作通过社区参与的方式进行，证明基于自然资源的生产方法可以非常有效，并且生产出差异化的产品。该项目还将该地区共同的历史、社会、环境、文化和经济特点考虑在内。高卡玛匡项目被认为是成功开发了南大河州南部一半地区内的差异化农业的项目。整个项目中巴西农业研究公司的参与旨在说明可以开发一种以家庭所有的土地结构为基础的经济活动方式。

第七章 大洋洲的世界名山

第一节 地质火山——澳大利亚甘比尔山

甘比尔山市位于南澳大利亚一座著名的火山两侧，人口总数27000人，是南澳大利亚最大的区域中心城市。它吸引着大量的游客从澳大利亚的东南和维多利亚港前往这里来购物、运动和享用美食。这座城市的土壤并没有直接与此火山相连，然而它的水源却与它相关。相对较浅的水源是吸引最初的定居者的主要原因，到今天，只有从更深层的蓝湖里取水才能够满足甘比尔山市日益增长的人口。甘比尔山是南澳大利亚最大的城市，距阿德莱德436千米，距墨尔本441千米，是理想的中转旅客地和袋鼠岛。这是澳大利亚最大的海陆城市，也是环绕整个区域自然和文化保存最好的最完美的旅游目的地，拥有许多洞穴和排水口、海岸线、河流、湖泊以及葡萄酒酿造厂。

一、生态环境

甘比尔山最初命名于1800年12月3日，彼时詹姆斯·格朗特上尉和尼尔森女士一起视察此地，看到两座美丽的高峰并将其中的一座命名为甘比尔山，以纪念圣甘比尔。1839年，第一位白人斯蒂芬·亨利，来自波特兰，来到此处发现了美丽的蓝湖。1841年他带着牛群回去，留下了他建在湖边的山谷里的小屋，看管员住在那里帮他看管留下的货物，市中心的山洞则是他们的水源。仓库后来在布朗湖干枯的河岸里凸显出来，是由于各种各样的瀑布使得此地的地下水层不断下降的结果。回溯至1859年，蓝湖的水量历史记载中就已干旱得不足让一个牛群饮用了。到1875年，水面有所回升，可以恢复蓝湖域的基本面貌了。19世纪后半部分，此地区主要是以其高耸壮丽的瀑布而闻名于世，这也导致地区植被环境的破坏，引致政府机构开始鼓励那些土地拥有者们重新种植植物。

南澳的东部有一些国有的富有生产性的农业、园艺、林业用地。大概有4.2%的南澳人口住在东南部并且主要定居在低地，特别是在甘比尔山。仅有大约13%的再生欧洲植被被剩余在这个地区，仅40%的再生植被在正常保护下，超过75%的植被认为是稀有或是受到威胁的，很多植被类型是这个地区的珍品。当地地区降雨等级从南部地区850毫米到北部的450毫米。

甘比尔山有着炎热的夏季和湿冷的冬季。这块区域位于海洋性气候和地中海气候的过渡带。

　　甘比尔山植被的繁茂不仅仅是因为丰富的年降雨量，它的生命之源是位于地表石灰岩下面楔形地块丰富的地下水。发源于洞穴和裂缝的地下水穿过石灰岩缓慢地向南流向海洋，丰富的地下水对美丽的城市公园和花园的形成还有乡村用水有很大的贡献。在海洋环境中形成的石灰岩是由化石和珊瑚构成的，并且不断地向墨累河河岸扩张，一块位于墨累河麦克唐纳港口的石灰岩厚度超过了 320 米。雨水渗透地表浸入石灰岩中，它就像一块巨大的海绵把雨水都储存在空隙之间，被称为无压含水层就是因为地下水在气压的作用下都储存在地下。甘比尔山著名的蓝湖、小蓝湖、文斯湖和皮卡里尼湖是一个提供进入地下水系统的"窗口"。

　　二、地貌景观

　　甘比尔山因其壮观的火山景区和一年变换两次颜色的蓝湖景区吸引着大量的国内外游客来此观光旅游。澳大利亚南部平原的西维多利亚区域和西澳大利亚的石灰岩海湾是澳大利亚最广阔的火山区域。甘比尔山市是新火山板块西部最重要的一部分，并且它位于澳大利亚最西端。主要有 17 个爆发点，还拥有此区域里最小的一个火山。甘比尔山的褶皱就是火山喷发的结果。其火山岩层厚度探测为 80 厘米，火山喷发覆盖面积为 65 平方千米。

甘比尔山位于著名的奥特维盆地。它形成于 700 万年以前，正值澳大利亚从甘瓦纳大陆板块分离的时期。这个板块每年向亚洲板块方向移动 5 至 7 厘米，最后形成了一块独立的大陆。3000 万年前这片陆地被大片的海洋覆盖，所以在海洋层里留下了鱼骨、扇贝和化石，形成了巨大的石灰岩层，现在广泛遍布整个区域。因此，它被命名为石灰岩海岸而甘比尔山成为石灰岩海岸的心脏。海洋已经冲刷澳大利亚板块三次，在穿过东南部的低处时，细沙的冲刷形成丘陵后停止了活动，现在这些沙丘覆盖的地质断层也是很出名的。这些断层控制着东南低处的火山运动，甘比尔山的断层比较脆弱，现在已经位移了近 80 米。冲刷的淤积物形成了南面的海域。

发源于文斯湖和皮卡里尼湖的小河流每小时携带上百万升的水流向海洋。从皮卡里尼湖流向海滩的地下水穿过沙滩时可以看到涌动的泡泡。

乡村工业从石灰岩孔隙不同深度抽取地下水的创举不仅丰富多彩，而且给这个地方带来了财富。石灰岩是一种重要的工业产品，是工业建筑的主要建筑石料，被广泛应用于铁路建设和其他特定用途包括农用石灰、玻璃、玻璃纤维、雕刻和钙质产品如药片、牙膏、爽身粉等。由于地下水慢慢延伸至海洋，从而导致了石灰岩的融化，因此在甘比尔山下的城市以及周边的地区形成了很多洞穴。

三、奇异蓝湖

世界上有许多著名的蓝湖，甘比尔山的蓝湖因其一年之中会改变两次颜色而著名。每年在气候变暖温度升高时，湖水的表面会变换颜色，逐渐由冬天沉闷的灰蓝色变成灿烂的湖蓝色，在三月之前湖水一直都会是冬天的色调。

为什么蓝湖是蓝色的？蓝湖颜色发生变化的一系列说法在 20 世纪被提出。一种说法是蓝色是溶解了一些荧光性的有机物而导致的，它使得湖水表层呈现季节性的颜色变化。另一种说法是湖水表层方解石吸收了除蓝色之外的所有明显的辐射而变成蓝色。大自然的水是蓝色的，同样天也是蓝

色的，因此，蓝湖（所有的蓝湖）应该是蓝色的，问题的关键就是：为什么蓝湖的颜色会在冬天变成灰蓝色？

冬天——八月：湖水的颜色是灰蓝色的，海藻与湖水从底部到顶部完全地融合在一起。湖水呈现出灰蓝色是因为水面表层的有机物质吸收了蓝色的光。低利率的方解石沉淀物不足以消除水中的腐殖植物，因此水是清澈的。

秋天——三月：水表温度低，方解石产物慢慢地引人注目，水表面的海藻增多了，颜色就变成了浅绿，新旧有机物从湖水下层开始混合到湖水顶部，这可能导致了湖水颜色的变化。此外，水中增加的有机物更多地吸收了蓝色的光。

夏天——二月：方解石继续形成，它继续剥去湖水顶部的有机物，通过一些化学反应，方解石和有机物沉入湖底。越来越多的有机物被消除，湖水变得越来越蓝。湖底和水表的有机物是不会混合的，因为湖水的层理会防止两种水的混合。

春天——十一月：湖水开始形成薄的分层，温暖的水切断了湖水的深层循环。二氧化碳的排放更改了水表的 PH 酸碱度从而保护了方解石的沉淀物，沉淀物在水表聚集，使得湖水呈现明亮的蓝色。这些方解石来自于附近的石灰岩与白云石含水层渗入到地下水。高层的方解石与来自水层的有机酸相互作用，春天湖水颜色的改变多来自于这种透明的方解石。

四、旅游休闲

旅游业能带给甘比尔山每年大约 1 亿美元的经济收入，这个城市作为旅游集散地，拥有很多吸引游客的景点，如蓝湖、湖谷野生动物公园以及甘比尔山洞、花园洞以及英吉布雷切特洞。甘比尔山区域还有一些冲水洞穴和灰岩坑，它吸引了众多来自世界各地的潜水员，最受欢迎的当属埃文湖和皮卡里尼湖。

这个城市在主要的交通干道上建立了一个景点，在其建筑内部通过电影的形式，来展示发生在这个古老城市里的故事，其中最吸引公众喜爱的有两部电影。其中一部电影讲述了火山历史位置的故事和山的起点；游览从褶皱山开始到甘比尔山结束；之后是对新火山位置的描述，讲述了南澳大利亚迁徙之前维多利亚火山的历史。

第二节　休闲之山——新西兰南阿尔卑斯山

新西兰位于太平洋南部，介于南极洲和赤道之间。西隔塔斯曼海与澳大利亚相望，相隔 1600 千米，北邻汤加、斐济。新西兰由北岛、南岛、斯图尔特岛及其附近一些小岛组成，面积约 27 万平方千米，专属经济区 120 万平方千米。海岸线长 6900 千米。境内多山，平原狭小，山脉和丘陵约占其总面积的 75% 以上。四季区分不十分明显，温差不大。绝大部分属温带海洋性气候，一年四季气候温和、阳光充足、雨量丰富，植物生长十分茂盛。水力资源丰富，全国 80% 的电力为水力发电。森林面积约占全国土地面积的 29%，生态环境非常好。北岛多火山和温泉，南岛多冰河与湖泊。总人口 470 多万人，其中欧洲移民后裔占 78.8%，毛利人占 14.5%，亚裔占 6.7%。75% 的人口居住在北岛，奥克兰地区的人口占全国总人口 30.7%。南阿尔卑斯山脉是位于新西兰南岛西部的一条山脉，是整个南岛的天然分水岭。"南阿尔卑斯山脉"一般是用来泛指整座山脉，组成这条山脉的其他众多小山脉有许多各自不同的名称。南阿尔卑斯山脉处于一个板块边缘区，是太平洋火山环的一部分，形成于 2500 万至 3000 万年前，西边的印度澳洲板块向东移，压下东边的太平洋板块，地质构造压力使得山脉不断地升举和产生地震。

南阿尔卑斯山是由库克船长在 1770 年 3 月 23 日所命名，用来描述此山脉"惊人的高度"。纵贯南岛中西部，全长 320 千米，呈东北—西南走向。西坡陡峻，直逼海岸。东坡较平缓，有宽阔的山麓丘陵，渐降为坎特伯雷平原。大部分山岭巍峨高耸，有 17 个 3000 米以上的高峰，最高的库克峰海拔 3764 米，是新西兰第一高峰。许多高山顶上终年积雪，有大小冰川 360 多处，其中以位于库克峰巅东侧长达 28.9 千米的塔斯曼冰川最有名。地形崎岖，多 U 字形谷和狭长的冰蚀湖，成为南岛东部大多数河流的发源地。在南岛西南部山脉逼至海滨，形成众多的峡湾。山区风景壮丽，建有国家公园和滑雪场地多处，为重要旅游区之一。南阿尔卑斯山又是南岛东西部的气候分界线。西坡雨水充沛，森林茂密；东部位于背风雨影地区，降水较少，林木稀疏，低矮的山麓丘陵只能生长草本植物。山区多湖泊和急流瀑布，水力资源丰富。因为山脉与西行风垂直，为波浪滑翔提供了极好的条件。强盛西风也产生一种称为西北云弧的气候现象，含水分的空气被推到山顶形成一片晴空中的一块单独云层，这种景观在坎特伯雷和北奥塔哥的夏季经常可见。还有一种称为西北风的焚风，被山脉挡住的强风迫使潮湿空气往上升和降雨，并在山的背风处形成干燥热风。唯一横贯山区的铁路，穿越长达 8 千米的"阿瑟山口"大隧道，连接东岸的克赖斯特彻奇和西岸的格雷茅斯两大港口城市，并在南阿尔卑斯山区形成了一些颇具特色的旅游城镇。

一、长白之云

库克山国家公园位于新西兰南岛中西部，从 450 千米长的西海岸向内陆延伸 40~90 千米，公园长达 64 千米，最窄处只有 20 千米，占地 70696 公顷，冰河面积占 40%。它南起阿瑟隘口，西接迈因岭，正处于南阿尔卑

斯山景色最壮观秀丽的中段。公园内共有15座海拔3000米以上的山峰,而海拔2000米以上的山峰则多达140座,山峰连绵起伏、气势磅礴、蔚为壮观。其中海拔3764米的库克山雄踞中间,它是新西兰最高峰,相对高度3000米,也是大洋洲第二高峰。屹立在群峰之巅的库克山顶峰终年被冰雪覆盖,而群山的谷地里,则隐藏着许多条冰川。在毛利神话中有传说:天父与地母结合,生出了大量子孙,他们来到新西兰,把巨型独木舟变成了南岛,把一群子孙变成了库克山群峰,其中有一个叫"Aorangi",意为"长白之云",泛指毛利人所见的群山冰河景况。

库克山国家公园由冰河、陡壁、温泉、山林及各种野生动物构成。公园的三分之二被南部的山毛榉树和罗汉松所覆盖,其中一些树的树龄已超过800年。公园里的

大鹦鹉是世界上仅有的高山鹦鹉、啄羊鹦鹉,这里还有一种巨大的不会飞的南秧鸟,也属于稀有的濒危品种。库克山上有美丽的高山植物花园,当地植物最值得一提的是库克百合花。

库克山被冰河侵蚀成Ⅴ字形的山谷前,有两个宁静而美丽的湖泊位于其间,即普卡基湖和太卡普湖。这两个湖的背景都是库克山以及周围的群峰,湖水源于冰川,水色碧蓝中含带着乳白,晶莹如玉、平洁如镜。在普卡基湖边,坐落着一个小小的教堂,还有一只牧羊狗的雕塑,它们都静静地守候在湖畔,记载着这里的故事。蓝天、白云、雪山、碧湖、绿色相间的原野和山林,五彩缤纷的花朵,没有人烟,只有大自然的风声掠过人们的耳际。

库克山国家公园是观赏南阿尔卑斯山的绝佳地点。这里有29座山峰都高于海拔3000米,所以这里也成为新西兰登山爱好者最渴望来到的地方。1894年首度由杰克·克拉克、汤玛斯·费夫、乔治·格雷汉等三位新西兰登山家登顶成功,但并非所有人都如此幸运,由于其气候变化莫测,突如其来的风暴或雪崩等潜藏的危险,都有可能夺走登山者宝贵的性命。

库克山国家公园最著名的步道是胡克谷步道,长9千米,来回约需3~4小时。沿途除了有库克山峰和周围群峰的美景相伴,春夏两季青翠的高山草地上,还有如库克山百合等无数美丽的花朵灿烂相迎。高山纪念碑是眺望山谷景色的绝佳据点,接近穆勒冰河时,还可欣赏高山与冰瀑的壮观景象。

胡克谷步道的尽头是终点湖,一般游客多半在抵达这座蓝色冰河湖后,即按原路折回;往前还有曲折的步道通往胡克小屋。山林间有无数的山径可作徒步健行,优良的滑雪道可供人滑雪,也可乘着小飞机游览山区,鸟瞰或降落在冰河上。

二、探险之都

皇后镇位于瓦卡蒂普湖北岸,是一个被南阿尔卑斯山包围的美丽小镇,依山傍水,其海拔高度为 310 米。人口相当稀少,只有约 18000 人,其中欧美人约占 80%,亚洲 10%,其他种族则为 10%。根据地理学家的研究,在距今 15000 年前的冰河世纪,皇后镇是被冰河所覆盖的。新西兰因其多变地理景观,被喻为"活地理教室",而皇后镇则是全国地势最险峻美丽而又富刺激性的地区,故该区以"新西兰最著名的户外活动天堂"而得名。

皇后镇拥有世界上第一个商业化的蹦极场地——卡瓦劳大桥,其经营历史可追溯至 1988 年。受到瓦努阿图葡萄藤蹦极运动的启发,新西兰的亨利·凡·阿希与 A.J. 哈克特创造了这种新西兰独有的旅游项目,并从此风靡全球。

此外,商业喷射快艇的发源地也在皇后镇。游客们可以在著名的休特弗河上观赏壮丽的峡谷风光,也可以在皇后镇码头乘坐"卡瓦劳号"喷射快艇,体验穿越休特弗河峡谷的惊险感觉。休特弗河与卡瓦劳河四季皆可进行漂流活动。甚至是在冬季,你也可以乘坐直升机前往休特弗河体验漂流的乐趣。卡瓦劳河是新西兰商业化漂流河流中流量最大的一条,也是初学者的理想选择。如果希望寻找更加刺激的感觉,休特弗河的船长峡谷将

是你真正的挑战。作为冬日度假的最佳胜地,皇后镇拥有多个滑雪场地,科罗奈特峰拥有南部湖群最古老的、也是最著名的雪场。无论是雪板滑雪、自由式滑雪,还是全家大小一起滑雪,科罗奈特峰多变的地形地貌都能够满足客人的要求。雪地开放时间为 6 月初,通常可持续至 10 月。冬季一过,科罗奈特峰上的滑雪道便成为自行车观光降滑道。

三、蓝宝之石

蒂卡波湖是新西兰南岛中部的湖泊,位于南阿尔卑斯山脉东麓,为冰川堰塞湖。长约 24 千米,宽 6 千米,面积 96 平方千米,水深约 190 米。蒂卡波湖犹如一块清澈透亮的蓝宝石,藏身在基督城与皇后镇之间的南阿尔卑斯群山中。新西兰最高峰库克山在远方巍然耸立,而温柔的蒂卡波湖则在一旁静静地陪伴,如同一面明镜映照着库克山伟岸的身影。湖水泄入蒂卡波河,建有水闸向下游各水电站供水,湖水水位变化可达 8 米。蒂卡波湖是 2 万年以来由南阿尔卑斯山脉冰河的侵蚀与冰矶侧堆石围积而成。因水源来自库克山等高山融雪,故水温一直保持在摄氏 7 至 10 度,不适合游泳,但适合鳟鱼生存。又因有水坝的调节,水面的海拔高度保持在 704 至 710 米之间,坝口即是湖的出口,向东流入南太平洋。美丽迷人的蒂卡波湖四周围绕着被金色灿烂的阳光笼罩的树丛和一望无际的雪山。这里最初只是一个未开发的冰河,由于冰河移动造成的细岩粉和尘埃悬浮在水中,形成湖底独有的青绿色的岩石,久而久之累积在湖底,在阳光的照射下,会形成如梦如幻的乳蓝色,使整个湖面呈现一种翠绿迷蒙的梦幻景象。

蒂卡波湖湖边生长着一种非常特别的花,完全成熟的时候会呈现出像薰衣草般的紫色。这种紫色的野花就是鲁冰花。在蒂卡波湖畔,鲁冰花成片,在碧蓝的湖水和青青的草地映衬下特别显眼,叫人难以忽略它的美。来到蒂卡波湖,不论是热情如火的夏天还是寒冷的冬日,都有让人欢喜不尽的

旅游活动，如乘坐飞机俯瞰秀美的蒂卡波湖全貌，在附近山脉骑脚踏车、骑马、乘坐皮船出海、鳟鱼垂钓，夏天在蒂卡波湖上滑水，冬日在附近库克雪山上滑雪，还可以在如同东方女子黑色长发的浪漫夜幕下用天文望远镜仰望繁星点点……

牧羊人教堂于1935年建造，以一只曾在开发高山地区的工程中立下大功的牧羊犬而命名，用石头砌成的古朴教堂已成为蒂卡波湖的标志。透过教堂的窗户，青翠的小草、紫色的鲁冰花、湛蓝的湖水和皑皑的雪山仿佛就如镶在画框里般精致。梦幻般的山水配上石头教堂的点缀，人如同走进了一幅画里。

四、生物天堂

凯库拉是位于新西兰的基督城与皮克顿之间的一个海边小镇，距南岛最大的城市基督城以北约2.5小时车程。它是前往南部海洋哺乳动物保护区的门户，也是少数几个可以在一天之内看遍鲸鱼、海豚、海豹、信天翁、企鹅和多种海鸟的地方。热带涌来的暖流与由南极而来的富含营养物的寒流交汇，营养物流入峡谷混合，然后被推上海洋表面，带来大量浮游生物，形成了浮游植物为浮游动物和磷虾提供食物，浮游动物和磷虾又是乌贼和小型鱼类的食物，然后乌贼和小型鱼类又是大型鱼类、鸟类、海豹、海豚、鲨鱼和鲸的食物的食物链。这个不大的半岛，坐落在新西兰风景如画的南岛东海岸，是海洋生物生活的天堂。

游客可以乘船出海追逐鲸鱼的踪影，在航程中还有机会欣赏到珍稀的暗色斑纹海豚、赫氏海豚、新西兰毛皮海豹等动物。在陆地上看起来笨头笨脑的海豹，在海里可一点也不含糊，借助海水的浮力，它们胖乎乎的身体出奇得灵巧。最激动人心的，当然还是抹香鲸。碧海蓝天之际，一条抹香鲸的身影显现出来，优美的流线体型，紧致光滑的皮肤，就如一位美丽的少女，翩翩起舞在太平洋的万顷碧波之间。暗斑海豚是凯库拉沿岸丰富的海洋生物群中的奇特动物，也是南大洋中最为欢快、活泼的精灵之一。因居住着各种鲸类和海豚而出名的凯库拉小镇上其实还有一群神奇生物，那就是形形色色的远洋海鸟。凯库拉是全球最大的信天翁聚居地，每年都有多达 14 个种类的信天翁飞来此处。

　　凯库拉的海岸线聚居着各色海洋生物，定能为您带来难忘的潜水体验。游人可以探索原始的海中森林和石灰珊瑚岩，那里栖息着奇异的八爪鱼、龙虾、长壳的海绵以及缠结的无脊椎动物，它们争先恐后，纷纷希望占据岩石和珊瑚上的领地。

参考文献

[1] 秦成逊,王杰.西部地区基于生态文明的山地经济发展研究[J].生态经济,2012(10).

[2] 徐斌,金伟.世界名山[M].长春:长春出版社,2007.

[3] 谢凝高.名山·风景·遗产——谢凝高文集[M].北京:中华书局,2011.

[4] 谢凝高.中国的名山大川[M].北京:商务印书馆,1997.

[5] 郑翔.基于产业集群理论的山岳型旅游景区战略创新研究[J].中国市场,2008(48).

[6] 卢云亭.论名山的特性、类别和旅游功能[J].资源导刊,2009(6).

[7] 刘强.文化景观视角下的中国名山风景区价值研究[J].安徽农业科学,2012,40(15).

[8] 卢劲杉,董树宝.世界名山[M].长春:长春出版社,2004.

[9] 唐千友.日本汉诗中的富士山形象研究[J].安徽大学学报(哲学社会科学版),2012(6).

[10] 葛晓音.中国文人与山水名胜,中华文化讲座丛书(第一集)[M].北京:北京大学出版社,1994.

[11] 杨乃运,雷发林.巧克力山和大眼镜猴[J].旅游,2007(1).

[12] [韩]韩相一.韩国雪岳山国立公园[J].中国园林,2005(11).

[13] 黎群笑.香山旅游经济研究[D].中央民族大学硕士学位论文，2012.

[14] 金丽娟.香山公园森林游憩资源价值评估与旅游管理对策研究[D].北京林业大学硕士学位论文，2005.

[15] 胡雯雯，张茵.二分型客源结构旅游目的地游憩价值评估——以北京香山公园为例[J].旅游论坛，2012（1）.

[16] 邱建平.南非桌山的地质景观[J].浙江国土资源，2010（1）.

[17] 臧敏.泰山旅游资源管理模式及旅游产业可持续发展策略研究[D].山东农业大学硕士学位论文，2010.

[18] 朱波，梁振民，国转英.泰安市泰山旅游业发展态势分析[J].广东农业科学，2010（5）.

[19] 杨坤.泰山旅游景区竞争力研究[D].中国海洋大学硕士学位论文，2012.

[20] 杨炯，孟华，王雷亭，牛健.基于公众认知的地质遗迹保护与开发——以泰山地质公园为例[J].资源开发与市场，2010（1）.

[21] 郑德亮，袁建华.泰山旅游产业SWOT分析及发展建议[J].山东工商学院学报，2009，23（1）.

[22] 马爱云，贾素红，姜红.泰山旅游资源的优势与生态环境保护[J].泰安教育学院学报岱宗学刊，2008，12（3）.

[23] 张慧，周春梅.山岳型旅游地旅游产品深度开发研究——以峨眉山为例[J].资源开发与市场，2007（8）.

[24] 李铁松，胡大鹏.峨眉山旅游资源类型与开发研究[J].四川师范学院学报(哲学社会科学版)，2000（4）.

[25] 李雪飞.峨眉山风景区旅游环境承载力研究[J].学术动态，2007（2）.

[26] 陈沙沙，孙克勤.中国的世界文化—自然遗产可持续发展研究——以峨眉山—乐山大佛为例[J].资源开发与市场，2010，26（12）.

[27] 罗晖.峨眉山世界遗产地保护规划的探索研究——以峨眉山风景名胜区总体规划为例[J].规划师，2007，23（3）.

[28] 胡善风，朱红兵.山岳型遗产地旅游可持续发展研究——以黄山风景区为例[J].合肥工业大学学报（社会科学版），2013，27（1）.

[29] 胡善风.黄山旅游资源开发与可持续利用研究[J].地理科学，2002.22（3）.

[30] 王娟，闻飞.黄山风景区国际旅游市场时空演替特征研究[J].旅游学刊，2007（8）.

[31] 刘淑珍，李友根.对黄山市旅游发展的SWOT分析[J].价值工程，2009（1）.

[32] 吴雁昭.黄山市旅游资源整合研究[D].中央民族大学硕士学位论文，2011.

[33] 王灏铮.危险的脚步：中国登山家攀登世界七大洲最高峰纪实[M].北京：中国社会科学出版社，2003.

[34] [日]张纪浔.日本名山——富士山的开发与保护.世界名山研究会发言稿，2013.

[35] 韩欣.世界名山（上下）[M].北京：东方出版社，2007.

[36] 百度百科.

与会人员名单

国家和地区	姓 名	时任职务
中国江西	黄跃金	江西省政协主席
	殷美根	九江市人民政府市长
	魏宏彬	九江市政协主席
	廖奇志	九江市人民政府副市长
	张知明	江西省外事侨务办公室副主任
	吕玉琪	江西省教育厅副巡视员
	杨 健	庐山管理局党委书记，世界名山协会秘书长
	卢 叶	联合国教科文组织代表
	陈 敏	江西省教育厅国际合作与交流处处长
	王丰鹏	九江市人民政府秘书长
	洪 华	九江市政协秘书长
	舒瑞鹏	九江市人民政府外侨办主任
	熊 伟	庐山管理局党委委员、宣传部部长
澳大利亚	杨 娜	世界名山协会大洋洲副秘书长
	阿曼达	阿什赫斯特国际旅行主管
美国	詹姆斯	美国阿姆斯特朗大西洋州立大学副校长助理&国际处处长
	劳 拉	美国阿姆斯特朗大西洋州立大学分管国际教育交流的副校长助理&人文学院院长
	理查德	美国阿姆斯特朗大西洋州立大学经济学教授
	盖瑞文	世界名山协会北美洲副秘书长&战略规划副总监&美国波特兰州立大学公共管理学及政策学博士
	罗 伊	原美国波特兰州立大学分管教务长、副校长
	那克斯	世界名山、地质公园及世界遗产研究专家

续表：

国家和地区	姓　名	时任职务
巴西	莫妮卡	世界名山协会南美洲副秘书长 & 巴西社会研究调查与科技部副主任 & 巴西塞阿拉州联邦大学教授
	罗密欧	巴西塞阿拉州联邦大学国际处处长
南非	温　蒂	南非国家公园好望角区域好望角研究中心区域生态学家
	迈克尔	南非西开普敦大学教授
德国	乌　特	德国欧洲森林艺术协会组织者发起者
	沃尔特	德国亚琛工业大学全职教授
中国台湾	陈隆升	中国台湾玉山公园交流协会荣誉理事长
菲律宾	那　罗	菲律宾圣名大学分管教学副校长教授
	玛　利	菲律宾圣名大学科研处处长
泰国	尼瓦斯	泰国清迈大学校长
	马如宝	泰国清迈大学语言学院院长、副教授
法国	菲利普	法国普瓦提埃大学管理学院院长
	郭宇纲	法国普瓦提埃大学孔子学院
中国香港	吴振扬	香港地质保护协会会长
	曹景钧	中国香港中文大学公共管理系教授
加拿大	约　翰	加拿大菲沙河谷大学执行理事
英国	谢维尔	英国伯恩茅斯大学设计工程电脑学院副院长
	芬　唐	加泽拉大学集团主管，北哈特福德郡大学校长
	柯瑞安	洛维奇城市大学校长
俄罗斯	艾比兹耶娃	俄罗斯人民友谊大学文学院副院长
意大利	毛利兹	意大利责任旅游协会主席，欧洲责任旅游及酒店联盟主席
日本	横山则夫	日本大和高田友好协会会长
	张纪浔	日本城西大学经管系教授
中国云南	丁文丽	中国云南师范大学副校长
	明庆忠	中国云南师范大学科研处处长
中国广东	唐晓春	中国广东商学院资源与环境学院院长
中国北京	孙忠权	中国华北电力大学副校长
中国山东	王庆功	泰山学院党委书记
	殷　敏	泰山学院党办院办主任
	彭淑贞	泰山学院旅游学院院长

续表：

国家和地区	姓　名	时任职务
公共外交论坛嘉宾代表	赵启正	前国务院新闻办公室主任、全国政协外事委员会主任，现中国人民大学新闻学院院长、上海公共外交协会等多家协会顾问
	华黎明	前中国驻伊朗、阿联酋、荷兰大使兼中国常驻禁止化学武器（OPCW）代表；中国国际问题研究所特约研究员、中国联合国协会常务理事
	吴正龙	中国太平洋经济合作全国委员会副会长，中国前驻克罗地亚大使
	吕凤鼎	原中国驻瑞典、尼日利亚特命全权大使，第十一届全国政协委员
公共外交学界代表	姜　飞	中国社科院新闻与传播研究所世界传媒研究所所长
	张毓强	中国传媒大学国际传播战略与发展研究中心常务副主任、传媒博物馆副馆长
	张洪忠	北京师范大学艺术与传媒学院院长助理、传播效果研究室主任
	刘　涛	西北师范大学传媒学院副院长
	陈　冠	中国人民大学商学院教授
	刘　蓉	北京外国语大学校友办
九江学院	郑　翔	九江学院党委书记
	甘筱青	九江学院党委副书记、校长
	吴桃娥	九江学院党委委员、副校长
	欧阳春	九江学院党委委员、副校长
	纪岗昌	九江学院副校长
	陶春元	九江学院副校长
	杨焱林	九江学院党委委员、副校长
	杨耀防	九江学院校长助理、临床医学院/附属医院院长
	雷蔚真	九江学院校长助理
	李宁宁	九江学院庐山文化研究中心主任
	李松志	九江学院旅游与国土资源学院副院长
	廖　亮	九江学院生命科学学院院长

后　记

　　世界名山是全世界共同的财富，是人类的精神家园。世界名山不仅体现了自然的雄浑、秀美，还包蕴着人类文化、知识、历史、智慧。保护好并永续利用世界名山，是摆在人类面前的共同课题。

　　2009年10月，首届"中国庐山世界名山大会"召开，来自五大洲近26个国家的嘉宾及各世界名山代表200多人共聚庐山，对名山保护、资源开发、交流合作等课题进行了广泛而深入的探讨，草签了"世界名山协会"章程，并发表了《庐山宣言》。这是世界名山交流合作与研究发展过程中的里程碑事件。

　　2013年5月，首届"世界名山学术研讨会暨高校公共外交论坛"在庐山脚下的九江学院召开。"友谊、合作、发展"成为架设在不同峰峦、不同文化之间的桥梁，名山成为不同国度、不同民族交流与合作的新渠道。此次会议成立了"世界名山研究会"，这是世界名山研究与保护利用过程中的又一重要里程碑。

　　不同国度、不同时空的人们都应有机会来了解、体味世界名山这一人类共同的宝贵财富。同时，世界名山作为一种特殊的综合资源，亦应发挥出其促进人类交流、合作与发展的社会功能。在此背景下，《走进世界名山》一书应运而生。

　　《走进世界名山》的编纂工作受到了九江学院党委书记郑翔博士的高度

重视，并为该书作序；得到了其他校领导的关心和帮助，得到了其他部门的有力配合，也得到了众多教职工的大力支持，在此对他们表示衷心的感谢！

　　《走进世界名山》主编为韩琨、李松志，副主编为桑龙扬、龚唯、魏伟新、熊云明。全书主要由九江学院旅游与国土资源学院老师撰稿，参编人员有李翔宇、贾超、姚丽娜、王燕华、张昕华、郭英、王丽霞；由外国语学院国学译馆老师翻译。在该书的编纂过程中，全体编写及翻译人员查阅了大量的资料、数据，数易其稿，希望尽可能全面地将世界名山的精华呈献给读者。因篇幅所限，本书所涉名山只是众多名山的一部分。书中部分图片由九江学院党委宣传部副部长、江西人民出版社九江学院分社执行社长陈晓松同志提供，部分来自网络，在此表示感谢。同时，由于编撰、翻译人员水平有限，加之时间仓促，不足之处甚至错误在所难免，恳请批评指正。

Preface

Famous mountains are the essence of the earth and the dreamlands of tourists. Through the ages, during process of our discovery, conquest, and protection of the nature, we have set up a complex relationship between humans and famous mountains: a relationship that has been renewed from materiality to spirituality, from exploitation to conservation. A famous mountain influences and shapes a city, a region, and even the history, culture, and spiritual symbolism of a nation. Meanwhile, there are endless scientific problems about world famous mountains demand us to discover, study, and share. Throughout the globe, many people agree there is a famous mountain in our hearts, mountains in which we all take pride.

What mountains can be qualified as world famous mountains in our minds? Firstly, it must be essence of the earth. Marked by towering peaks, magnificent spectacle, various shapes and harmonious colors, world famous mountains are masterpieces of the nature. These mountains, as the source of rivers, warehouse for plants, and paradise for animals, are the origin of life and the eternal basis for the survival of human, which deserve our constant admiration. Deep snow, thick vegetation, inexhaustible waterfalls, and sedimentary geological structure are the typical outward expression of its vitality and a world famous mountain is also a life itself. From the material world to the spiritual one, they become symbols of loftiness, strength, toughness, munificence and eternity.It is fair that every continent owns its own world famous mountains around the globe.

Secondly, world famous mountains are a Mecca for tourists. By virtue of the above mentioned characteristics, over thousands of years, they become irreplaceable destinations for visiting, esthetics appreciation and experiencing life as well as the places for exploring nature, being close to nature, enjoying nature and relaxation.They also become preferred locations for people to go sightseeing, have a holiday, go outside for amusement, play sports, and even settle down. Therefore, to an increasing extent, world famous mountains turn into tourist resorts accommodating hundreds of millions of tourists every year. People with different races, languages, colors of skin or dresses get along amiably and peacefully in every famous mountain to admire and enjoy the splendid works by nature and also by our ancestors.

Thirdly, famous mountains are the places where the career of their administrators lies. Commissioned by all humanity to manage and protect the famous mountains, we are the administrators and guardians of these mountains. We have the good fortune to work for the famous mountains, we are willing to bustle about the famous mountains, and we work overtime for the famous mountains without complaints, because they are our service object and where our duty and honor lie. We meet each other by putting ourselves out of the way and travelling far from five continents. What is so attractive to bring strangers like us together? What is the strength to unite us on earth? The answer is: the common sense of responsibility for the world famous mountains.

Nowdays, snow melting starts early in famous mountains with global warming; garbage is increasing due to an influx of visitors with heightened demand, and pollutants of scenic spots need to be disposed in a more scientific and economic way; diversified service is necessary with rising number of incoming tourists and man-made environments, etc. It requires us to appreciate these famous mountains from three perspectives to overcome difficulties: first, a scientific perspective; second, an aesthetic perspective; third, a philosophical one. With rich academic achievements,talents and resources, universities as a major force in generating knowledge of world famous mountains and also the front lines of researching these mountains, are irreplaceable. Study on the world famous mountains is the glorious mission of an university.

At present, any famous mountain chosen in this book should be a mountain and important tourist destination, which has its own administrative organization, and most importantly, should be a member of World Famous Mountains Association. Thus there are totally 27 famous mountains listed in *An Overview of the World Famous Mountains*, which will introduce a wide range of topics concerning world famous mountains, including natural sceneries, cultural customs and characteristics of local civilizations, and mountain tourism. This book will enable you to appreciate the majesty of these mountains, different tourism landscapes, and various folk customs around the world while remaining indoors.

Zheng Xiang

Contents

141	**Preface**

◀ Chapter 1   **World Famous Mountains:
New Angles to Understand the World**

152	*Section 1 Open the Magnificent Scroll of World Famous Mountains*
152	I. World Famous Mountains: New Concepts of Civilization
153	II. World Famous Mountains:Multidimensional Value
154	III. World Famous Mountains: Important Carrier of Heritage
155	*Section 2 Focus on "The World Famous Mountains Research Institute"*
155	I. Background
156	II. The Founding
157	III. Principles and Tasks
157	IV. Constitution
159	*Section 3 The Sustainable Development of World Famous Mountains Tourism*
159	I. Tourism Functions of Famous Mountains
161	II. Characteristics of Famous Mountain Tourism
162	III. Sustainable Development of Famous Mountains Tourism

Chapter 2 World Famous Mountains in Asia

166	**Section 1 Lushan—Sacred Mountain**
166	I. Geological Features
167	II. Remarkable Value
170	III. Recommended Scenic Spots
176	**Section 2 Mount Tai—Head of the Five Most Famous Mountains in China**
176	I. Geomorphologic Landscapes
177	II. Main Scenic Spots
180	III. Six Scenic Areas
182	**Section 3 Mount Emei—Delicately Beautiful Buddhist Mountain**
182	I. Geomorphologic Landscapes
183	II. Four Spectacles
185	III. Main Tourist Areas
190	**Section 4 Huangshan—The Picturesque Scene in China**
190	I. Geomorphological Landscapes
191	II. Main Scenic Areas
194	III. Four Wonders and Three Waterfalls
196	**Section 5 Fragrant Hills—The Garden Behind the Hill**
197	I. Historical Changes
197	II. Four Seasons Scenery
198	III. Main Scenic Spots
202	**Section 6 Mt. Jade—Taiwan's Holy Mountain**
204	I. Ecology of Mt. Jade
205	II. Features of Mt. Jade
205	III. Tourism of Mt. Jade
206	**Section 7 Mount Fuji—The Holy Mountain of Japan**
206	I. Mount Fuji

208	II. Deifying of Mount Fuji
210	III. Leisure of Mount Fuji
212	*Section 8 Seoraksan—Eastern Fairyland*
213	I. Beautiful Landscapes
213	II. Scenic Spots
215	III. Tourism and Sighting
216	*Section 9 The Chocolate Hills—Eastern Wonderful Hills*
216	I. Legend and Origin
217	II. Main Attractions
218	III. Tarsiers

◀ Chapter 3   World Famous Mountains in Africa

220	*Section 1 Kilimanjaro—Snow Peak in the Equator*
220	I. Scenery
221	II. Legends
222	III. Tourist Attractions
222	*Section 2 Table Mountain—The City of Lape*
223	I. Geological Features
223	II. The Beautiful Scenery
224	III. Legend of Odd Cloud

◀ Chapter 4   World Famous Mountains in Europe

226	*Section 1 The Alps & The Eisenwurzen Geopark—The Backbone of Europe*
226	I. Ecological Landscapes
227	II. Tourism and Leisure
229	III. Geopark
229	*Section 2 Cozia Mountain—Ecological Homeland*
230	I. Beautiful Ecological Landscapes
230	II. Cultural Attractions
232	III. Tourism Activities
232	*Section 3 Gaina Mountain—A Love Fairyland*
232	I. Curious Legend
233	II. Single Party Folk
234	III. Tourist Experience
234	*Section 4 Covasna Mountain—The Pearl of Hot Spring*
235	I. Fascinating Attractions
236	II. Unique Hot Spring Resources
237	III. Tourists Activities
237	*Section 5 Bergstrasse-Odenwald Mountain—Geological Wonder*
237	I. Unique Stratum
238	II. Tourism Resources

◀ Chapter 5   World Famous Mountains in North America

240	*Section 1 Mount Hood—The Landmark of the North America*
240	I. Volcanic Activity
240	II. Glaciers

242	III. Tourist Attractions
244	IV. Recreations
244	Section 2 Mount Rainier—Winter Resort
245	I. Geographical Setting
246	II. Volcanic Activity
247	III. Glaciers
247	IV. Recreations
248	Section 3 The Shasta Mount—Wonderland of Oz
249	I. Natural Ecology
250	II. Lakes and Rivers
250	III. Recreations
251	Section 4 Blue Ridge Mount & Shenandoah National Park—Blue Ridge Lizard
251	I. Geological Landscapes
252	II. Formation of the Park
253	III. Attractions

◀ **Chapter 6**   **World Famous Mountains in South America**

256	Section 1 Araripe Mountain—Plateau Fossil
256	I. Tourism Facilities
257	II. Typical Landscapes
259	III. Development Strategy
260	Section 2 Guaramiranga Mountain Chain—Ecological Forest
260	I. Natural Features
260	II. Leisure and Tourism
261	Section 3 Mt. Quixadá—Paradise of Paragliding
262	I. Natural Landscapes
262	II. Tourism Development

263	Section 4 Mt. Ibipaba—Paradise of Skydiving
263	I. Climate and Vegetation
263	II. Leisure and Tourism
263	Section 5 Kamaqua Highland—Ecological Highland
263	I. Ecological Tourism
264	II. Tourism Development

◀ Chapter 7   World Famous Mountains in Oceania

266	Section 1 Mount Gambier—Geological Volcano
266	I. Ecological Environment
267	II. Geomorphologic Landscapes
268	III. The Blue Lake
270	IV. Travel and Leisure
270	Section 2 Southern Alps—Mountain for Leisure
272	I. The Misty Cloud
273	II. The City of Adventure
274	III. The Blue Treasure—Lake Tekapo
276	IV. Paradise of the Wild Life

277	**Bibliography**
280	**Participants**
285	**Postscript**

Chapter 1

World Famous Mountains: New Angles to Understand the World

In the culture of nations, the mountain exists as a magical image because of its sky-high and profound. However, most of the time mountain like a great philosopher, silence but full of splendid things. A grain of gold sand released occasionally by mountains may quietly passing out prehistoric information. If people can understand the language of a mountain, then they can find the clue of the earth's mystery and the origin of the human civilization.

The great philosopher Confucius once saw the profoundness and lenience of a mountain and praised, mountains are like the benevolent; the poet Li Bai thoroughly understood the ease and grace of a mountain when meditating in front of torrent waterfall of Lushan; the poet Du Fu comprehended the majesty and grandness of a mountain and wrote, "one would see the other mountains all appear dwarfs under the sky"; the poet Su Shi noticed the rule of constant changes of mountains and depicted, "from the side, a whole range; from the end, a single peak". In the hustle and bustle of modern urban life, people walk through concrete forests and engage themselves with busy and prosperous social activities. It has become more and more difficult to find time to retreat to natural landscapes. The ideal life—"find a moment of leisure in a busy life"—which was respected by our forefathers has become more and more distant.

Throughout the history of human, famous mountains around the world are nature gifts, but they also contain infinite treasure of human civilization. Since the born of the earth, mountains stand majestically, mutely waiting for human's exploration.

Section 1 Open the Magnificent Scroll of World Famous Mountains

On the surface of the earth there are many winding, towering, and peculiar mountains, rising and overlapping each other and forming a large mountain family. Diverse in surface morphology, some run parallel to each other for thousands of miles, and others stand as magnificent and lonely sentries. Mountains can be very frequently seen, especially on the Eurasian and American continents. A famous mountain is a unique geographical entity with many rich connotations surrounding its name. Such connotations are formed under specific historical conditions, and serve as a reflection of different eras.

I. World Famous Mountains: New Concepts of Civilization

Famous mountains were masterpieces in the eyes of man during the agricultural age, when life was at the mercy of the nature. Humans placed complicated emotions on nature, such as awe, worship, affinity, praise and prayer. Famous mountains were protected and taken as representative of the holiness of nature, serving as special places to meet people's spiritual and cultural needs in nature, such as sacrifice, religion, tourism, education, seclusion, aesthetic appreciation, and artistic creation. Thus, famous mountains were the bond for spiritual relationships between humans and nature and the unique landscapes of famous mountains were protected in ancient times. During the industrial age, many national parks or national scenic spots were formed using scientific and aesthetic values, and served as regional spaces that integrated nature and culture to meet people's needs for spiritual and cultural activities. These parks created enormous social, economic and ecological environmental benefits for their regions and their countries. Next, came the ecological age, when the ecological safety of the "global village" and the cultural heritage of humans encountered unprecedented threats. In 1992, the United Nations Conference on Environment and Development in Brazil approved Agenda 21, in which the importance of, and vulnerability of, mountain ecosystems were explicitly expounded and the need for responsible research and development of mountains was raised to a state of high concern alongside climatic change, biodiversity protection and wetland conservation. Our task now, for the ecological age, is to ensure that the world's famous mountains are developed and maintained with responsibility by paying more attention to the sustainability of development, ecological balance, industry diversity and systematicness, with intra-regional and inter-regional circulation. These famous mountains provide not only unique and magnificent natural landscapes, but also colorful human landscapes, and have the potential to be the sites of the harmonious unification of natural beauty and humanistic beauty. It will be impossible to protect these natural spaces and human heritages without a globally united world. The core issue for famous mountains today is that of protection. So, let's protect the authenticity and integrity of such heritages so that they can be sustainably passed on and appreciated for many more generations to come.

II. World Famous Mountains: Multidimensional Value

Famous mountains can satisfy people's spiritual and cultural needs for nature with their unique cultural histories and natural landscapes. These types of mountains have three major characteristics and functions: aesthetic value, scientific value, and physical landscapes that carry certain historical and cultural value.

1. The Aesthetic Value of Famous Mountains

Famous mountains are natural landscapes rich in complex beauty derived from nature, and every mountain has its own beauty which is shaped by its particular geologic evolution and geomorphologic development.Mountains, especially famous mountains, are recognizable to those that know them by their unique identifying characteristics, such grandness of Mount Tai, the oddness of Mount Huang, and the grace of Mount Emei, in China.

2. The Scientific Value of Famous Mountains

Famous mountains are not only valuable for their beauty alone, they also offer significant opportunities for scientific study and discovery. They offer sites for researching and understanding the history of the earth, the progression of geological changes, and natural laws of geography. For example, Mount Gambier in Australia, which possesses both typical volcanic landscapes and rare volcanic environments, is an ideal site for researching volcanic geomorphology.Huangshan in China is famous for its beautiful granite, and Lushan, also in China, is named as natural geological museum and natural botanical garden because of its raised cracks, complete stratums and characteristic frameworks and rich flora.

3. The Historical and Cultural Value of Famous Mountains

Famous mountains typically have long histories and correspondingly rich cultural heritages. The term "World Famous" rarely applies to modern mountains, it is instead used in connection with mountains that possess a long and ancient history. In China, Mount Tai and Huangshan have histories that have been developing since the Qin and Han dynasties. Many famous mountains have around twelve hundred years of recorded history. These mountains are covered in rich cultural landscapes and monuments, such as ancient architecture, religious artifacts, and cliff inscriptions. The contents of these numerous cultural landscapes are valuable for their contributions to art, architectural, and engineering history. It is no wonder that these places are famous for being "historical and cultural treasures".

III.World Famous Mountains: Important Carrier of Heritage

What is a "World Heritage"? A great creation of mankind, or the magical beauty of nature? The majestic pyramids of Egypt or the ancient Great Wall of China? Both of these sites are World Heritage sites, but they are not the only kinds of World Heritage sites.We know what constitutes a World Heritage

Site in accordance with international law, and that the approval process for declaring a site a World Heritage site is strict. The UNESCO General Conference of November 1972 introduced the "Protection of the World Cultural and Natural Heritage Convention", which is often referred to as "the World Heritage Convention". To become a World Heritage site, a location must produce a series of scientific reports, and undergo a certification process. If we study the current "World Heritage List", we can generalize the three main categories of World Heritage sites:

(1) A site created by mankind.

(2) A natural site.

(3) A site which shows the co-evolution of man and nature. A combination of World Cultural and Natural Heritage sites, such as the Chinese Huangshan, Mount Tai, and Lushan.

Section 2 Focus on "The World Famous Mountains Research Institute"

I. Background

The world famous mountains are the spiritual home of mankind as well as the common wealth of the world. Today, the earth is suffering more and more damage, and natural resources are being over-exploited. The common problem now facing humanity is that of studying and protecting the world famous mountains with natural and cultural landscapes of scientific, aesthetic and humanistic values so that they can be sustainably used and appreciated for generations to come.

Initiated by the former Party Secretary of the Lushan Administrative Bureau, Dr. Zheng Xiang, the first World Famous Mountains Conference was held on October 13, 2009 on Lushan in China. The representatives from 12 famous mountains such as Lushan, Mount Tai, Mount Hood, Mount Gambier and the Alps were invited to the conference as well as the representatives of 10 countries from the UNESCO Beijing Office, officials of embassies and consulates from 10 countries and more than 260 guests of 26 countries. The theme of the first conference was, "Friendship, Cooperation and Development", a theme closely related to the two eternal issues of protection and development concerning the world famous mountains today. The conference focused on the opportunities and challenges surrounding the healthy development of mountains in relation to the topics of global economic development and environment protection. Also discussed were aspects of cooperation in terms of environment protection, tourism, and cultural education. The representatives from 6 mountains including Lushan, Mount

Hood and Table Mountain signed a friendly agreement for further exchanges and cooperation in the areas of environmental protection, tourism, culture and education. Lushan representatives initiated the establishment of the World Famous Mountains Association, a permanent platform for mutual exchanges and cooperation amongst the representatives of mountains around the world, aimed at promoting the responsible development of famous mountains and the cultivation of harmonious international relationships.

In 2012, Dr. Zheng Xiang, who initiated the World Famous Mountains Conference and the World Famous Mountains Association, became the Party Secretary of Jiujiang University, which is located at the base of Lushan, in the Jiangxi Province of China. Since his instatement at Jiujiang University, Dr. Zheng Xiang has been actively negotiating with the deputy secretary generals of the World Famous Mountains Association, in preparation for the creation and development of a World Famous Mountains Research Institute, aimed at expanding and continuing the central mission of the World Famous Mountains Association.

II. The Founding

Through the joint effort of various parties, the first World Famous Mountains Research Conference and Public Diplomacy Forum embraced its grand opening at Jiujiang University on May 13th, 2013. The theme of the conference was, "Communication, Discussion, and Sharing", with focuses on four main tasks: First, the establishment of the World Famous Mountain Research Institute (WFMRI), with the intention of building an academic platform for universities and institutes to share information and research concerning famous mountains; Second, to encourage university research of famous mountains; Third, to strengthen cooperation between the regions where the famous mountains are located around the globe; And fourth, to help involved universities find roles in public diplomacy. During the conference, over 60 experts and scholars from Australia, America, Brazil, South Africa, Germany, The Philippines, Thailand, France, Canada, Britain, Russia, Italy, Japan, Mainland China, Hong Kong and Taiwan held discussions on a series of problems that included questions on how best to utilize involved universities in the creation of a research platform for famous mountains, how to accelerate the research on famous mountains, and how to encourage increased diplomatic communication and cross cultural communication surrounding these issues. In the conference, over 30 representatives from 5 continents signed the Manifesto of World Famous Mountains Research Institute and initiated the establishment of the World Famous Mountains

Research Institute. The institute is an academic, non-governmental, non-political, and non-profitable organization. Jiujiang University has functioned as the standing organization of the institute since its inception.

III. Principles and Tasks

The principle task of the WMFRI is to provide sustainable utilization and scientific research of world famous mountains. What is sustainable utilization? Dr. Zheng Xiang, the Secretary General, clarifies it with 3 sentences: First, the intent to leave our descendants with convenience, not trouble; Second, to leave our descendants with complete sites, not regrets; Third, to leave our descendants with profits, not losses.

There are three main tasks of the research institute: First is that of research and publication; The second is research and training; The third is research and consultation. The WMFRI will begin publication with an introductory series covering the history of the organization and introducing a number of associated famous mountains. Following this publication, it will pursue the publication of existing studies, and will focus on the publication of specific research and areas of study related to famous mountains, with disciplines ranging from hydrology to tourism. The WMFRI aims to focus particularly on the topics of conservation, tourism, and the promotion of local economic development in the regions surrounding famous mountains.

IV. Constitution

On May 15th over 60 experts and scholars from universities and research institutions of 16 countries and regions attended the symposium held by Jiujiang University in Jiangxi, China. Together they decided to create the World Famous Mountains Research Institute to address the countless questions about world famous mountains yet to be shared and explored.

1. General

The organization is named "World Famous Mountains Research Institute", and is abbreviated as WFMRI. Jiujiang University functions as the headquarters of the research institute. The WFMRI will comply with the WFMRI Constitution and with the laws of the People's Republic of China. It is a non-governmental, non-political, and non-profit organization of academic fellowship (NGO). It aims to promote the protection of mountains; mountain tourism; local economic development in areas surrounding famous mountains; the harmonious development of man and nature; global sharing and exchange, and the sustainable use of the world famous mountains.

2. Work Content

The overall work of the WFMRI includes: research and publishing; training and consulting; integration of academic strength; promotion of scientific research on famous mountains; strengthening exchange and cooperation among universities and colleges; and the promotion of public diplomacy and cultural exchanges. In order to facilitate exchanges between members of the WFMRI and its researchers, a research website has been established within which research databases of the world famous mountains have been created as well as a research journal column, a space for research papers, and a home for research information on mountains. Friendly and cooperative relations can be established among universities in the places where famous mountains stand so as to promote talent training and discipline construction, and share high-quality educational resources and research results. All members of the research institute should give full play to their advantages, effectively take responsibility of making studies on the famous mountains, conduct researches on the research projects listed by the research institute or the research direction of their own, actively write and submit academic papers. Academic seminar should be held every two years to publish the research achievements. Classified special researches should be carried out, such as research on water resources protection of famous mountains, research on tourist behaviors in famous mountains, research on governing bodies of famous mountains, and so on. The training and consulting institutions of world famous mountains should also be established, which can play full use of the advantages in talents of the member units of the World Famous Mountains Research Institute and organize experts and scholars of the member units to offer training to the governors of world famous mountains. Meanwhile, it can do some tourism planning and management for some world famous mountains waiting to be developed, provide advisory services, and so on. The research institute introduces books about basic situations and basic knowledge of world famous mountains, anthologizes all sorts of scattered present research results to determine status in the academic community. All research findings should be made to play their due roles in promoting the protection of world famous mountains, realizing natural resources value, historical and cultural value, and aesthetic value of famous mountains, promoting the sustainable use of famous mountains and promoting regional economic development, etc.

Section 3 The Sustainable Development of World Famous Mountains Tourism

With the increasing interest of tourists and improving cultural attainments, people's requirements for the appreciation of tourism destinations are continuously extending into pursuing naturalness, pursuing the cultural grade, pursuing aesthetic value and the desire of obtaining Information. In the new century, people prefer such tourist locations where can bring them back to the nature for recreation and vacation. By virtue of differences in the geological conditions of formation, the composition of rock properties, the climate, rivers and other geographical factors, as well as historical and cultural backgrounds, every mountain has its unique image and charm, which attract tens of thousands of domestic and international tourists. Famous mountains with unique value in tourism are priceless treasures in the world, besides, the development and construction of these mountains all around the world also provide us with some experiences and lessons.

I. Tourism Functions of Famous Mountains

1. A Place to Cultivate Aesthetic Senses

Tourists can experience many kinds of beauty when touring mountains and the difficulties in climbing the mountains, which make the journey more colorful and exciting. While maneuvering through the mountains which are potentially steep, tall, quiet, beautiful and even bizarre, people can be nurtured to enjoy the beauty. The experience of touring mountains is especially poignant when visitors reach the top of a mountain, with the unique atmosphere of beholding the world from a potentially great height. The Tang Dynasty poet Du Fu's feeling of "overlooks any other mountains" is a concentrated reflection of the experience of scaling a mountain and viewing the world from that particular vantage point. Perhaps, the more times people climb mountains, the richer and profounder the enjoyment can be. Mountains can be commonly shared and appreciated sites of aesthetical appreciation and education.

2. A Good Place to Relax

Many World Famous Mountains share the common characteristics of dense forests, fragrant clusters of flowers, agreeable climates, fresh air, and natural landscapes that haven't been too heavily touched by the hand of industry and modernity. These characteristics create an atmosphere that can contribute to human physical health, mental health, and the rehabilitation of the spirit and of vitality. In recent years, an activity known as a "forest bath" has even become popular in Europe, the United States, and Japan; it includes climbing mountains for the view, and wandering in the forest while walking in the shade.

3. Cultural Tourism

Many famous temples, ancient city walls, village forts, battlefields, cliff inscriptions, and statues, are distributed throughout the world's famous mountains. These cultural relics are of interest to tourists searching for cultural histories, and are also important as sites of scientific study. These places contribute to the understanding of regional histories, opening up horizons of study and enriching our knowledge. Many famous mountains, such as Lushan, Mount Fuji and Mount Tai, are the bases of scientific education concerning landforms, biology, pharmaceutical innovations, botanical gardens, architecture, painting, and other artistic aesthetics.

4. A place of Summer Relaxation

As the temperature in the mountains is generally far lower than the towns and cities around them, especially in the summer season, many famous mountains serve as places of harbor for city dwellers trying to escape the heat of summer. This is especially important in countries where summer heat indexes can reach extremes.

5. A Variety of Unique Tourism Activities

Many mountains provide a variety of tourism activities, and many of these activities are unique to mountains. For example, in the aspect of sightseeing, visitors can appreciate not only crags, waterfalls, trees and flowers, birds and animals, but also clouds, sun sets and sun rises in the mountains. In addition, people also can develop tourism activities such as sports, skiing, mountain climbing, fitness rehabilitation, escaping the heat and enjoying the cool, scientific research, bird watching, glacier tourism, and so on.

6. Build up a Good Physique and Improve One's Health

According to mountain physiological research, mountain climates are very beneficial to human health. In order to adapt to the alpine environment, the human body will undergo a series of physiological changes such as pulmonary ventilation and the increase of vital capacity, stimulation of blood circulation, increase in cerebral blood flow, increase in urine acidity, increase in glucosamine urinary excretion, and a decrease in blood sugar. In addition, mountaineering is also beneficial to the stomach, the thyroid and adrenal glands. Mountain climbing can also cultivate perseverance, open mind, and nurture the soul.

II. Characteristics of Famous Mountain Tourism

1. Remarkable Characteristics and Natural Scenery Advantages

Mountain tourist areas are mainly famous for their various natural landscape resources and rich cultural landscape, which have very high aesthetic, historical, and scientific research values. Many tourist resources with famous mountains playing the dominant role are national tourist attractions, some are even world-class.

2. Limited Touring Ground and Fragile Ecological Environments

The areas of many scenic spots, which are mainly mountains, are wide and huge; however, there is little flat ground which makes touring spaces relatively small. Moreover, these scenic landscapes are always located in mountainous areas which are mostly economically and culturally underdeveloped. Therefore, people have a very strong desire to speed up the development in these areas to attract and encourage the flow of tourism, which is tend to exert negative impacts on the ecological environments of the mountains and the regions surrounding them.

3. Crossing Different Administrative Regions and Complex Multilateral Interests

Due to the mountain areas are quite large, some scenic areas span several counties, some span several villages and towns, and they are mostly spread across several village committees, thus the administrative divisions related to mountain scenic area are complex. It is difficult to clearly define respective rights and adjust complicated relations when addressing the governing of these areas.

4. Inconspicuous Tourism Images and Large Differences in Tourist Seasons

Tourism products of different types follow different elasticity of demand in different seasons. Commonly, products based on natural tourism resources are sold in large quantities in tourist flow seasons, while places of historical interest are in contrast. If there is only single industrial structure of mountain scenic spots with strong homogeneity, it will strengthen the intensity of tourist flow in certain seasons; the converse situation holds if the products are composited with strong complementariness and reasonable spatial layout.

III. Sustainable Development of Famous Mountains Tourism

1. Concept Innovation and Building an Overall Competitive Advantage

At present, the developers and constructors of tourism resources in famous-mountains-oriented-scenic-spots are mainly the governments of the administrative area, the departments of tourism and part of the scenic area operators. Since the ownership and part of the managerial rights belong to the government of administrative area, who takes its own interest as the premise, it brings fierce competitions in tourism resources, tourist source market and tourism projects. With the deepening of the concept of "Great Tourism" and "Great System", breaking the administrative boundaries and integrating the tourism resources is imperative, that is, to solve the common problems of each stakeholder, and give sufficient consideration to the feature of each stakeholder, so as to fulfill powerful combination.

2. Expanding the Chain of the Tourism Industry, and Building a World Famous Mountains Travel Brand

It is necessary to promote world famous mountains tourism from sightseeing tours to tours for leisure and recreation, from resource development to brand building, and market development. This extensive and resource-based industry should be turned into energy-saving and efficient industry and also tourism should be combined with many other activities and areas of interest such as: relaxation, sports and fitness, shopping, entertainment, and business activities. It is better to vigorously develop the different potential aspects of tourism such as sightseeing, ecology, culture (including cultural relics), countryside, forest, leisure, fitness, etc., and mindfully continue the construction and improvement of tourist resorts. Industrial chain need to be extended, which will create several influential, efficient, large-sized products and brands. Developing the handicraft manufacturing industry, the tourism supplies manufacturing industry and tourism food processing industry will be a focus. Besides, there is a need to encourage the research and development of scenic spots and characteristic tourist commodities and souvenirs develop the cultural entertainment industry, and excavate local cultures, develop and bring in renowned performance groups, strive for undertaking various large-scale cultural, physical and artistic activities. Moreover, to build movie/video shooting bases, literary and artistic creation bases, water sports bases, educational and scientific research bases are also necessary.

3. Promoting Innovative Tourism Marketing Techniques and Improving Integration of Network Resources

We should adhere to the principle of "government-led, marketing operation, media guide, enterprises follow-up", and "unified promotion caliber, unified promotion management, unified promotion advertisements, unified promotional action" to perfect the government and enterprises coalition, department union, upper and lower linkage promotion strategy, and the reward system of tourism market development and products research, mobilize all positive factors, integrate all resources, gather the funds to the important things, jointly promote the market image, and promote the tourist products. It is necessary to pay more attention to the overall promotion of tourism products and publicity of tourism city image, and segment the tourist market. We need to target at the major tourist market, comprehensively utilize radio, movies, television, internet, newspapers and other media, and explore to set up the tourist information center. Through the establishment of intermediary organizations, associations, information center, we can provide various training, consulting and information, or organize an entrepreneur exchange party purposefully, promote exchanges and cooperation between the tourism enterprises, and generate tourism enterprise collaboration network. In addition, through forms such as business connection, resource sharing, exchange of experience, we can reduce operating costs, improve the efficiency of the whole tourism industry, and produce 1+ 1> 2 external economic benefit.

4. Standardization of Famous Mountain Management and Optimization of Tourism Environment

The tourism enterprises should be guided to strengthen the tourism brand protection awareness, actively carry out tourism brand trademark registration. It is also necessary to promote tourism standardization work, guide and supervise tourism enterprises to fully implement international standards. All kinds of related local industry standards should be improved; guides for travel agencies, tour guides, tourist attractions, and reception units should be classified as well. People should adhere to market access and exit mechanism, and who graded last in the performance evaluation will be laid off. Methods of inspection, examination, inspection, rectification and other means can be employed to strengthen the supervision of main body of tourism market, and try to employ "all-in-one card system" for regional tourism. Tickets prices of tourist attractions should be supervised and controlled, the span of control should be determined as well. It is necessary to actively build civilized scenic spots to improve the service quality and service level, and also to build local tourism reputation and improve the handling of complaints and coordination mechanism. Examination systems, dealing with skills identification, qualification and certification of tourism practitioners, can also be carried out and skill training should be focused on. Relative affairs should be managed according to the law and tourism market supervision regulations. It is urgent to crack down slaughtering or cheating customer, buying and selling by coercion, various unfair competition acts, illegal and criminal activities. It is necessary to attach great importance to tourism security, improve the tourism emergency system, involving social security, traffic safety, fire safety, device safety, food safety, health and epidemic prevention, and emergency rescue work. It is necessary to improve the scenic area tourist service center system as well as information consultation system, and improve bilingual or multilingual sign systems. "Green passage" policy for tourism should run smoothly, and nobody has absolutely unrestricted access to check and detain foreign tourist vehicles. In addition, the whole society should be mobilized to concern, participate and support tourism, and create a good environment for accelerating the development of tourism industry.

Chapter 2

World Famous Mountains in Asia

Section 1 Lushan—Sacred Mountain

Lushan is situated in Jiujiang City, Jiangxi Province, People's Republic of China, adjacent to the Yangtze River to the north and Poyang Lake to the east. It is a horst block mountain, inseparably standing between the Yangtze River and Poyang Lake. Since ancient times, it has been reputed as a top scenic mountain in China, as in the old saying "East or west, the landscape of Lushan is the best". It is famous for its "magnificence, precipitousness, marvelousness and beauty".

On December 6, 1996, Lushan was approved to be included on the World Heritage List as World Cultural Landscape. In 2002, it ranked as one of "Ten Famous Mountains in China", and the film "Love Story on Lushan" has been listed in the "Guinness World Records". In 2004, Lushan became a member of the first batch of Global Geoparks in China. In 2005, it passed the assessment as one of the world's "United Nations CCC/UN Prominent Eco-Tourism Scenery" sites and was nominated as the sole China's "World Heritage Protection Management Unit". In January, 2006, it became a member of the first batch of "National Civilized Scenic Areas". In 2007, it was officially approved as "National AAAAA Scenic Area". In 2008, it was among the first batch of "National Tourism Business Card" and "Top Ten Famous World Heritage Sites in China". In 2009, it won its reputation as one of the "Top Ten Summer Resorts in China" and the "Top Ten Beautiful Mountains in China". In the same year, the 1st World Famous Mountains Conference was successfully held in Lushan, which became the permanent registered location of the World Famous Mountains Association. It is the first that has won all the three top honors as a scenic spot: World Cultural Heritage, World Natural Heritage and World Geopark.

I. Geological Features

Lushan stands near the southern bank of the Yangtze River and to the northwest of Poyang Lake. Covering an area of 302 square kilometers with 171 named peaks, it is 29 kilometers long from north to south and 16 kilometers wide from east to west. The tallest peak, Big Hanyang Peak, is 1474 meters above sea level. The average elevation of Lushan is over 1000 meters. Lushan, the Yangtze River(the longest river in China) and Poyang Lake(the largest fresh lake in China) compose a special geographic location, which has produced geological and geomorphologic landscapes with outstanding value.

In geomorphological terms, Lushan is called a "horst block mountain".

It began developing around 1 billion years ago, and in the process recorded the evolution of the earth's crust and witnessed the earth's amazing changes. Lushan is situated at the joint area of the anticline of Jiangnantai and the hidden part the Yangtze plate continental earth crust. Its layers have all been systematically exposed, (with the exception of the Triassic period), with clear structures, showing the main process of the evolution of the earth's crust.

The continual replacements of land and ocean, the slow deposition of the crust, the alternating coldness and warmth of the climate, the evolution of the life and death of many creatures, the mountains' rise of Yanshan Movement, and the significant influences of Quaternary Glaciers, all of these factors and more have made Lushan the geological wonder it is today.

In the past, some western geologists once asserted that there had been no Quaternary Glaciers in China, to which, however, the Chinese geologist Li Siguang was opposed. He firmly believed that many of Lushan's peculiar geomorphologic landscapes were the carved "masterpieces" of Quaternary Glaciation.

Lushan has been approved as one of the first World Geoparks with its unique features of geological structure, significant geological characteristics, extraordinary and beautiful sceneries, and geological sites of rich cultural and historical connotation.

II. Remarkable Value

Lushan's historic sites uniquely combine the mountain's natural beauty to create a cultural landscape with a high aesthetic value, a landscape which is closely linked to the spirit of the Chinese nation and culture. Its prominent geological structure, as well as the richness of animal and plant life helps it win compliments like "the magnificent", "the unique", "the steep", and "the glorious". These characteristics blend perfectly with the richly-connotative historic remains, thus help creating a unique cultural landscape. Lushan is amazing because of its close contact with nature and culture as a whole, which embodies and displays the spirit of Chinese people and their cultural life. The prominent values of Lushan are mainly displayed in its culture, aesthetic, science and ecology.

1.Cultural value

Lushan is inseparable from Chinese cultural history and is an outstanding representative of Chinese culture of mountain-water landscape. Tao Yuanming, the great thinker and pioneer of Chinese pastoral poetry, wrote the famous essay "The Legendary Peach Blossom Paradise" in Lushan in 418 AD. In this essay he describes the ideal kingdom, which is a magnificent chapter in the history of human thought. Many poets and scholars have been attracted to Lushan to make academic researches and compose their masterpieces. Among them are Hui Yuan, the pioneer of Chinese Buddhist thought; Lu Xiujing, the founder of the first Taoist Scriptures; Xie Lingyun, the pioneer of Chinese landscape poetry; Gu Kaizhi, the first Chinese landscape painter; Zong Bing, the first Chinese landscape-painting theorist and Wang Xizhi, a great calligraphy master. More than 1500 noted figures in the fields of literature, politics and arts, such as Li Bai, Bai Juyi, Su Shi and Wang Anshi ever visited and even lived on Mount Lushan, leaving behind some 10000 pieces of verses as well as other writings, paintings and calligraphic works, all of which contribute to the fact that Mount Lushan has become the representative of Chinese landscape culture.

As the center of cultural activities in the south of China, Lushan is a model of Chinese Academy Education and the blending focus between Chinese and Western cultures. The significant cultural evolutions and political events that took place in the history of Lushan have influenced the development of Chinese history. Since ancient times, there have been three periods in the history of Lushan that reflect the trends of Chinese history. In 1928, Hu Shi, the famous scholar, noted that three historic remains in Lushan respectively represented three historical trends: Donglin Temple for the great trend of Chinese Buddhist-styled and Buddhism Chinese-styled; White Deer Cave Academy for the great trend of Song Dynasty Learning for seven hundred years in the pre-modern times; and Guling Town for the great trend of western cultural invasion.

2. Aesthetic value

Lushan is endowed with exotic sceneries and natural landscapes, producing an aesthetic feeling by way of perception and cognition. The most direct manifestation of its aesthetic value is to be found in poems and paintings of Lushan, and in particular those of a scenic nature. The aesthetic feeling of the spirit that rises from them is one of the carriers of the beauty of Lushan.

3. Scientific Value

In the 1930s, Chinese geologist Li Siguang discovered quaternary glacial relics in Lushan, thus entitled Lushan to be the birthplace of the theory of quaternary glaciation of China. The typical quaternary glacial relics of eastern China, such as precious metamorphic nuclear rock structures and spectacular complex landforms, have high value in geological scientific researches. Furthermore, in the East Valley Villas Region of Lushan, there are more than 600 villas built by original owners from the US, the UK, Sweden, Italy, France, Portugal, Finland, Canada, Australia, Norway, Austria, Switzerland, Denmark, Ireland, Russia, Holland, and China, etc. With all kinds of different styles, you can see churches of both Romanesque and gothic styles, Byzantine architecture that combines eastern art forms with western ones, Japanese architecture, Islam mosques, and other flavors of foreign architecture, which could be called the masterpieces of architecture in the world and have remarkable value of scientific research.

4. Ecological Value

Due to its superb natural conditions, Lushan is rich in vegetation, which distributes in vertical zonality. Lushan is typically very pleasant with a humid climate, plenty of rainfall, abundant vegetation and luxuriantly green vegetation. Located in an area that experiences subtropical monsoons, it has an average annual precipitation of 1950-2000 milliliters with seas of clouds enshrouding its peaks throughout the year. With the increase of altitude, surface water heat is vertically distributed. Evergreen broad-leaved forests, and evergreen and deciduous broad-leaved mixed forests grow respectively from the foot to the top of the mountain. Lushan is a natural botanical garden. According to incomplete statistics, the plants in Lushan nurtures 210 families, 735 genera, 1720 species, classified into seven types of temperate zones, tropical zones, subtropical zones, that share similarities with climate zones in East Asia, North America and China.

III. Recommended Scenic Spots

Lushan's dream-like spring, refreshing summer, invigorating autumn and snowy winter have long impressed its visitors. Many ancient poets have expressed their love for Lushan. Bai Juyi, a famous poet of the Tang Dynasty, described the natural beauty of Lushan in his verse "East or West, the landscape of Lushan is the best". Lushan became a world-famous summer resort as early as at the end of the 19th century because of its pleasant weather and natural beauty.

1. Valley of Splendor

The Jinxiu Valley (Valley of Splendor), according to a legend, was the place where Hui Yuan (a famous monk during the Jin Dynasty in ancient China) gathered flowers and herbs. Jinxiu Valley was so named because the flowers there are very beautiful and splendid like brocade and silk in the four seasons. The sceneries of Lushan unroll like a splendid and intoxicating picture scroll.

The Splendid Immortal Cave is so named because of the Immortal Cave hidden in the cliffs at the end of the plank road along the cliffs in Jinxiu Valley. The cave is widely known for Mao Zedong's famous verse: "It is nature that chisels a cave for immortals antique, the unmatched beauty dwells on the lofty and perilous peak." As a natural cave, the Immortal Cave is 7 meters high and 14 meters deep. The Immortal Cave is also known as "Bergamot Rock" for the uneven front stones at the top of the cave, like five outstretched fingers. The Immortal Cave is a Taoist holy place, which, according to a legend, is the site where Lu Dongbin, one of the Taoist "Eight Immortals" tried to make pills of immortality and cultivate vital energy before becoming an immortal. Chunyang Temple, which is made of stone, is in the Immortal Cave, and is where Lu Dongbin's stone statue stands with a sword on its back.

The oddness of the Tianqiao Bridge is not in the bridge itself. It is over the deep valley, in which there are many cliffs and rocks which are very spectacular from a bird's eye view. When clouds or mists rise continuously from the bottom of the valley, surging like rolling silver waves, and leaping onto the bridge, you will feel extremely happy and relaxed. In a moment, a gust of wind comes from the north, blowing away the clouds, then the Jinxiu Valley and the Tianqiao Bridge appear again with their extraordinary splendor.

2. Rising Sun at Hanpokou

The best spot for observing the morning sunrise on Lushan is Hanpokou which lies in the middle of Hanpo Peak in the East Valley of Lushan. The huge canyon between Hanpo Ridge, Jiuqi Peak and Hanyang Peak stand right to the face of Poyang Lake, just like a large open mouth holding Poyang Lake, and heartily sucking water. In Chinese, one of the meanings of "Kou" is mouth, and "Han" means to hold, so the valley is called "Hanpokou", the mouth that holds Poyang Lake. Hanpokou is a huge U-shape valley that was formed during the Quaternary Glaciation Period.

The diverse beauty of Hanpokou, the capacious space, vast field of vision, low verdant hills, stationary mountains, flowing water and so on—all reflect and connect each other, integrating into a breathtaking whole. Miraculousness and openness are the subtlety and charm of the place. Before dawn, if you ascend the Hanpo Ridge, and overlook Poyang Lake from the Wang-Po Pavilion (a pavilion for viewing Poyang Lake), you will be amazed by the whole process of sunrise: at the beginning: the sky is shallowly blue, then in a moment, flushes with crimson clouds in the horizon, and brightens slowly; as the sun rises slowly on the surface of the water, the lake is dyed orange, sparkling. The glistening light on the waves of the lake are especially dazzling and particularly bright. Sometimes it seems as if the sun jumps out of the lake, making everything crimson. This sunrise lightens the green mountains, and dyes the water red; so the morning sun, the lake, and mountains constitute the magnificent scenery of "Seas of rosy clouds seem to be beautiful clothes".

3. Five Old Men Listening to the Waterfalls(Wulao Peak)

The spectacular scenic area of "Five Old Men Listening to the Waterfalls" consists of two scenic spots: The Five Old Men Peaks (Wulao Peaks)—the five grandest peaks of Lushan, and the Three-step Waterfall—the most magnificent waterfall of Lushan. Seen from afar, the five peaks look like five old men sitting by Poyang Lake side by side, so these peaks are known as

"The Five Old Men Peaks"; while "the Three-step Waterfall" earns its name because the torrents dash down in three steps. The scenic area of "Five Old Men Listening to the Waterfalls" is the essence of Lushan's scenery.

4. The Bailudong Academy

The Bailudong Academy (The White Deer Cave Academy) was the earliest established institute of higher education in China and was the top of the four great ancient Chinese academies. By the time of the Song Dynasty, the prestige of "the Four Chinese Ancient Academies" had prevailed. The Bailudong Academy, Suiyang Academy, Yingtian Academy and Yuelu Academy—these four academies are known as the academic origin of Chinese higher education.

The founder of The Bailudong Academy was Li Bo, a poet of the Tang Dynasty. During the years of Zhenyuan period (785 AD—805 AD) of the Tang Dynasty, Li Bo lived in seclusion in Lushan for learning. He raised a white deer for fun, and thus acquired the nickname of Mr. White Deer. During the years of Changqing (821 AD—824 AD) of the Tang Dynasty, Li Bo was appointed as an official of the Prefectural Governor of Jiangzhou (now Jiujiang city). He built pavilions and planted trees and flowers at the spot of the White Deer Cave.

In the middle period of Kaiyuan, the Southern Tang Dynasty (937AD—975AD), a school known as "Lushan Guoxue(Chinese Culture)Academy" was set up in Lushan. In the Song Dynasty, when Zhu Xi, the famous neo-confucianism master and educator, was appointed as the chief of Nankang (now Xingzi County), he reconstructed the academy buildings and gave lectures. He made rules and set the goals of the academy and wrote them on the horizontal inscribed board. The academy became famous and attracted many renowned scholars from home and abroad to give lectures there. Since then, as a cultural center in China, it became a model of "lecture-style" academy for several hundred years from the late Song Dynasty to the early Qing Dynasty.

5.Kingdom of Plants

Lushan Botanical Garden, the "Kingdom of Plants", founded in 1934, was the first official botanical garden in China and has an important position in the history of Chinese and International botanical gardens. The people who founded the Lushan botanical garden were Dr. Hu Xiansu of Harvard University, who was a giant in Chinese botanical circles, and his assistants, the famous botanists Qin Renchang and Chen Fenghuai. They worked very hard and made painstaking efforts to create the first formal botanical garden in this valley.

The Botanical Garden covers an area of approximately 5000 acres, divided into the Pine Area, the Flowery Area, the Medicinal Garden, the Rock Garden, the Tea Garden, the Kiwifruit Garden, the International Friendship Azalea Garden, the Natural reserve, the Green House and Nursery. The garden collects more than 5500 species of Chinese and foreign plants, including more than 150 kinds of rare and endangered plants under state protection. There are about 600 varieties of conifers in the world, with 250 varieties in this garden, which is known as a living specimen park of the pine, cypress, fir and juniper.

6. Huajing Michun (Seeking for Spring in Flowery Path)

The full name of the scenic spot Huajing Michun is "Bai Sima Flowery Path". In 815 AD, Bai Juyi, the famous Tang Dynasty poet, was banished to Jiujiang city as an official Sima (Magistrate). He was unhappy about being banished, and in the following early summer, he climbed up to Lushan and stayed in Da Lin Temple. Seen from the hillside of Da Lin Temple, the peach trees were in full bloom, while spring flowers on the bottom of the mountain had already withered away. Shocked by this beautiful scene, he was pleased and composed a famous seven-character-quatrain, "Da Lin Temple Peach Blossoms":

"All flowers in late spring have fallen far and wide,
But peach blossoms are full-blown on the mountainside,
I often regret spring's gone and I can't find its trace,
Without knowing it's come up to adorn this place."

With attractions including the Flowery Area, Rock Garden, Greenhouse and Peach Forest, and the beautiful Ru Qin (violin-shape) Lake in the cove, Bai Sima Flowery Path has become a famous scenic spot for tourists. In 1987, the thatched cottage built in the foothill by Bai Juyi himself was moved into the Flower Path Park by relevant departments. Some materials, calligraphy, and paintings about poet Bai Juyi are displayed in the cottage. In front of the cottage stands his statue, which is a good memory of the great poet by the later generations.

7. Meilu Villa

The history of villas in Lushan dates back to 1895. The villas are all quite different, but most of them belong to European mountain villa architectural styles, and, to a certain extent, reflect a variety of house building arts from around the world. These fantastic villas, integrating western architectural art and culture, and the unique natural landscape of Lushan, are the perfect combination of culture and nature.

Of the many villas on Lushan, Meilu Villa is the most famous one. It is located in the middle of the Changchong river, facing south, with the main building area of 996 square meters and the garden area of 4928 square meters. It leans against the hills with a zigzag spring flowing through its garden. The garden is full of vitality with many blooming flowers and valuable evergreen Chinese trees such as golden larch trees, ginkgo, magnolia, liriodendron and conifers; and other rare trees including spruce, red maple, Platanus and Campasis radicans. Meilu villa, with a Western architectural style and garden layout that blends Chinese and Western sensibilities, not only reflects the characteristics of the interaction between Chinese and Western cultures and aesthetic orientations, but also reflects a people-oriented emotional appeal. It fully demonstrates the unique charm of architectural and garden-based art and creates a strong aesthetic pleasure with ingenious combinations of colours and a unity and collaboration of reserved beautiful melodies and natural environment. Meilu villa, known as the only building where Chiang Kai-shek and Mao Zedong, the top leaders of KMT and CPC, have ever lived, is the most wonderful one among the villas in Lushan.

8. Huang Long and Bao Shu

Huang Long and Bao Shu is a tourist attraction consisting of Huang Long Temple, Huang Long Pool, Wu Long Pool and Three Precious Trees. It is a natural oxygen bar in Lushan known for its quietness and classicality. There are three towering trees in front of Huang Long Temple, known as the San Bao Trees (Three Precious Trees)— two cedars, and one gingko. According to legend, these three towering trees were planted by a famous monk Tan Shen in the Jin Dynasty and have a history of over 1500 years.

9. The Street Market in Clouds

There is a unique Chinese mountainous city surrounded by towering peaks in clouds on top of Lushan. In the center of this city, a street market winds its way like a fairytale through the mountains, amazing tourists with a fascinating view alongside.

As the most bustling place in Cooling Town, "The street market in clouds" runs from the east to the west in the form of a curve. It is shaped like a clear half-moon or a charming flower in shyness. Along the street, there are row upon row of shops and restaurants, cafes and bars on one side, and the elegant and cozy park on the other side. Tourists can have a good taste of the unique Mount Lu's snacks in these restaurants and enjoy buying some souvenirs in the shops or relax themselves in the bars. The park is ideal for visitors' relaxation. In the park stands a bull statue. On the substrate are written two Chinese characters meaning "Cooling Street" by the famous calligrapher Qigong.

10. The Five Religions Praying Park

Lushan is a famous holy mountain, of various cultures, politics and religions. A unique phenomenon of Lushan is that there are five religious sects co-existing harmoniously on the mountain. In order to enrich Lushan's religious culture, under the supervision of the Administration Bureau of Lushan, the Five Religions Praying Park was completed in 2010. The park is located in Qinglian Valley in the scenic area of Wulao Peaks(The Five Old Men Peaks). The theme of the project is "The Heaven calls and the earth answers", and the expression style is "The bell makes sounds for the world and the gospel prevails", and the focus is the scenic design of the praying route. The most distinctive feature of the Five Religions Praying Park of Lushan is the praying bell with a weight of 38.5 tons. The overall height of the bell is 476 cm, indicating 40076 km of the equator. The height of the bell is 365 cm, representing 365 days a year. Its circumference is 960 cm, standing for the total land area of China. There are five religious signs and blessing words on the bell, representing five religions, including Buddhism, Taoism, Catholicism, Islam and Christianity. The bell is cast with pure copper and its sounds can be heard as far as ten kilometers away.

Section 2 Mount Tai – Head of the Five Most Famous Mountains in China

Mount Tai (Taishan), known as the head of Five Mountains in China, is situated in the north of Taian city in central Shandong province. It was originally named Dai Shan(岱山) and Dai Zong(岱宗), meaning the head of mountains of China, and Mount Tai or Tai Shan(泰山) had a more than two-thousand-year historical standing. The Jade Emperor Peak(the highest peak), about 200 km in length and 50 km in which, stretching through 3 cities— Taian, Jinan, and Laiwu, with about 200 km in length and 50 km in width. The whole mountain chain runs across the central part of Shandong and covers more than ten counties, and intersects in the north-south passageway of North China Plain and the west-east watercourse of the middle and lower reaches of Yellow River. This unique geographical location has played important roles in expanding its influence and carrying forward its culture. Over thousands of years, above 10 ancient emperors held their worship ceremonies on Mount Tai, of which Confucious and many famous poets also sang high praises. In 1987, Mount Tai was listed in the World Heritage Sites by UNESCO, as the first World Cultural and Natural Heritage site in China.

I. Geomorphologic Landscapes

With the Jade Emperor Peak 1545 meters (5029 ft) high, Mount Tai enjoys a distinct vertical change in weather, which contributes to the rich natural landscapes. The abundant rainfall creates numerous springs, waterfalls, brooks and ravines including 72 famous springs, 64 waterfalls and ponds, as well as 130 brooks and ravines. Moreover, the changeable weather causes many weather phenomena, such as rime and other meteorological spectacles. It is the weather's variability that makes Mt. Tai a spectacular and marvelous place.

The landforms of Mt. Tai can be identified as four types: alluvial-proluvial terrace, denudation-accumulated hills, tectonic denudation low mountains and tectonic-erosion middle and lower mountains. In spatial image, the whole mountain area goes from low to high with towering peaks standing one after another, taking on a collection of lofty terrains.

As one of the World Geoparks, its rich geological resources have been widely researched by experts and scholars both at home and abroad. The scientific values contained in these resources have attracted geologists and tourists to learn the Earth changes and popularize the knowledge of geography and geology. At present, many geological resources can be learned by visiting the Museum of Mount Tai Geopark and some geological relics, such as hydro geological relics, geologic structure relics, rock sites, and stratum sites. Most landscapes gather around the following scenic spots: Aolai Peak, Peach Valley, Fan Cliff, Tianzhu Peak, and Zhongtian Gate.

II. Main Scenic Spots

The scenic spots on Mount Tai center around the main peak and have been protected and reconstructed for thousands of years. Mount Tai lies among Shangdong Hill with the main peak standing upright and held up by surrounding peaks rising up one after another. On the top, we can hold all mountains in a single glance. Human landscape of historic figures and cultural heritage lay out from the southwest Sheshou mountain where sacrifices were offered to the earth, and Haoli mountain to Mount Tai's highest Jade Emperor Peak (Yuhuangding), which creates triple spaces of "Hell", "Human World" and "Heaven". Dai Temple is the main architecture of the city's central axis, connecting front Heaven Street and back Winding Path. From Dai Temple, tourists can ascend along the path leading from "Human World" to "Heaven" to come into more and more delightful stages.

1. Stone Carvings on Mount Tai

Stone carvings on Mount Tai are not only famous for their number and variety but also for their long history and high aesthetic taste. They are valuable materials for studying the history of Mount Tai and also calligraphic and engraving art and they are historical, cultural, aesthetic and of great artistic value. At present, the existing stone carvings were preserved since 1687. They are mainly distributed on both sides of Dai Temple and Eighteen Winding Bends of mountaineering path. Among them, 273 are in Dai temple, 222 in the Hongmen scenic area (from Daizong Arch to Hutian Pavilion), 188 in the area of Middle Heaven Gate (from Hutian Pavilion to Chaoyang Cave), 358 in the area of South Heaven Gate (from Chaoyang Cave to Houshi Cove) and 165 in the area of Bamboo Forest (including Puzhao Temple, Wuxian Shrine, Martyr Memorial Temple, Sanyang Taoist Temple and Fan Cliff).

2. Eighteen Winding Bends (Shibapan)

Shibapan is the steepest section along the path to the top, making it one of the main symbols of Mount Tai. A steep winding path is embedded among the steep cliffs on both sides, like a heavenly ladder in the distance. Shibapan is usually divided into three sections according to the dip angles: the gradual Shibapan from Kai Hill to Longmen Archway, half-steep Shibanpan from Longmen Archway to Shengxian Archway and steep Shibapan from Shengxian Archway to South Heaven Gate. The huge hanging rock on the west cliff of the steep Shibapan is called Greeting Buddha. Its silhouette is like a bald head of a Buddha with high nose bridge and smiling face lying on its side. The obliquity of the steep rocks on Shibanpan is from 70 to 80 degrees.

3. South Heaven Gate

The end of the Eighteen Winding Bends was called Santian Gate or Tianmen Pass at an altitude of 1460 meters. The mountain here is the steepest in the low place between Feilong Rock and Xiangfeng Ridge just like an open heaven gate. It was built by the Taoist Zhang Zhichun in 1264 (the fifth year of Zhongtong in Yuan Dynasty). The gate is of attic type with its arch made of stones and "South Heaven Gate" written in the center of the arch. Red walls and coloured-glaze-tile roofs make it magnificent. On the side of the gate there is a Chinese couplet depicting the places of interest and numerous steps overlooking all mountains at the top. Du Renjie in Yuan dynasty carved the *Tianmen inscription* to record this: "There are no houses beside the South Heaven Gate. Zhang Zhichun first built it in several years." The stone carvings are still well-preserved in the western stone houses of South Heaven Gate.

4. Dai Temple

Dai Temple is the progenitor of all the ancient temples in Chinese famous mountains. It was built during the Qin and Han Dynasty, repaired and expanded in Song Dynasty, and was the previous imperial palace for several dynasties. Every emperor who came to Mount Tai to offer sacrifices to heaven and earth would first hold a ceremony in Dai Temple and then climb the mountain. As a famous royal ancestral temple in the center of Tai'an City at the southern foot of Mount Tai, covers an area of nearly 100000 square meters. And as a national cultural relic protection unit, the number of the first-class cultural relics in it ranks the 60th in more than 2000 museums across China.

Tian Kuang Hall, the main architecture of Dai Temple to the north of Ren'an Gate, was built in 1009 AD (the second year of Da Zhong Xiang Fu in Song Dynasty). The hall, built on a rectangular stone terrace with carved fences surrounding thee sides, is 48.7 meters long, 19.73 meters wide and 22.3 meters high. The double-eaved gable roof, colour-painted bucket arches, coloured tiles and eight bright red posts make the hall majestic and magnificent. It is "one of the three famous ancient palaces" in China, among which the other two are Beijing's Tai He Temple and Da Cheng Hall in Qu Fu (Shandong Province).

5. Sunrise and Sunset

The best time to visit Mount Tai is from May to November. Its four wonders are known as: Rising Sun from the East, Jade-plate Clouds, Sunset Afterglow and Golden-belt-like Yellow River at Sunset. The "Rising Sun from the East", one of the wonders on the top, is spectacular and impressive and an important symbol of Mount Tai. At dawn, when visitors look to the east from the top, the morning sunshine goes from grey to yellowish, and then to orange. The clouds in the sky turn red and violet while the rosy clouds and the vast sea of clouds on the horizon form a giant canvas in the sky. On the horizon, the sun rises in the faraway east like a floating palace lantern. Soon the mountains glow with the golden sunshine. What a spectacular and magic sunrise on the horizon.

The "Sunset Afterglow" is another wonder. At sunset, if you look up to the west on the top of Mount Tai just after rain, you will find peak-and-mountain-like clouds and the golden sunshine piercing the clouds and mist and pouring down on the earth. Against the afterglow, the clouds are seemingly beset with bright edges glittering with brilliant lights, which are so wonderful and unpredictable. If clouds appear at this time, the sunset rays will strike in the "sea". The magnificent scenery and vivid nature are more charming. Sunset Afterglow and Golden-belt-like Yellow River at Sunset will change with seasons and climate. To appreciate and enjoy the beauty of the scenes, visitors should choose proper travel time. Autumn is the best choice because of the high bright blue sky and delightful sunshine. To travel after a heavy rain is a second choice because of lingering residual clouds, fine weather, little dust, green hills and clear waters. You can open your eyes glazing in all directions to enjoy the beautiful landscapes.

III. Six Scenic Areas

Mountain Tai is famous for its six large tourist areas.

The first is the central district of Mount Tai and the most popular route for tourists to reach the top on foot. The path winds its way from the Yitian Gate to the Zhongtian Gate and then to the South Heaven Gate with 6250 stone steps covering over 5.5 kilometers. All the way the path winds along mountain ridges and there stand high peaks and thick forests with a mixture of ancient trees and fantastic rocks. The major scenic spots here are Daizong Arch, Guandi Temple, Yitian Gate, the Arch of Confucius, Hongmen Palace, Wanxian Tower, Dou Mu Hall, Jingshi (Scripture Stone) Valley, Hutian Pavilion, Zhongtian Gate, Yunbu (Soaring) Bridge, Guest-greeting Pine, Face-to-face Pine Peak, Five-Pine Pavilion, Mengxian Shrine, Shengxian Arch and the Eighteen Winding Bends, etc.

The second area, also known as the West Stream Scenic Area, is the west district of Mount Tai. There are two routes for tourists to choose. One is a twisting mountain highway leading directly to the Middle Heaven Gate; the other is a winding path with beautiful ridges, deep ravines, high waterfalls, deep pools and gurgling rivulets on both sides. In the area, the major scenic spots are the Huangxi River, Longevity Bridge, Wuji Temple, Primus Temple, Fan Cliff, Tiansheng Village, Black Dragon Pool and White Dragon Pool, etc.

Climbing from the first area, through the Eighteen Winding Bends and South Heaven Gate, you will arrive at the third area, the top scenic spot. Here the tourists can not only enjoy the natural beauty and the ancient ruins, but also experience the feeling of "dwarfing all peaks". The major scenic spots here are the South Heaven Gate, Moon-Viewing Peak, Sky Street, White-Cloud Cave, Confucius Temple, Bixia Temple, Tangmo Cliff, Jade Emperor Peak, Tanhai Rock, Sun-Viewing Peak, Lu-Viewing Platform.

The centre of the fourth area is Houshi Cove, where you can see mighty cliffs, fantastic rocks, awesome ancient pines, singing birds and fragrant flowers. The beautiful scenery is beyond description. After getting to the mountain top, tourists can take a cable car to the major scenic spots—Eight Immortals Cave, Grandma Temple, Duzu Plate, Tianzhu Peak, Nine-dragon Hillock, Yellow Flower Cave, Lotus Cave and Yaoguan Platform, etc. Even more amazing natural beauty are Double Pine, Crouching Dragon Pine, Flying Dragon Pine, Sister Pine and Candle Pine growing in rocks.

At the foot of Mount Tai, the main spot inside the City of Tai'an is the fifth area, where you can enjoy the scenery of Mount Tai before climbing it. The major scenic spots are Double-Dragon Pool, Yaocan Pavilion, Dai Temple, Daizong Arch, Wangmu Pool, Guandi Temple, Puzhao Temple, Wuxian Memorial temple, Hanming Hall, Sanyang Taoist Temple, etc.

The sixth area is located at the western foot of Mount Tai and is composed of two tourist resorts, the Peach Valley and Cherry Park. The Peach Valley is beautiful and quiet, with cable cars taking tourists directly to the main peak. The Cherry Park is just outside of Tai'an City, with the harmony of chirping birds and babbling streams. To the Tai'an people, this area is a good recreational place.

Section 3 Mount Emei—Delicately Beautiful Buddhist Mountain

Mount Emei, 7 kilometers west of Emeishan City, 37 east of Leshan City, is located in Leshan City, the southwest of Sichuan Basin. The mountain, covering an area of 154 square kilometers, consists of four sections, namely, Da'e, Er'e, San'e, Si'e mountains. Its highest peak, Wanfo Top, is 3099 meters above sea level.

Due to the height geographical location of the Mount Emei, the weather and the seasons are quite different in different positions in the mountain. The hosts of heaven and infinite space have made Mt. Emei very mysterious. Mt. Emei commands immense natural heritage and an abundant range of species and unique landform. Thus it gets such titles as "Kingdom of Plants", "Animals' Paradise" "Geological Museum", and "Buddhist Celestial Mountain", which is the ashram of Samantabhadra Bodhisattva and Chinese Buddhist Holy land. In 1982, Mt. Emei was approved in the name of Mount Emei scenic area in the first list of state-level scenic spots by the State Council. On December 6, 1996, Mount Emei—Leshan Giant Buddha was added to the List of World Heritage by UNESCO as a cultural and natural heritage. In 2007, the Mount Emei Scenic Area was officially approved as National 5A tourist attractions by the National Tourism Administration.

I .Geomorphologic Landscapes

The geological evolution history of Mt. Emei is summarized as, "800 million years of gestation, 70 million years of growth, 2 million years of spring breezes and seasonable rain and imperceptible changes". In the process of millions of years of evolution, different kinds of geological structures have been formed in Mt. Emei through numerous strong crustal movements. Stratigraphic depositon occurred in 13 different international divisions of geological eras except the middle late Ordovician, Silurian, Devonian and Carboniferous eras. Thus it has been hailed as the "Museum of geology". The Yanshan movement at the end of the Mesozoic period outlined the geological structure of Mt. Emei, which was formed by the Himalayan mountain-building movement in the neotectonic period and the later uplift of the Qinghai-Tibet Plateau.

At the top of the mountain a large mass of Paleozoic whinstone ejected and its rock foundation was under protection, which could maintain the mountain's height. In addition, the waterfall of the mountain cut deep gorges through it, resulting in more than 2000 meters of stunningly magnificent canyons and striking peaks. Along the mountain, various landscapes coexist according to different stratum, such as cave landforms in limestone formation, like Jiulao-dong, by way of the areas of moorstones and metamorphites to steep gorges and basalt platform at the top of the mountain. It was naturally endogenetic processes and external agency that produced numerous spaces of scenic beauty on Mt. Emei.

II. Four Spectacles

1. A Sea of Clouds

When it is fine and clear, white clouds rise slowly among the mountains. The unbroken cloud plains appear above the horizon like a snowy white woolen blanket, smooth, clean and thick. Buddhism calls a sea of clouds "a silver World". The cloud plains of Mt. Emei are made up of low clouds. When wind comes, the sea of clouds is wafted in all the directions and then the mountains become small islands floating in an ocean. When the sea of clouds gathers together, the peaks are invisible again.

2. Sunrise

Mt. Emei lies on the west edge of Sichuan basin. Looking down the wide stretch "Tianfu basin" and watching the sunrise on the top of mountain one can broaden one's outlook and open one's mind, which makes one think about the relationship between human beings and nature. After the sunrise, millions of sun rays shoot onto the ground and Mt. Emei seems to wear a golden cloak from the head to the feet, showing all her glamour to the visitors.

3. Buddha Rays

The Buddha ray is also called the glory of Mt. Emei. Buddhism considers Buddha rays as the dazzling light from the brow of Samantabhadra Bodhisattva. As a matter of fact, a Buddha Ray is a natural phenomenon of light. Various airborne compounds scatter the sunlight and make these rays visible, due to diffraction, reflection, and scattering. In the afternoons of the summer and early winter, at the foot of the Sheshen Rock, a radius of around one to two meters appears with seven colors of the red, orange, yellow, green, black blue, blue and purple. It looms and shines in the center like a mirror. Back against the sunlight from the west, sometimes people can find their own shadow in the aura. And their every body movement is followed by their figures in the aura, as if they were facing a bright mirror. Even if millions of people were looking at it, they could only see themselves.

4. Saint Lamps

In the dark nights of Golden Summit, occasionally, one can see a point of fluorescence flowing between the valleys, then changing into several points and step by step into numerous ones. "Sometimes they are spreading out, like dancing stars; sometimes they gather together and surround each other." This dazzling phenomenon is called "worship of thousands of saint lamps to Samantabhadra Bodhisattva" from ancient times. The phenomenon of saint lamps is very fantastic. About its origin, someone says that it is wildfire. But others think that it comes from glowworms. It has also been said that it is the light coming from the honey fungus when the humidity of air is higher than 100%.

III. Main Tourist Areas

1. Shengji Curfew

Shengji Temple, formerly known as Cifu Temple, 2.5 kilometers south of Emeishan City, is the first and biggest temple on Mount Emei. Outside the temple, there are two ficus virens that cannot be encircled by several persons without their hands joined together. In ancient times, a copper bell hung over the pagoda of the temple and so was called Shengji copper bell. The bell was cast in the Jiajing Period of the Ming dynasty. It was paid by donation and built by Buddhist monk Biechuan. This bronze bell is strong and weights 12.5 tons. It is said that it's the biggest copper bell of Sichuan Province.

In 1959, Shengji Temple became abandoned and the copper bell was deserted beside the road. In 1978, the bell was removed to phoenix hill opposite to the Baoguo Temple and was maintained by building a pavilion above it. On phoenix hill, it is an integral whole and a unified entity of the towering cedar and cypress, the solemn and elegant octagonal pavilion, the ancient forest of steles surrounded by hundreds of inscriptions and the huge bell. This is an amazing landscape, blending natural beauty and humanistic beauty.

2. Sea of Clouds on the Luo Peak

Luo Peak, 0.5 kilometers of the right side of Fuhu Temple, is a small hill at the foot of Fuhu Mountain. Luo Peak is famous for beautiful trees and bamboo, winding mountain streams, old and towering Nanmu trees and quiet and secluded alley. Luo Peak is also the rare gathering place of pine trees on Mt. Emei. On the hill, there are hundreds of oddly-shaped pine trees which are tall and straight. When the wind blows, the sound of wind among the pine trees, like waves, resounds through the valley. After it rains in the summer, stream curls up slowly from valleys or floats across the blue sky. Looking from the thick pine trees, the clouds show their changing beauties which are light, graceful and unpredictable. Clouds rise from the stones and springs flow among them. These fantastic sights are feasts for the eyes. Luo peak nunnery, also called Luo peak temple, is an elegant and small temple which was rebuilt in June, 1987. This temple is quiet, tasteful and otherworldly, amid green bamboos and tall trees. Behind the nunnery, there is a newly-built pagoda forest for monks. All the senior monks in Mt. Emei may choose Luo peak as their resting places after Parinirvana.

3. Pinnacle Lingyan

The site of Lingyan temple is on the left side of Gaoqiao, 5 kilometers southwest of Baoguo temple. It was built in the Sui and Tang dynasties. The Ming Dynasty was the Linyan temple's heyday. The old temple collapsed in the 1960s, but the natural scene of Pinnacle Lingyan stills remains as before. Enjoying the sight of dense jungle and verdant rocks on Lingyan hill, you will feel that you cannot get enough of the beautiful view. Lingyan is on the piedmont behind the three peaks of golden summit. Looking out to the north from the site of Lingyan temple, you can see that, nearby, rolling hills are interspersed with thick jungle and bamboo; in the distance, wanfo, qianfo and golden summits are just like three huge green screens which are tall and straight, soft and distinct. From high to low and from near to far, the color of the hills changes from viridis to deep green and from grayish blue to gray, extending to far layer upon layer and beyond the boundary between the hills and the blue sky. With layer after layer of palaces amid thick jungle and verdant rocks, the temple is magnificent and is one of the ten famous scenery spots of Mt. Emei.

4. Double Bridges of Qingyin Pavilion

Qingyin Pavilion is in the middle part of Mt. Emei, and, together with the Longmen Grotto, are always called "two pizazzy showplaces of water". The whole area of the pavilion is a fine picture with green hills and blue water. Exquisite and refined pavilions occupy a commanding position and two gloriettes called Jieyu and Zhongxin stand in the middle of the region. There is one stone bridge crossing on the Black River and the White River on each side of the gloriette. The two bridges are like a pair of wings, so a beautiful name was given to them: Double Flying Bridges. At the lower point, you can see the Black River on the right of the Cattle Heart Pavilion and White River on its left. The Black River is also called Black Dragon River, which is derived from the Black Dragon Pool and rounds the Hongchun Plain and the color of the water is dark green. The White River is derived from Sancha River which is at the foot of Gongbei Mountain and rounds Wannian Temple. Because the color of the water is ivory, it is also called White Dragon River. The two rivers merge into billowing waves, striking the huge Cattle Heart stone in the middle of the green pond, which is a specific temple garden environment. Watching the Black river and the White River in Zhongxin gloriette, you will feel that mountains are moving along with water. Experts of landscape architecture acclaim it as a sound poem and a stereograph.

5. Autumn Wind on Baishui Pool

The whitewater autumn is named after the autumn in Wannian Temple which is located in Lion ridge, 1020 meters above the sea-level. Wannian Temple was constructed in the Eastern Jin Dynasty. Then the Chan Master Hui Tong in Tang Dynasty, preaching there, changed its name to White Water Temple. When the autumn comes, colorful trees leaves in the wood, white water swimming in the green pool, the singing frogs, fragrant sweet-scented give relaxation and freshness to tourists. So comes the name Autumn Wind on Baishui Pool.

6. Morning Rain at Hongchunping

Hongchunping, known for its quietness and grace is surrounded by the hills, where you can not only see low clouds, thick mist, and verdant ancient trees, but also hear the sound of crashing waves and high-pitched singing of birds. Hongchunping Temple, formerly called Qianfo Temple (Thousand-Buddha Temple), was built in 1573 (Ming Dynasty) and renamed because of the three Hongchun trees planted in front. The air is particular fresh with a little cool after a shower in a spring or summer morning and the courtyard of the temple is very clean and tidy. At the moment, the pavilions, terraces and towers seem to have been all enveloped in "the light rain", partly hidden and partly visible, like a mirage in the desert. The tourists who are in the pavilion or walking outside seem to have been dampened. But if you stroke your clothes, you will not find out a wet trace but a cool and comfortable feeling.

7. Snow Landscape of Daping

Daping, the isolated hill, rises between the Black Water and White Water and is located in the middle of Mt. Emei. On its left are Huayanding Temple, Zhanglaoping, Xixin Temple, and Guanxinpo; On its right are Tianchi, Baozhang Peak and Yunv Peak; Zhongxin Temple is in front of it and Jiulao Cave is behind it. Daping Mountain, 1450 meters above sea level, is cliffy and thrusts into the sky alone with steep slopes only in the east and north sides of it. Every late autumn, snow falls on Golden Top and after the beginning of winter, Daping is covered with snow, where the upright evergreen trees stand like a white tower. In severe winter, snow-covered trees and ice flowers are everywhere in which is like a silver world. Daping and its surrounding peaks become white pure lands. After the snow is over, quite special and marvelous snow scenery will spread in front of you when you are standing on the top of mountain.

8. The Fairy Land of Jiulao Cave

Xianfeng Temple and Jiulao Cave are collectively called the Fairyland of Jiulao Cave. Jiulao Fairy Cave is the full name of Jiulao Cave, 0.5 kilometers away from the right of Xianfeng Temple. Story has it that Jiulao Cave is a rendezvous for immortals. Because of the story, Jiulao Cave has a magical aura. Jiulao Cave is located in the right side of mountain next to Xianfeng Temple. Clusters of wisterias are inverted around the cave cliff abyss under it. The mouth of the cave is herringboned with 4 meters high. The cave is wet and gloomy. Inside, there is no more than 100 meters' tunnel to walk upright. Go further, Bifurcated tunnels staggered, deeply and mysteriously, which stop people from entering without ascertaining the direction.

After the joint investigation of a geographical team in Sichun and related experts in 1986, the secret of Jiulao Cave was revealed. Jiulao Cave is a very famous karstic cave in Mt. Emei. There is a fully blocked watching space in a 1500-meter passage extended down. The space offers the beauty of multivariate shape. The first stage of the cave is a shallow part. There are spacious hall and corridor-like cave. The second stage is in the middle as the main part of Jiulao Cave. Bifurcated caves begin to appear in this part with the shape of crossed net. That is, a cave is in a cave, overlapping, criss-cross and the bigger caves or shafts only are in the staggered junction. The third stage is the deeper, mainly crack-like caves. A hidden stream is sometimes oozing through the crack, and sometimes winding its way into the bottom of cave. The roof and wall of the cave is rich in karstic shapes such as stalactites, stalagmites, stone pillars, clints and lime-flowers and so on.

9. Moonlit Night at Xixiang Pool

Moonlit scenery in Mt. Emei has been renowned since ancient times. The perfect places of moon watching are Baoguo Temple, Luofeng Temple, Wannian Temple, Xianfeng Temple and Xixiang Pool. On a moon night, the clouds and fog come together; the sky is particularly blue. Everything is in silence. A bright moon is shining in the clear sky and the fir trees stand in the moon-lit night, whistling. The moon light shines through the dense green bushes and the Hall of Daxiong, Half-Moon Pavilion, Xixiang Pool, Chuxi Pavilion and Yinyue Tower are all in the moonlight. In the moonlight, the ancient temple strongly resembles the elephant's head. The profile is so clear, set against the blue sky. The Great Hall looks like elephant's forehead and the wing-room in each side is just like the elephant's ear. Besides, the Zuantian Slope stone steps under the Banyuetai are like the elephant's long trunk. It's not simple coincidence but the inventive mind of the building architects. The silver moon is high overhead and reflected in the pool. Changes in the sky and the jade hare in the pool are in echoes. Heaven and earth become the whole.

10. Auspicious Light of the Golden Summit

The Golden Summit is the symbol of Mt. Emei. The Auspicious Light of the Golden Summit serves as Mt. Emei's top scenic site of the ten marvels. It is the essence of Mt.Emei, composed of Four Marvelous Spectacles, namely the Cloud Sea, the Sunrise, the Buddha Rays, and the Saint Lamps.

Section 4 Huangshan—The Picturesque Scene in China

Located in the Huangshan District of Huangshan City in the south of Anhui Province, Huangshan Mountain (directly under the jurisdiction of Huangshan City), is about 40 km long from north to south and 30 km wide from east to west. The mountain has a total area of 1200 square kilometers, and the core scenic area is 160.6 square kilometers. Huangshan Mountain, formerly known as "Yi (Black) Mountain", was the place where the legendary ancestor of the Chinese Yellow Emperor cultivated himself and became an immortal. On June 16 of the 6th year of Tianbao of the Tang Dynasty (747AD), it was named as Huangshan by Emperor Xuanzong and the day has become the mountain's birthday. Huangshan Mountain, as one of China's most famous mountains—Mount Tai, Huashan, Hengshan (Hunan province), Songshan, Hengshan (Shanxi province) and Huangshan, Lushan, Mount Yandang, is renowned as "the first marvelous mountain". The 72 peaks in Huangshan Mountain, which are towering, powerful, beautiful and steep, have a naturally unique layout. The pines, rocks, sea of clouds and hot springs, are all known to be the "four unique features" of the mountain, which are such a miracle of nature that the trip to Huangshan always gives travellers the impression of "trips to China's five great mountains render trips to other mountains unnecessary, and a trip to Huangshan renders trips to the five great mountains unnecessary".

Huangshan Mountain is one of China's top ten scenic spots, and on December 12, 1990, it was listed by UNESCO as a "World Natural and Cultural Heritage" site. The evaluation of the World Heritage Committee on Huangshan Mountain was, Huangshan Mountain, in the heyday of Chinese literature and art history (16th century AD, the "landscape" style) was widely praised, being famous for "Auroral State, First Wonder". In 2004, it became the first geological park in the world, the world's first access to the world cultural and natural heritage and a world geological park (three highest honors for resorts). The United Nations World Heritage stamp series were issued on April 11, 2013, among which the World Cultural and Natural heritage site Huangshan was listed.

I. Geomorphological Landscapes

Huangshan has formed the unique forest-like-peak structure after a long orogeny, crustal uplift, glacial movements and natural weathering. It is said that it has 72 peaks among which there are 36 great peaks and 36 small peaks. Lianhua Peak, the flat-top Bright-top Peak, and the steep Heavenly Capital

Peak (elevation of 1810 m, one of the Three Peaks of Huangshan Mountain along with Bright-top peak and Lianhua Peak, and one of the great peaks of the 36) all sit in the scenic center, around which dozens of more-than-1-kilometer-high peaks organically form a rhythmic, magnificent, breathtaking stereoscopic screen.

Huangshan is mainly composed of granites. The long-term erosion by water makes the various granite caves and tunnels magnificent. The front range's rock joints are sparse, the weathering rocks is spherical, so the whole mountain looks spectacular and vigorous; The back range's rock joints are intensive, the weathering rocks are vertical, and the whole mountain looks high and steep. So Huangshan Mountain has such a geomorphic feature as "the front ranges are grand and the back ranges are pretty".

In the quaternary glacier period, Huangshan successively experienced three glacial epochs, and the glacier movement, glacial ploughing and eroding left many glacier vestiges on the mountain's granite, creating glacier landscapes all over Huangshan and finally forming the grand natural marvelous sights after their outcropping surface and receiving the nature's billion year's of chiseling.

II. Main Scenic Areas

1. Jade Screen Scenic Spot

It has Jade Screen Tower as its centre and the Lotus Peak and the Heavenly Capital Peak as its main body. Along the way there are some wonderful scenic spots such as "Penglai Three Islands", "Ladder on the Clouds", "Thin Strip of Sky", "New Thin Strip of Sky" and "Turtle Cavern". The Jade Screen Tower is located between the Lotus Peak and the Heavenly Capital Peak, which epitomizes most of the wonders of the Huangshan Mountain, and therefore it is called the best of the mountain range. On its left is the famous Guest-Welcoming Pine; on its right is the Farewell Pine. At the front are the Guest-Escorting Pine and the Monju Terrace; at the back is the Jade Screen Peak. On top of the peak is the famous "Jade Screen Sleeping Buddha", with its head on the left and feet to the right. The rock is engraved with Chairman Mao Zedong's cursive, "How wonderful the landscape is!" On the East Cliff is engraved Marshal Zhu De's calligraphy "Picturesque is the landscape!" and Marshal Liu Bochen's poem describing the scenery of Huangshan.

Located one kilometer away to the south of the Jade Screen Peak, the Heavenly Capital Peak is the steepest of the three main peaks, with an elevation of 1830 meters.

The Lotus Peak, located to the north of the Jade Screen, is the highest peak in the area, with an elevation of 1864.8 meters. It looks like a blooming lotus, hence the name. The way from the Lotus Ridge to the summit is about 1.5 kilometers, which is called the Lotus Stem. Along the way are some wondrous pines such as the Flying Dragon Pine and the Upside-down Pine and Huangshan azaleas. The Lotus Peak rises high, overtopping other peaks around. Standing on its top in clear weather, you can even see Mt. Tianmu in the east, Mt. Lushan in the west and Mt. Jiuhua in the north. Or after rain, you will see the sea of clouds surging around you.

Downhill from the Lotus Peak, over the rocks of Turtle and Snake, the Ladder on the Clouds, through the Turtle Cavern, there is the Turtle Peak (1780 meters high). Down the Turtle Peak is the Heavenly Sea, which is located in the middle of the Front, the Back, the East and the West Seas and right at the center of the Huangshan. In this 1750 m high mountain basin grows a great number of rare plant species. Taking advantage of the unique climatic conditions, the Botanical Department of Huangshan has built an alpine botanical garden.

2. North Sea Scenic Spot

Situated among the Bright Summit Peak, the Begin-to-believe Peak, the Lion Peak and the Goose Peak, the North Sea is at the heart of the Huangshan scenic area. To the east is the Cloud Valley; to the south, the Jade Screen; to the north, the Pine Valley. With an area of 1316 hectares, it is a high-mountain open area at the elevation of 1600 meters. The North Sea features peaks, with a perfect combination of peaks, rocks, stone bridges, docks, terraces, pines and cloud wonders. It is grotesque and imposing. It represents the scenic windows of the mountain. There is an array of many scenic spots such as the Lion Peak, Refreshing Terrace, Monkey Gasping at the Sea, Dream Flower Brush, Flying-over Rock, and Eighteen Buddha Saluting to the South Sea. There is also an array of many peaks such as the Shimen Peak and the Gongyang Peak, both at an altitude of 1800 meters, shaped like a barrier separating the north and south. There is also the Lion Peak, at an altitude of 1690 meters above the sea level, crouching within the scenic area. The Refreshing Terrace over the Lion Peak is the best place to watch the sea of clouds and sunrise. The Begin-to-believe Peak, though not as tall as the Heavenly Capital Peak or the Lotus Peak, nor in the row of the 36 Peaks, is known for its precipitous cliffs, which represents the grandness of Huangshan Mountain.

3. Hot Springs Scenic Spot

It is one of the tourist reception centers with an elevation of 650 meters. With the Lansheng Bridge as its hub, it has the Peach Blossom Stream and Xiaoyao Stream flowing through. Main hotels include Taoyuan Hotel, Hot Spring Hotel, Mount Huang Hotel, etc.

4. White Cloud Scenic Spot

Located in the western part of the mountain, it covers 16.5 square kilometers, stretching from Xugu Bridge over the Yunmen stream in the south till Funiu Ridge in the north, from Yunji, Shiren peaks in the east till Shuanghekou bank in the west. With an elevation of 610 meters, the scenic area centers around Diaoqiao Buddhist convent, which is located under Shiren Peak, the confluence of Baiyun and Baimen streams. This area enjoys a tranquility and elegance of rounding ranges of hills, fantastic pines and rocks, and spring waters merging into an organic whole.

5. Pine Valley

Huangshan is known for its steep front and beautiful back, and the back mountain refers to the Pine Valley, the north gate of the Huangshan. Located in the north slope, it has a fall in altitude of 1100 meters made up of over 6500 steps. Arriving at the north gate of Huangshan, tourists could start from the Furong Ridge to visit the mountain. Rocks and ponds are the highlights. Among this refreshing world, the Emerald Pool, the Five-Dragon Pond, and the rock of Guan Gong Resists Cao Cao (both were famous generals during the Three Kingdoms Period) are the main scenic points. The Emerald Pool is surrounded by rocks, with a crystal stream from the Pine Valley flowing into it. The reflections of the mountains and trees create another fairy world in the water. In the rainy season visitors can enjoy the famous landscape "listening to the ripple water in valley".

6. Cloud Valley Scenic Spot

Located in the east of Huangshan, it is a low-lying, slightly open valley, only 890 meters above the sea level. The Song Dynasty Prime Minister Cheng Yuanfeng once studied here, thus it got the name as the cradle of prime minister. The Ming Dynasty scholar Fu Yan once came by, asked by "throwing the bowl" monk for calligraphy "Cloud Valley", since then the Buddhist temple was renamed "Cloud Valley Temple", it is still used nowadays. The main tourist attractions are the Cloud Valley Villa, old trees, oddly shaped rocks, the Nine-Dragon Waterfall and the Baizhang Spring.

III. Four Wonders and Three Waterfalls

1. Four Wonders

(1) Fantastic Pines. They are seen in every corner of the mountain, 800 meters above the sea level. The seeds fall into the crevices where they take root and grow with great vigor. The uneven terrain prevents them from growing upright. Instead they become crooked and even downward. Their leaves are like needles, sharp and short, thick and green. Some pines lean on the shore, tall and straight; some stand firmly at the summit of peaks, withstanding rain and wind; others stand upside down on the cliffs, going through or around the stones of the mountain. You can see "no trees rather than pines, no pines without rocks, no pines no fantastic".

The Huangshan pines are a variant of Chinese pines due to Huangshan's unique landform and climate. They generally grow at 800 meters above the sea level, usually on the north slope of Huangshan around 1500-1700 meters high, and 1000-1600 meters in the south slope. There is a great relationship between Huangshan pine in different poses and with different expressions and natural environment on the mountain. The pine seeds can be carried by the wind to the cracks in the granite, and they take roots and grow with vigor.

The most famous pines are: Guest-Greeting Pine, Guest-Goodbye Pine, Sea Exploring Pine, Cushion Pine, Black Tiger Pine, Lying Dragon Pine, Kylin Pine, Couple Pine, Harp Pine and Drago-claws Pine—they are Huangshan's ten famous pines.Someone once compiled a "Pine Spectrum", including a large number of Huangshan pines, each of which is of unique, beautiful, and elegant style.

(2) Grotesque Rocks. Grotesque rocks, one of the four wonders of Huangshan, are characterized by their rareness and large quantity. More than 120 breathtaking grotesque rocks of a great variety of shapes have been named. Seen from different positions or in different weather, grotesque rocks in Huangshan Mountain are utterly different, which can be described as "ranges or peaks from different views, near and far from different level". The rocks are scattered throughout all the ridges and peaks; some stand upright at the summit, some at the sloping fields, and some partner pines, constituting a

picture scroll of natural sights.

Huangshan rocks, when viewed from different angles, have different shapes. Inside the chains of peaks in Huangshan, there are no places without rocks, no stones without pines and no pines without rareness. The fantastic pines and grotesque rocks form a delightful balance.

(3) Sea of Clouds. Huangshan is home to clouds and mists. The sea of clouds has a fairy tale beauty. Winter is the best season for this spectacle. According to their locations, the seas of clouds are divided into East Sea, South Sea, West Sea, North Sea and Sky Sea. If you climb up the Lotus Peak, the Heavenly Capital Peak and the Bright Summit Peak, you will find yourself over the clouds and they appear as a sea beneath you.

It is true that a sea of clouds can be seen in many high mountains but those of Huangshan are unique with oddly shaped rocks and old pines. Peaks, large and small, hidden and visible, are reappearing in the boundless waves of clouds. The Heavenly Capital Peak and the Bright Summit Peak look like isolated islands within this white cloudy sea. At sunrise or sunset, the glistening clouds assume every hue from red to purple. You will be amazed by the beauty when all the red leaves are floating on the white clouds in autumn, when the clouds gush between the peaks like a raging river while the red leaves flutter delicately in the breeze. You had better go to the Jade Screen Pavilion to view the South Sea, the Refreshing Terrace for the North Sea, the Paiyun Tower for the West Sea, the White Goose Ridge for the East Sea and the Legendary Turtle Peak for the Sky Sea.

(4) Hot Springs. As one of the four wonders of Huangshan, run out of the Purple Peak (850 meters high). Bicarbonate is largely contained in the spring, which is drinkable and bathable. Legend has it that the Yellow Emperor, the ancestor of the Chinese nation, bathed here for 49 days before he ascended to heaven and became immortal. Therefore the Springs here are also called "Ling Spring".

The hot springs run from the Purple Peak, on the other side of the Peach Blossom Peak, are the first stop following the entrance. The outlet water quantity is about 400 tons every day. The water stays at 42°C all year and is said to help prevent digestive, nerve, cardiovascular metabolism, movement and skin illnesses.

2. Three Waterfalls in Huangshan

Three large waterfalls are worth a visit. They are Renzi (like the Chinese character " 人 ") Waterfall, the Baizhang (100 zhang, over 1093feet) Waterfall and the Nine-Dragon Waterfall. The Renzi Waterfall, also known as the Feiyu Waterfall (Flying Rain Waterfall) in ancient times, is situated between the Ziyun Peak (Purple Cloud Peak) and the Zhusha Peak (Cinnabar Peak). The water drops down in two streams from the two peaks in a shape of " 人 ". The best place for viewing the waterfall is Viewing Floor. The Nine-Dragon Waterfall is situated between the Luohan Peak and the Xianglu Peak, hanging down from cliffs thousands of meters high. It has nine curves, each forming a pool underneath. Therefore, the waterfall is made up of nine cascades and nine pools, known as Nine-Dragon Waterfall. After heavy rain, the rushing waterfall looks like nine white dragons, flying down from the sky. Therefore, among a number of waterfalls found in this Mountain, the Nine-Dragon Waterfall is the most spectacular one. Baizhang Waterfall is located between Green Lake and Ziyun Peak, hanging down from cliffs thousands of meters high. Near the waterfall is Baizhang Stand, in front of which there is a viewing pavilion.

Section 5 Fragrant Hills—The Garden Behind the Hill

Fragrant Hills Park (Xiangshan Park) is located in the east of the Western Mountains, in the northwestern part of Beijing, China. It covers 1.6 km² (395 acres), 20 km far from the city. It is a famous big mountain forest park with Royal Garden Characters. Fragrant Hills, 557 meters above sea level, the highest peak with a huge stone, is shaped like an incense burner. From morning to twilight, the clouds and mist rolled up like smoke trails, so it is called Incense Burner Hill, and also referred to as Fragrant Hills. Fragrant Hills saw human landscapes as early as in 1186 and the Fragrant Hill Temple has ranked first in the Jingxi Temples. In the Qing Dynasty, Emperor Qianlong built 28 scenes of Jingyi Garden in this location. Since 1949, most of the historical relics have been gradually restored. Nowadays, the cultural relics and historic sites are rich and precious. The pavilions are interspersed among the mountain forest like stars in the night. In 2002, it was rated as the first boutique park in Beijing. In 2004, it passed ISO9001 international quality management system and ISO14001 international environmental management system certification. On 12th October, 2012, it was awarded the title of "World Famous Mountains" at the 24th Beijing Fragrant Hill Red Leaves Culture

Festival Opening Ceremony.

I. Historical Changes

　　Fragrant Hills Park has a long history which dates back to the Jin Dynasty. Emperors Jin Shizong and Zhang Zong built Fragrant Hill and named the temple Da Yong An Si (Big Eternal Peace Temple). In 1312, Emperor Renzong allotted funds to rebuild the temple and renamed it Ganlu Temple(Sweet Dew Temple).In 1331, Yelu Chucai's descendant, Yelu Elemi, built Biyun Temple(Blue Cloud Temple), forming eight scenes of Fragrant Hills and ten scenes of Biyun. In 1441, Fan Hong, a court eunuch, contributed about 700000 yuan to rebuild the temple. The giant temple became grand and splendi in which halls, pavilions, corridors, galleries, and worship idols took on an altogether new look. In the Qing Dynasty, Emperor Qianlong expanded the construction on the basis of the original temple and spent only nine months to build about 80 large and small gardens, of which there were 28 scenes named and described in poems by Emperor Qianlong, which were popular in Beijing. These 28 scenes were titled Jingyi garden by Emperor Qianlong. In 1860, Anglo-French allied forces looted a great number of treasures in Jingyi Garden and destroyed almost all the buildings. On 12th March, 1925, Sun Yet-sen died in Beijing and his coffin was kept in Biyun Temple for four years. After his coffin was moved to Zijin Mountain in Nanjing, the memorial and tomb containing his personal effects were built to be respected by people. In 1956, the park was open to the public as people's garden. From 1993 till now, the Fragrant Hills Park has been appraised as the model unit of Beijing city and rewarded as the AAAA scene by the National Tourism Administration in 2001 and one of the first excellent gardens of Beijing city in 2002.

II. Four Seasons Scenery

　　The Fragrant Hills Park (Xiangshan Park) is noted for its precipitous peaks and ridges, abundant water and exuberant green trees, with its main peak Xiang Lufeng known as Guijianchou (notoriously cliffy) towering at an elevation of 557 meters. In the park, there are more than 260000 trees of different kinds, over 5800 of which are ancient and rare, covering a quarter of Beijing Distinct. Since its total forest coverage reaches 98%, it is proved to be one of the anion-richest places in Beijing. In the park, songbirds and frolicking squirrels share a harmonious world between man and nature. There is carpet of flowers in the spring, air of cool in the summer and blanket of snow in the winter, notably in the autumn, mountains and plains of fiery red leaves, Cotinus coggyria mainly grows widely and vigorously, presenting the most well-known and magnificent scene to the tourists.

On the Fragrant Hills, melting snow, sprouting grass and swimming catkin signal the arrival of spring. Shady ancient woods, ravine streams and tasty green grass mean the growing of hot summer. When the tourists step into the gates, all the summer heat will be relieved. They will feel fresh and cool no matter whether walking on the tree-lined path or resting at any places of Fragrant Hills. As summer merges into autumn, pine and cypress dotted with some maple and goldenrain trees colour the hills brightly. The household red leaves of Fragrant Hills, Cotinus coggyria with egg-shaped leaves especially, are turning redder and redder with the heavy frost until the whole hills and mountains are tinged with red. In the deep autumn, the fiery red leaves spreading over the South Mounts captivate the tourists' eyes and lure the people from all over the world. When the winter comes, the withered wild grass, darkened pine and cypress, frosted streams and sharp wind appear lifeless and depressed superficially whereas various silver-edged pavilions, towering snow-covered peaks, tranquil white hills against fascinating red walls of temple and lofty pine in the snow take on another poetic and picturesque scenery.

III. Main Scenic Spots

1. Fragrant Hill Temple

The site of Fragrant Hill Temple was once Big Yong'an Temple, which was built in the 26th year according to the Da Ding calendar in the Jin Dynasty (1186) and was originally the palace of the Jin Dynasty. According to the records, there were five halls, in front of which were Shifang, gate, bell tower, walls and red tile nestling in the pines and cypresses. And it is one of the 28 famous Fragrant Hill scenic spots. But after the two catastrophes caused by the British and French Allied Forces and the Eight Power Allied forces, only the stone screen in front of the main hall, stone tablet, stone steps and some other stone products survived. The stone screen itself has high artistic value. On its front is carved "Diamond Sutra" in the middle, with "Heart Sutra" on its left and "Guanyin(a Buddism godness) Sutra" on the right. And on its back are carved three figures of the Buddha: Randeng, Guanyin, and Samantabhadra.Inside the gate there are stone tablets carved with Emperor Qianlong's "Sal Tree Song" respectively in Han, Manchu, Mongolian, and Tibetan. There are several famous monuments outside the gate:(1) The Pine Listening to Buddha Dharma: there is one old vigorous and lush pine tree on either sides of the gate whose shape is like people listening attentively to Buddha dharma. (2) Rooster Crowing: If you stamp on the bricks under the above-mentioned pine tree, you can hear the clank sound as if the Rooster crows. (3) Zhile Pond: under the stone bridge in front of the gate, there is a square pond with white marble railings. And a dragon head stands on its south with spring running out. Thus it is called Zhile pond (It means understanding joy). (4) Green Pavillion: The pavilion is built on top of the cliff. When you climb to the pavillion, you will find yourself surrounded by boundless green, thus it is named Green Pavillion. In the 28th year of Wanli calendar (1600), Emperor Wanli returned after visiting the ancestor's tombs, passed by the plaque and considered it too small. Then he wrote three big characters prounouced as "Lai Qing Xuan" in Chinese with its diameter of about one foot. Until now there are still some related monuments such as Escorting Pine and Danjing Wells etc.

2. Censer Peak

The highest point of Fragrant Hills Park is 557 meters above the sea level. Because of its steep terrain, it is very difficult to climb and thus it has a nickname prounouced in Chinese as "Gui Jian Chou", which means "sorrowful to a ghost". Three distinctive pavilions have been built on the peak of Fragrant Hills. "Double Ninth Pavilion" means that one can climb the mountain and see a bird's eye view of the whole city on the Double Ninth Festival. "On Cloudy Pavilion" is named in such way because it is always surrounded by clouds before spring rain or after the autumn rain and people seem to walk through clouds. "Purple Smoke Pavilion" gets its name from one famous poem Cataract on Lushan since there is faint purple cloud on occasional mornings and evenings. Standing on the jade viewing platform, you can see Kunming Lake which is just like a pot of water and all kinds of buildings are scattered here and there. Then you will have a new understanding of Beijing.

3. Temple of Azure Clouds

Temple of Azure Clouds is the most exquiste temple in the Xishan Scenic Area. This monastery was founded in the 2nd year of Zhishun Calendar in the Yuan Dynasty (1331), which has a history of over 600 years. It was then known as the Nunnery of Azure Clouds. Then in Zhengde years of Ming Dynasty (1514), Yu Jing, an eunuch, built tomb erected for himself while his alive in the mountains behind the nunnery and renamed it Temple of Azure Clouds. Later in Tianqi years, Wei Zhongxian repaired and extended Temple of Azure Clouds. But in the 40th year of Kangxi Calendar, Zhang Yuan, the patrol officer of South of the Yangtze River, burnt and leveled it when he learned that Temple of Azure Clouds was the tomb of Wei Zhongxian, an evil minister. In the 13th year of Qianlong calendar (1748), the Temple of Azure Clouds was greatly expanded and an Indian-style pagoda with a diamond throne built in the back. And on the right a new Arhat Hall was built in imitation of Jingci Temple in Hangzhou. Thus the symmetrical pattern along the axis formed and laid its scale for the present temple. Temple of Azure Clouds is built by the mountain, which rises with the mountain slope. Its six layers of courtyards form its distinctive pattern. The architectural style of the temple combines the features of Zen and Tantra. There is a plaque on the gate with golden characters against blue background and it says "Temple of Azure Clouds" in Han, Mongolian, Manchu and Tibetan, which were handwritten by Emperor Qianlong. Two grand stone lions with fine carving stand on both sides of the gate and they fortunately remain well-kept from the Ming Dynasty. The Temple of Azure Clouds was destroyed during the Cultural Revolution and was later rebuilt.

4. Sun Yat-sen Memorial Hall

Sun Yat-sen Memorial Hall is located in the Temple of the Azure Clouds on the Fragrant Hills. In the center of the memorial hall is the white marble statue of Mr. Sun Yat-sen, offered respectfully by the KMT Central Committee and the Sun Yat-sen schools across the country. The wall has been inlaid with Mr. Sun Yat-sen's to the Soviet Union, which was carved out of white marble. In the northwest corner of the main hall, a glass cover steel coffin has been set forth, delivered by the Soviet people on 30th March , 1925. Mr. Sun Yat-sen's manuscripts and literary remains are also displayed in the memorial hall.

To commemorate the temporary resting place of Mr. Sun Yat-sen, the National Government founded Prime Minister Memorial in the Hall of Puming Miaojue and Prime Minister Cenotaph on the wall of the arched gate of the Five Pagoda. After 1949, the Temple of the Azure Clouds was rebuilt by the people's Government and renamed Sun Yat-sen Memorial Hall (inscribed by Soong Chingling, his wife) and Sun Yat-sen Cenotaph for the sake of posterity.

5. The Red Leaves on the Fragrant Hills

The spectacular red leaves on the Fragrant Hills are of eight families, including fourteen tree species, like acer mono, acer buergerianum, acer palmatum, persimmon tree and so on, and more than 200000 trees. Cotinus coggygria, nearly 100000 trees, are the majority of the park. The leaves of the trees contain a great quantity of chlorophyll, xanthophyll, carotenoid, carotene and anthocyanidin. In spring and summer time the plants photosynthesize with chlorophyll and the leaves appear for green. In late summer, since the colder weather and larger daily temperature extremes hinder the synthesis of chlorophyll, with chlorophyll disappearing gradually, and the amount of carotenoid, carotene and anthocyanidin increasing, the leaves turn a beautiful reddish yellow and orange red. The longest-living tree species of cotinus coggygria represent the Fragrant Hill best. See a thousand hills crimsoned through by their serried woods deep-dyed. In the autumn sun, with the dazzling scenery of the pure and powerful red leaves of acer mono, flowers in gold, blue, white and purple, silver-white trunks and golden leaves, it smells like fairyland in this place.

The red leaves on the Fragrant Hills roughly present various prospects in three periods. The first stage, bright-colored trees: from mid to late October, the park seems a wondrous and breathtaking mountain spectacle with the mixture of green, gold and red plants. The second stage, deep-dyed serried woods: from late October to early November, with the first frost and the falling of temperature, the red leaves get more intensively and brilliantly colorful, and the hills are crimsoned through with deep-dyes, majestic and magnificent. The third stage, floating red leaves: from early November to mid November, with the temperature lowering and cold winds, the red leaves float and scatter all over the mountains, like rain of flowers, bringing the pathos of farewell. Tourists could choose their favorite to take in according to their own preferences. Geographically, the red leaves color first on Yu-sum Wat and the slope of the southern hill. In the middle the finest view is on the cableway and along the north way. In November, despite red leaves falling throughout the hill, the leaves of acer truncatum still attach tightly to the late autumn of Beijing in Tranquility Green Lake and the Valley. Since 1989, Red Leaves Festival on the theme of red leaves, has been held for twenty years.

6. Shuangqing Villa

To the southeast of Fragrant Hills Temple, on the hillside, there is a fine and quiet courtyard, namely Shuangqing Villa. Formly Qiyun House of the famous 28 Scenes of Providence Park, now it is noted as red tourism spot of the park. In it two fresh springs keep running all the year, one down to Zhile Moat and the other into Tranquility Green Lake. There are an octagonal pavilion and towering ginkgo tree standing by the pond in the yard. In 1917 Hebei Province flooded, Supervisor Xiong Xiling founded Xiangshan Loving Comprehensive School here and built the villa, called Shuangqing Villa. On 25th March, 1949, Mao Zedong came to Peiping from Xibaipo, Pingshan County, Hebei Province with the Party Central Committee, and lived in the villa. It was once the residence of Mao Zedong as well as an early sight for the headquarters of the Central Committee of the Chinese Communist Party. In 1998, approved by the Beijing municipal, government and Beijing municipal Bureau of cultural relics, this Villa was in Beijing Municipal Museum's list. In 2009, it ranked as national patriotism educational base.

Section 6 Mt. Jade—Taiwan's Holy Mountain

Yushan (Mt. Jade) is situated in central Taiwan, China which extends to Sandiaojiao in the north and Pingtong Plain of South Taiwan, stretching over approximately 300 kilometers. Yushan Peak— the dominant peak in Yushan Mountain ranges 2.3 kilometers north of Tropic of cancer—stands aloft 3952 meters above sea level , the highest peak in Taiwan and in Eastern Asia as well. It is also regarded as one of the China's ten best-known mountains.

Covering a total of 105490 hectares across the four counties of Nantou, Chiayi, Kaohsiung and Hualian, Yushan National Park is the second largest national park in Taiwan Province after the Dongsha Marine National Park. It is the geology of a typically subtropical mountain mainly with high mountains and river valleys. Yushan Mountain, together with Mt.Xueshan, Mt.Hsiukuluan, Mt. Nanhuda and Mt. Beidawu, called the "Five Sacred Mountains", is the most representative of Taiwan. Yushan Mountain or Mt. Jade, a towering mountain, is impressive for its great height and grandeur, which is named due to its snow-capped peak shining like jade. Its Perpetual snow has become one of the eight sights in Taiwan.Yushan Mountain is one of the symbol of contemporary Taiwan as well as the holy mountain of Bunun people and Tsou people. On April 10 of 1985, Yushan Mountain and its surroundings were delimited to the newly established national park-Yushan

National Park.

    Similar to the Himalayas, Taiwan mountain range, as one of the youngest mountain ranges in China, rose gradually in the tertiary period. Yushan lies where Taiwan crust went up and axis passed with complicated structure and many dislocations. A large tectonic line respectively on its east and west sides adjacent to Central Mountains and Ali Mountains. Yushan belongs to the aqueous rock mountain, with very peculiar landform and folding stratum like waves. Due to the weathering of water and wind, rugged and steep sandstone and shale, Yushan is totally different from the general mountains. Towering and lofty cliffs, cloudcapped peaks, and perpetual snows offer marvelous scenery.

    Surrounding the dominant peak, east, west, north and south peaks constitute majestic Yushan peaks where the gorgeous scenery is pleasing, such as Snow-covered Landscape, Seas of Clouds, Iridescent Cloud of High Mountain and etc. Mt. Xiuguluan at an elevation of 3860 meters is the highest among central mountain range, facing Yushan peak. And Xiugu plain at the foot of the mountain is covered with arrow bamboo, alpine rhododendron, and white deadwood. Tafen hill, a gently sloping hill, is as magnificent as a Pyramid with two lakes named Tafen Pond at the south side of it. Mabolasi Mountain, Xiuguluan Mountain, Xinkang Mountain, East Peak and South Peak of Yushan, are the four of Taiwan's Ten Major Summits, all of which create precious ecological environment besides nurturing the splendid geographic landscape.

I. Ecology of Mt. Jade

Yushan National Park has contained rich ecological resources. With the transmutation of topography, geology and climate, the primitive forest and rare wildlife present diversity, which make the park the most integrated ecological environment. Varied topography and climate have created a natural paradise for various kinds of plants. From the foothills to the top, vegetation come into sight, ranging from the tropical zone, subtropical zone, temperate zone to frigid zone. Alpine vegetation is much more colorful and unique, in which over 20 kinds of plants are named after Yushan. Yushan juniper is a kind of needle-leaved tree at the highest altitude in Taiwan and can form a giant tree group. However, the strong wind in the draught and the northern peak prevents upward growth, resulting in a vast expanse of low shrubs and a tremendous spectacle. In May or June of every year, large and white Yushan rhododendrons dress up the whole mountain and valley as a wonderland. From July to September, a tiny crucifer named alpine cress, unique to Yushan grows at the highest point, scattering across the rock debris of Yushan summit and the draught zone.

It is counted that there are 28 species of mammals, accounting for half of all mammals in Taiwan, of which eight species are endemic to Taiwan, including Alpine white-bellied rat, Apodemus semotus, Formosan rock macaque, Formosan shrew, bottlenose mustached bat, agouti, Taiwan Vole and three endangered animals-Taiwan scales carp, Taiwan black bear and Sika deer. The hynobius formosanus, which remained from the Ice Age are rare creatures and can only live in a high-altitude alpine area.

II. Features of Mt. Jade

The first feature is the attitude with steep stretching mountains. There are 30 majestic mountains in the Yushan national park, which are over 3000 meters high. The dominant peak in the middle is as high as 3952 meters. The five peaks look forbiddingly precipitous as a whole, so Yushan Mountain can be referred to as the King of mountains, followed by Mount Emei and Mount Tai.

The second feature is the snow. Yushan Mountain is so high that the temperature there is very low, the frost existing throughout the year. And the dominant peak had ever a record of -17.5°C. It begins to snow every October and ends till the next March. In the summer, there is still snow in the shade of the mountaintop, which is a rare wonder called "tropical snow mountain" and placed on the list of the eight sceneries in TaiWan.

The third feature is its perilousness. The peaks rise one after another with perpendicular cliffs and deep gully. As a result, nobody can arrive at the summit unless an experienced climber.

III. Tourism of Mt. Jade

In Yushan National Park there are three tourist centers: Tatajia centre on New Zhongheng Road, Meishan center on Nanheng Road, and Nanan center in the eastern area. They are the best places for the tourists to have a general understanding of the park. The climbing activity concentrates on Yushan Mountain section, two exits respectively from Dongpu on Batong ancient road to Batongguan and from Nanan to Walami, Guanshan, Taguanshan, Guanshanling and Xiangyangshan. Yushan Mountain landscape can be divided into four parts:

The northwest area is seated at the northwest of the park, including the New zhongheng road, Tatajia, Dongpu, the main peak of Yushan Mountain and Nanxilindao etc, where there are geographical sceneries consisting of the main peak, Tatajia watershed, Nanzixian stream, Jinmendong escarpment, Batongguan watershed and so on, virgin forest and alpines including white wood, fir, hemlock and others, in addition, kinds of birds, butterflies, deer, and Taiwan monkeys. Cultural landscapes comprise God temple at the west peak, Yushan Weather Bureau at the north peak, the Batong entrance and aboriginal residence of the Bunong minority.

The south area is seated at the southwest of the park, including Nanheng Road, Meishan, Tianchi, Zhongzhiguan, Yakou, and Guanshan etc, where tourists will appreciate a variety of landscapes such as mountain topography, Laonongxi valley, cypress forest, precious birds, other mammals, lakes, and some cultural landscapes.

The east area is seated at the southeast, including Nan An, Shanfeng, Walami area and so on.

The core area is seated at the northeast and the central of the park, including Dashuiku, Mt. Xiuguluan, Mt.Mabolasi and so on.

Section 7 Mount Fuji—The Holy Mountain of Japan

I. Mount Fuji

As the highest peak in Japan, Mount Fuji, 3775.63 meters above the sea level, is one of the largest active volcanoes in the world. It stretches across Shizuoka-ken and Yamanashi-ken, about 100 kilometers from Tokyo, near the Pacific coast. The name "Fuji" can often be heard in traditional Japanese poetry "Waka". Mount Fuji is also hailed as "the Holy Mountain" by Japanese for its worldwide fame and the symbol of Japanese nation's pride.

The name "Fuji", meaning "eternal life" now, was derived from the Ainu Language, which meant "mountain of fire" or "the fire spirit". In the shape of a cone, the mountain soars into the sky, capped with snow, just like a fan. Some Japanese poets ever praised it as a jade fan in their poems, then, it gained another name "Jade fan". On top of Mount Fuji, there is a big crater like an alms bowl, 800 meters' diameter and 200meters' depth. It is the largest conical mountain in the world with about 40 km in diameter at the bottom. Perpetually covered by snow, its beautiful form has captivated people. Since 1990, the UNESCO was asked to add Mount Fuji to the list of the Cultural World Heritage Sites. On June 22, 2013, Mount Fuji was finally registered on the UNESCO World Heritage List at the 37th session of the World Heritage Committee.

1. The Mountain's Formation

As the most important symbol of Japan's natural beauty, Mount Fuji was formed by the bumps between the Izu Peninsulas (which was originally an island) and Honshu Island due to the movements of the earth's crust dating back about 10000 years ago. Mount Fuji is a standard cone volcano in shape. The forming process of Fuji can be roughly divided into four stages, i.e., Sen-Komitake, Komitake, Old Fuji and New Fuji. Lava streams, volcanic ashes and gravels were piled into the main body of the mountain, which includes eight peaks, among which the Peak Sword is the highest.

2. Potential Threat of Volcanic Activity

Mount Fuji is an active volcano. The first outbreak was documented in 800 AD, and the latest one was on December 16th, 1707, which emitted volcanic ashes, spreading over vast areas, and even reaching the ancient capital of Edo (i.e. Today's Tokyo), almost 100 km away. It lasted over two weeks. The whole city was overwhelmed by a thick layer of volcanic ashes, over 5 cm. Two older volcanoes were buried by the ejected magma. At present, unusual mountain changes are increasingly discovered in Mount Fuji, water in the mountain lakes has decreased and cracks of 300 meters long have been found on the flank of the mountain, and groundwater has poured out in several areas, all of which make the local people upset.

3. The Picturesque Ecological Environment

In the northern foothills of Mount Fuji lie five lakes—Lake Yamanaka, Lake Kawaguchi, Lake Sai, Lake Shoji and Lake Motosu. Lake Yamanakako is the largest one of five lakes, and 6.75 square kilometers. There are many sports facilities and people can play tennis and water skiing, go fishing, go camping and go boating, etc. Lake Kawaguchiko was developed earliest among the five lakes, which has become a tourist sightseeing center due to its convenient transportation. The Unoshima Island in Lake Kawaguchiko with a shrine dedicated to bless pregnant women who want a safe delivery is the unique island among the five lakes. And there is a 1260 - meter - long bridge across the lake. The image of Mount Fuji reflected in the lake is known as one of the wonderful scenes of Mount Fuji.

There is a vast plateau in the southern foothills of Mount Fuji. In summer, people can see herds of sheep and cows grazing the grass there. The Shiraito Waterfall and the Otodome Waterfall are located in the southwestern foothills of Mount Fuji. The Shiraito Waterfall flows off the edge of a 26 meters high cliff in more than ten thin white streams, which forms a spectacular curtain of rain over 130 meters wide. Compared to the Shiraito Waterfall, the Otodome Waterfall is like a giant pillar pounding from the top with a sound of thunder. Mount Fuji is also called a natural botanical garden. There are a variety of plants up to more than 2000 species with apparent vertical distribution, including the subtropical evergreen forest below an altitude of 500 meters, the temperate deciduous broad-leaved forest from 500 to 2000 meters, the cool-temperate mixed coniferous forest from 2000 to 2600 meters and the elfin wood belt above 2600 meters. Every year there are 130 kinds of wild birds, various kinds of animals and insects were seen around the mountain.

II. Deifying of Mount Fuji

As the highest peak of Japan, Mount Fuji is regarded as the source of artistic inspiration and pilgrimage. It also has countless legends and mysteries. They have mainly been manifested in the following three aspects: First, the origin myths are related to the territory of the country and the origin of the nation. Second, karma myths are related to the Buddhism. Third, the myth of the immortal mountain is related to the origin of the name of Mount Fuji.

1. The Legends of Fuji

Mount Fuji has always been the symbol of Japan, which is a good theme for literature and art creation. In Japanese Waka and Haiku, the good works praising Mount Fuji can be found everywhere. Japanese folktale Taketori

Monogatari (The Tale of the Bamboo Cutter) is considered as a legend of Mount Fuji.

The name of "Mount Fuji" may have direct relationship with these legends. In addition, Katsushika Hokusai, Japanese Ukiyo-e painter of the Edo period, created the Woodblock printing series "Thirty-six Views of Mount Fuji". It actually consists of 46 prints (10 of them were added after initial publication). This set of works shows the 46 expressions of natural changes of Mount Fuji.

2. Xu Fu Becoming a Crane

In Japan, there are more than 20 places possessing sites and legends about Xu Fu, nearly spreading across the country. The north foothill of Mount Fuji is one of the most concentrated sites about the legends of Xu Fu. It is said, the descendants of Xu Fu have still lived there up to now. The ruler of the Qin Dynasty and the first empror of China, Qin Shi Huang, sent his official Xu Fu, with a thousand virgin boys and girls, to the island of Penglai where Mount Fuji is located (the Japanese pronunciation of which is similar to "Fuji"). In the holy mountain, Xu Fu found a plant named Hamanasu (Rugosa rose or Japanese rose), which was a specie of rose relying on mountain fog. It could extend man's life by bearing red fruits. Xu Fu felt excited about it. Unfortuately, the emperor Qin Shi Huang passed away. Then, he took the elixir and settled down in the beautiful foothill, spreading Chinese culture. Several years later, Xu Fu died. After his death, he became a crane soaring over the fields of Mount Fuji. The crane did not die until the Genroku era (1688—1704), resting in the Fuyuan Temple nearby. Local people built a crane tomb in the temple to show sacrifices to it. People called the surrounding area of Mount Fuji "Crane City". This story was widely spread among Japanese.

3. The Fuji Belief

Japanese have adored Mount Fuji ever since the ancient time. They respected Mount Fuji as "the Abundant Mountain" and "the Holy Mountain". It was believed that many gods lived there guarding Japan, and then the Fuji Belief was formed. The worship towards the mountain has been long-standing religious mentality. So the holy shrine was built on the top of the mountain. The pilgrims gathered in crowds, wearing white gowns, and with Suzuki canes, step by step, piously climbed up to the top of the mountain for a whole night to show worship, where, there is Fujisan Hongu Sengen Taisha, which is a Shinto shrine to sacrifice the gods of Mount Fuji. This shrine is not only a sacred place for the pilgrims, but also a good resort for visitors. The pilgrimage troops have still been a famous scene in the summer.

III. Leisure of Mount Fuji

1. Mountaineering Activities

Since ancient times, Japanese have regarded Fuji as the Holy Mount which is always guarding their nation. In this sense, they just fantasy and worship Fuji down the ages. There is a popular sentence in Japan: one who fails to climb Mount Fuji is an ignorant man. In the mid Heian period (794—1192), people began to climb Fuji. With the combination of the faith in Mount Fuji and Confucianism, their climbing was on the rise in more areas. In the Edo period (1603—1867), it became very important in the lives of Edo people. It was said that the first person, Monk Yusoga, who climbed on the top of this mount at the risk of his life, came down the mountain with his eyebrows burned. From then on, other monks kept on climbing Mount Fuji year by year and built up the first group of log cabins on top of the mountain. In Meiji Restoration period (1868—1912), climbing Fuji became an activity of solemn ritual. With the changing climates and various mysterious phenomena in the nature and biology, Fuji deserved much respect and worshipping of people, whose enthusiasm in climbing was so high that some of them may take a pride in reaching the top for many times.

Every July and August are good seasons to climb Mount Fuji, which is closed other time instead. Now that there are more typhoons in August, July will be the best time to do it. From the foot to the top of Fuji, there are four mountaineering lines including the Yoshida-guchi, Subashiri, Gotemba-guchi, and Fujinomiya-guchi routes and other ten rest places. Most of people return after they stop at the fifth rest place which can be reached by bus and it needs four hours to reach the top of mountain from here.

2. Watching the Sunrise on the Top of Fuji

Watching the sunrise on top of the mountain, called "Go rei kou" in Japanese, is the best wish of every tourist climbing Mount Fuji. In order to watch the sunrise, climbers accommodated themselves on the mountainside have to get up at 4 a.m. and climb on the climax along the winding path. Before the sunrise, they can lean on a balcony at a sight of the distant quiet mountains and billowing clouds like a plain Chinese Brush Painting. Through the vast sea of clouds, they may catch a sight of the city lights shining as if they were in a fairyland world. As the first morning twilight rose slowly, rosy clouds like silks and satins come to emerge in the east. While the red sun drives thin clouds, all over the mountains and plains are dyed by the morning sunlight, which immediately turns into a profusion of colors and extraordinarily beauty.

3. Watching the Sea of Clouds on the Mountain

The unpredictable weather is also a major feature of Mount Fuji. Within the short ten hours from climbing to going down, it may be azure, bright and breezy, then suddenly blanketed with fog and even begins to pour with heavy rain. The temperature on the mountain is ten or twenty degrees Celsius different from the one under the mountain. This is caused by its special geographical environment. The local people observe the change of "clouds like bamboo hats" on top of Mount Fuji to predict the local weather based on years of experiences. "Clouds like bamboo hats" are formed when steam and atmosphere go over the top of the mountain and suddenly encounter cold air, then change into cloud particles and finally form with the wind. People conclude that when the clouds like bamboo hats circle the mountain peak, it will be sunny. When clouds like bamboo hats rise up, it is sunny. when clouds like bamboo hats are like crest, rainy. When clouds like bamboo hats go down the mountain, it is windy. When clouds like bamboo hats roll up the top of the mountain, it is windy and rainy. When clouds like bamboo hats are like lines, it is rainy. If clouds like bamboo hats are like hats, the meteorological rule is rainy.

4. Group of Alpine Lakes

On the top of Mount Fuji, there is a huge crater lake with a diameter of 800 meters and a depth of 200 meters; and at the northern foot of Fuji, There are Fuji Five Lakes. They are respectively Lake Yamanaka, Lake Kawaguchi, Lake Sai, Lake Shoji and Motosu, among which Lake Yamanaka is the largest one. In the Patient Nomura of the southeast of Lake Yamanaka, there are eight ponds including access pond, mirror pond, etc., which are collectively called "Nomura eight seas" and interlinked with Mountain Lake. On the shore of West Lake, there are Fugaku Wind Cave, Aokigahara Sea of Trees, Koyodai, Nakisawa Ice Caves, Mount Ashiwada Yama and other scenic areas. Since these lakes have an elevation of above 820 meters, there is a good integration of the landscape of lakes and mountains when yachts shuttle here, which is the famous scenic spot of Mount Fuji.

Section 8 Seoraksan—Eastern Fairyland

Seoraksan, is located in the east coast of Sokcho in Gangwon-do which is the highest mountain in the Taebaek Mountain range with an altitude of 1708 metres. The mountain was named Seorak ("Seol" meaning "snow" and "Ak" meaning "big mountain") because the snow would not melt for a long time keeping the rocks in a permanent state of white. Seoraksan is considered to be the most famous natural landscape. The government designated the area as a nature reserve in 1965 and also the first Korean national park in December 1973. It is also the second largest national park in South Korea with an area of about 375 square meters. There are more than 500 kinds of wild animals and 1000 species of rare animals. So it was designated by UNESCO as "South Korea's only plant preservation region" in August 1982 and maple leaf is the most famous.

I. Beautiful Landscapes

As Korean representative landscapes of mountains, Seoraksan is the most beautiful national parks in rock landscape with a variety of rocks. Valleys have beautiful natural landscapes which is centered on 12 fairy soup, zigzag Lake and valleys formed by numerous waterfalls, Marsh, pond and rocks. From the geological point of view, the majestic mountains and diverse landscape of Seoraksan is mainly due to the invasion of massive granite to form a spectacular landscape. Granite peaks such as Ulsan rock show a relatively flat, broad and rounded terrain; and porphyry type form a rough and rugged landscape. The difference is derived from diversity of rocks and the development of the joint. The top of Seoraksan has a rich Alpine plant community which is not only the Southern limit of Northern plants as well as the Northern limit of Southern plants.

Since ancient time, it has not been easy to get near Seoraksan. Its cultural resources is relatively rare in South Korea's national parks. Cultural landmarks in the national park include the Buddhist temples Baekdamsa, Sinheungsa, Seongguksa temple, and so on.

II. Scenic Spots

Seoraksan is located in the city of Sokcho which centers on the highest mountain, Daechongbong Peak with 1708 meters. The ridges extending north and south from Daecheongbong divide the park into Nae (inner) Seorak and Oe (outer) Seorak. The Outer Seorak of the park is the most accessible entrance to visitors. Cheonbuldong Valley is formed by water of Daechongbong Peak flowed from north.

Follow Suryeomdong valley and you will reach Waryong and Ssangpok waterfalls. Further up is Bongjeongam. Once you arrive at Daecheong peak you can view the magnificent mountain range. South NaeSeorak directs the valley from Oknyeotang area to Hangyeryeong. Daeseung Waterfall north of Jangsudae is the most beautiful site of NaeSeorak. South of Yongdaeri valley is the twelve fairy bathing spring, Oktang Falls, and Yongtang Falls, along with several other traditional relics.

The scene of Seoraksan is not only changed with seasons, but also with different administrative regions, landscape, climate and culture. If Cheonbuldong Valley of outer Seorak shows male bold beauty, Kaya cave of inner Seorak shows female soft deep beauty. In southern Seoraksan, you can enjoy the majestic of Daechongbong Peak and the elegance of Osaek Mineral Water. The climate of Taebaek Mountain on both sides are very varied that west side is inland climate and east side is oceanic climate.

1.Alpine Ski

The Alpine Ski Resort is located in Fuling Chen Plateau Basin. It has the large amount of snowfall and longest snowfall period. There is a unique Ski Museum to tell the history of skiing. It can offer many facilities such as ski field, indoor swimming pool, bowling alley in winter, golf, driving range, lawn sled, survival games, drifting in summer.

2.Shinheungsa Temple

Shinheungsa Temple, sometimes spelled Sinheungsa, was built in the sixth year of Queen Jindeok (654)of Silla Dynasty, by Jajang, a great Buddhist Master. It is located just a short walk from Seorak National Park's main entrance. The temple was first constructed to the east of Norumok, with a nine-story pagoda to enshrine the sarira of Buddha, and it was named Hyangseongsa, which was later changed to Sinheungsa.

3. Osaek Mineral Water

Located within Mt.Seoraksan National Park, it is a natural hot spring at about 650 m above sea level. There is a legend that the angels went to heaven after bathing in this very water. Osaek means five different flavors that may be tasted in this special water. The water has strong iron content and is highly carbonated, which makes it difficult to drink the first time. Osaek Hot Spring is famous for efficacy in treating neuralgia, muscle pains, arthritis, skin irritations, diabetes, blood circulation problem and digestive maladies. In particular, it is dubbed the "Beauty Hot Springs" for doing wonders for the skin. People from all over the country comes to Mt. Seoraksan just for access to it.

4. Jujeongol Valley

Situated in the southern Seoraksan Osaek region, Jujeongol Valley is where the old yeopjeon coins were made during the Joseon Dynasty. As one might expect of a valley in which the national currency is produced, Jujeongol lies deep between high mountain ridges where the glorious tints of the autumn foliage are said by many to be the most beautiful in all the Seoraksan Mountains. The path leading to Osaek Mineral Springs is the most popular hiking course in all the park.

III. Tourism and Sighting

Seoraksan is adjacent to east coast. In summer, a lot of tourists who come to east coast to avoid heat will visit here; in winter tourists who spend time in the surrounding ski resort and Spa will also come to this place; autumn is peak season for Seoraksan, strangely shaped rocks and valleys and all kinds of maple leaf form a beautiful scenery; spring, under the interaction of maritime and mountain climate, forming a unique landscape, will give you a chance to enjoy both flowers of summer and snows of winter at the same time attracts many visitors.

Many tourists like to enjoy the wild nature of the scenery. There are about 5 million visitors a year, most visitors do not climb mountains. They only walk around the outer Seorak area, staying nearby the temple and the top of the cable car. The Ulsan rock, the Dragon Waterfalls and Cheonbuldong Valley are the furthest they would go. If in South Seorak, the final destination of the tourists is generally colored syrup hot springs or fairy soup falls. Short distance tourists would like to visit in low altitude areas.

There are several restaurants in the park, including on some trails. Many snacks are quite famous in Sokcho such as sashimi, squid, rice sausage, soba noodles, cold noodles, tofu, etc. April, May, October, November are the best to taste sashimi each year. There are many sashimi shops in Dapu port and Dongming port. Try the Ojingeo Sundae (pronounced soon-dai), otherwise known as Squid Sausage. The casing of a squid is stuffed with tentacles, rice and herbs and is only available in this particular region of Korea. Uncle sausage is a snack originally from DPRK. It is walleye Pollack stuffed with kimchi, pork and other materials.

Section 9 The Chocolate Hills—Eastern Wonderful Hills

The Chocolate Hills is a geological formation in Bohol Province, Philippines. There are at least 1268 hills spreading over an area of more than 50 square kilometres (20 sq mi). They are covered in green grass that turns brown (like chocolate) during the dry season, hence the name. These cone-shaped or dome-shaped hills are actually made of grass-covered limestone. During the dry season, the grass-covered hills dry up and turn chocolate brown, turning the area into seemingly endless rows of "chocolate kisses". The branded confection is the inspiration behind the name, Chocolate Hills.

I. Legend and Origin

Two legends explain the formation of the Chocolate Hills. The first tells of a giant named Arogo who was extremely powerful and youthful. Arogo fell in love with Aloya, who was a simple mortal. Aloya's death caused Arogo much pain and misery, and in his sorrow he could not stop crying. When his tears dried, the Chocolate Hills were formed. The second tells the story of two feuding giants who hurled rocks, boulders, and sand at each other. The fighting lasted for days, and exhausted the two giants. In their exhaustion, they forgot about their feud and became friends, but when they left they forgot to clean up the mess they had made during their battle, hence the Chocolate Hills. The Chocolate Hills are conical karst hills similar to those seen in the limestone regions of Slovenia, Croatia, northern Puerto Rico, and Pinar del Río Province, Cuba. These hills consist of Late Pliocene to Early Pleistocene, thin to medium bedded, sandy to rubbly marine limestones. These limestones contain the abundant fossils of shallow marine foraminifera, coral, mollusks, and algae. These conical hills are geomorp hological features called cockpit karst, which were created by a combination of the dissolution of limestone by rainfall, surface water, and groundwater, and their subaerial erosion by rivers and streams after they had been uplifted above sea level and fractured by tectonic processes. These hills are separated by well developed flat plains and contain numerous caves and springs. The Chocolate Hills are considered to be a remarkable example of conical karst topography. The origin for the conical karst of the Chocolate Hills is described in popular terms on the bronze plaque at the viewing deck in Carmen, Bohol. This plaque states that they are eroded formations of a type of marine limestone that sits on top of hardened clay. The plaque reads: The unique land form known as the Chocolate Hills of Bohol was formed ages ago by the uplift of coral deposits and the action of rain water and erosion. The plaque also makes reference to a fanciful explanation of the origin of the Chocolate Hills that is unsupported by any published scientific research, i.e. either Hillmer or Travaglia and others, when it states: the grassy hills were once coral reefs that erupted from the sea in a massive geologic shift. They have been formed over millions of years of weathering and erosion.

II. Main Attractions

Viewed from the air on ordinary days, the chocolate hills look like odd green lumps spreading across the plain. Summer, however, brings out the hills' best colors as the velvet green foliage dries and the hills take on a chocolate brown hue, hence the name. The hills have long aroused a sense of curious wonder to those who have seen them. The Chocolate Hills are all in the same shape, but differ in the altitude. They are covered with grass, which, at the end of the dry season, turns chocolate brown, hence the name. At other times, the hills are green, and the association may be a bit difficult to make.

III. Tarsiers

A reason to visit the main island Bohol, is that Bohol still has tropical rainforests in the higher parts of the island. Moreover, If you want to meet the smallest monkey on earth, the Tarsier, you'll have to visit Bohol! The average size of this little creature is between 90 to 160 mm (3.5 to 6.25 inches). The weight is between 70 to 165 grams. Tarsiers are lemur like in being nocturnal and having a well-developed sense of smell. However, like monkeys, ape, and humans, the nose is dry and hair-covered, not moist and bald as is that of lemurs. The eyes and placenta are also similar form in structure.

The tarsier's small brain has an enormous visual cortex to process information from the large goggling eyes, the animal's most striking feature. The size of the eyes and visual cortex is probably made necessary by the absence of a reflective layer (tapetum) that the eyes of most other nocturnal mammals possess. The tarsier is also unusual in having especially long ankle bones (tarsals, hence the name tarsier), a short body, and a round head that can be rotated 180°. The face is short, with large, membranous ears that are almost constantly in motion. The fur is thick, silky, and coloured gray to dark brown. They also have a slender tail from 20 to 25 cm long. Their fingers are also elongated, with the third finger being about the same length as the upper arm. Most of the digits have nails, but the second and third toes of the hind feet bear claws instead, which are used for grooming. Tarsiers have very soft, velvety fur, which is generally buff, beige, or ochre in color. Bohol is home to an exotic range of flora and fauna you'll hardly find elsewhere. These shy, little nocturnal creatures with long tails, large round eyes, and fuzzy bodies are extremely difficult to keep and breed. Tarsiers are threatened with extinction due to wide spread poaching and deforestation.

Chapter 3

World Famous Mountains in Africa

Section 1 Kilimanjaro— Snow Peak in the Equator

Kilimanjaro is located in northeast Tanzania and 160 kilometers from the Great Rift Valley at south.It is a large strato-volcano between the equator and 3 degrees south latitude, the highest mountain in Africa. Kilimanjaro, with its three dormant volcanic cones, Kibo, Mawenzi, and Shira, extends nearly 80 kilometers from east to west, covering an area of 756 square meters. Uhuru Peak, 5892 meters high, is the highest summit on Kibo's crater rim and is called "the king of Africa" by many geologists. In 1861, the German officer Baron Carl Claus von der Decken and the young British geologist Richard Thornton made a first attempt to climb Kibo. In 1887, during his first attempt to climb Kilimanjaro, the German geology professor Hans Meyer reached the base of Kibo, but was forced to turn back by not having the equipment necessary to handle the deep snow and ice on Kibo.

I.Scenery

Being an Afromontane sky island, Kilimanjaro has an enormous biodiversity while low in endemic species. However endemics include the giant groundsels in the bunchgrass tussock grasslands, and other flora adapted to living in alpine plant conditions. Kilimanjaro has a large variety of forest types over an altitudinal range of 3000 m (9843 ft) containing over 1200 vascular plant species. Montane Ocotea forests occur on the wet southern slope.

Cassipourea and Juniperus forests grow on the dry northern slope. Subalpine Erica forests at 4100 m (13451 ft) represent the highest elevation cloud forest in Africa. In contrast to this enormous biodiversity, the degree of endemism is low. However, forest relicts in the deepest valleys of the cultivated lower areas suggest that a rich forest flora inhabited Mt Kilimanjaro in the past, with restricted-range species otherwise only known from the Eastern Arc mountains. The low degree of endemism on Kilimanjaro may result from destruction of lower elevation forest rather than the relatively young age of the mountain.

Another feature of the forests of Kilimanjaro is the absence of a bamboo zone, which occurs on all other tall mountains in East Africa with a similarly high rainfall. Sinarundinaria alpina stands are favoured by elephants and African buffalos elsewhere. On Kilimanjaro these megaherbivores occur on the northern slopes, where it is too dry for a large bamboo zone to develop. They are excluded from the wet southern slope forests by topography and humans, who have cultivated the foothills for at least 2000 years.

This interplay of biotic and abiotic factors could explain not only the lack of a bamboo zone on Kilimanjaro but also offers possible explanations for the patterns of diversity and endemism. If true, Kilimanjaro's forests would serve as a striking example of the large and long-lasting influence of both animals and humans on the African landscape.

II. Legends

Uncounted stories, thousands of myths and legends are told about Mount Kilimanjaro. Locals on the slopes, the Chagga people, are telling us of pygmies said to be no larger than human children, and who dwelt on the mountain's caves and ravines. These ravines, which have never been explored by tourists, are said to have been inhabited by mountain pygmies who survived by hunting and gathering.

Stories on Mount Kilimanjaro tell of mountain gorillas who once lived inside the dense, rainforest surrounding its slopes many years ago. Tales from locals, though no scientific data yet available to confirm this, have occupied the minds of tourists climbing the mountain today.

Folklores dominate Mount Kilimanjaro as well. The awesome feature of the mountain with its snow on the peak had attracted locals to connect the mountain with heavens, believing that it was the seat of God, glorified by the whitish color of the snow.

During dry seasons in the past, locals blamed the mountain's demons for taking away the rain, but when the rain was too much, they turned their faces to the mountain, bowing, asking God to forgive them.

III. Tourist Attractions

There are many African style star-hotels to meet demands of tourists from all over the world. Full equipped Kilimanjaro International Airport has advanced communication means, and has 14 international air routes opened up to other parts of the world. Tourists will be arriving at the foot of the mountain directly.

There are seven official trekking routes by which to ascend and descend Mount Kilimanjaro: Lemosho, Machame, Marangu, Mweka, Rongai, Shira, and Umbwe. Of all the routes, Machame is considered the most scenic, albeit steeper, route. It can be done in six or seven days. The Rongai is the easiest and least scenic of all camping routes. The Marangu is also relatively easy, but this route tends to be very busy, the ascent and descent routes are the same, and accommodation is in shared huts with all other climbers. People who wish to trek to the summit of Kilimanjaro are advised to undertake appropriate research and ensure that they are both properly equipped and physically capable. Though the climb is technically not as challenging as when climbing the high peaks of the Himalayas or Andes, the high elevation, low temperature, and occasional high winds make this a difficult and dangerous trek.

Section 2 Table Mountain—The City of Cape

Table Mountain (Afrikaans: Tafelberg) is one of the oldest mountains in the world and has existed about three hundred and sixty million years. It lies at the northern end of a sandstone mountain range that forms the spine of the Cape Peninsula, with Atlantic coast in front. It is a flat-topped mountain forming a prominent landmark overlooking the city of Cape Town and Table Bay harbor (named after Table Mountain) in South Africa. The view from the top of Table Mountain has been described as one of the most epic views in Africa.

The main feature of Table Mountain is the level plateau approximately 3 kilometers from side to side, edged by impressive cliffs. The plateau, flanked by Devil's Peak to the east and by Lion's Head to the west, forms a dramatic backdrop to Cape Town. This broad sweep of mountainous heights, together with Signal Hill, forms the natural amphitheatre of the City Bowl and Table Bay harbor. Table Mountain is close to downtown and featured in the Flag of Cape Town and other local government insignia. The mountain's Cape Floral Region protected areas are listed in World Heritage Sites.

I. Geological Features

The upper part of the mountain mesa consists of Ordovician quartzitic sandstone, commonly referred to as Table Mountain Sandstone (TMS), which is highly resistant to erosion and forms characteristic steep grey crags. Below the sandstone is a layer of micaceous basal shale, which weathers quite readily and is therefore not well exposed.

The basement consists of heavily folded and altered phyllites, and homfelses known informally as the Malmesbury shale. This has been intruded by the Cape Granite. Both rocks are of late Precambrian age. The basement rocks are not nearly as resistant to weathering as the TMS, but significant outcrops of the Cape Granite are visible on the western side of Lion's Head.

II. The Beautiful Scenery

Standing on the top of Table Mountain, you can have a panorama of visible Lion's Head, Signal Hill, Robben Island, the Cape Town city centre, Table Bay, and Devil's Peak. The highest point on Table Mountain is towards the eastern end of the plateau and is marked by Maclear's Beacon, a stone cairn built in 1865 for trigonometrical survey. It is 1087 metres above sea level. The flat top of the mountain is 1500 meters long, 200 meters wide, just like a big table. It is often covered by orographic clouds, formed when a south-easterly wind is directed up the mountain's slopes into colder air, where the moisture condenses to form the so-called "table cloth" of cloud. All kinds of rocks makes Table Mountain a natural museum.

Table Mountain has an unusually rich biodiversity. The mountain's vegetation types form part of the Cape Floral Region protected areas. These protected areas are a World Heritage Site, and an estimated 2200 species of plants are confined to Table Mountain. Many of these species, including a great many types of proteas, are endemic to the mountain and can be found nowhere else. The most famous protea here is the national flower——King Protea, which is colorful and bloom from May to December.

III. Legend of Odd Cloud

Legend attributes the Table Mountain's clouds to a smoking contest between the devil and a local pirate. There is an interesting story about it. One day, a local pirate called Van Hunks ran into a devil near Table Mountain. They had a chat while smoking. The Devil in good mood told Van Hunks where the only warm cave for a devil was to be found. The pirate was very clever and suggested that they had a contest of smoking and whoever won would own the warm cave. Since the clouds are always seen, the contest between the devil and the pirate is lasting.

Chapter 4

World Famous Mountains in Europe

Section 1 The Alps & The Eisenwurzen Geopark
—The Backbone of Europe

The Alps are great mountains ranges in the central south of Europe, covering the north border of Italy, the southeast of France, Switzerland, Liechtenstein, Austria, the south of Germany and Slovenia. The Alps stretch from the Atlas Mountains of North Africa across southern Europe and Asia to beyond the Himalayas. They extend north from the subtropical Mediterranean coast near Nice, France, to the Geneva before trending northeast to Vienna on the Danube. Most rivers in Europe originate from the Alps, which are rich in water resources, and are famous scenic spots for touring, holidaying and convalescing.

I. Ecological Landscapes

The main parts of the Alps extending southwest are the Pyrenees Mountains, extending south are the Apennine Mountains, extending southeast are the Dinara Mountains, extending east are the Carpathian Mountains. The Alps can be divided into three segments. The west segment: the west Alps spread from Mediterranean coast across the southeast of France and northwest of Italy to nearby Great St. Bernard Pass, the border of Switzerland. This segment is the narrowest, and the most concentrated peaks as well. The blue sky sets off spotlessly white Braun ("Braun" means white in French) Peak (4810 meters), the highest one of the Alps, which is situated on the border between France and Italy. The central segment: the central Alps lie between Great St. Bernard Pass and Boden Lake. They are the widest, having Matterhorn (4479 meters) and Monte Rosa (4634 meters). The east segment: the east Alps are at the east of Boden Lake. The altitude is lower than the west and central segment of the Alps. Europe is separated into several areas by the ridge of the Alps, which is the sources of many European rivers (such as Rhone, Rhine and the Po River) and of many tributaries of the Danube. The water flows from the Alps finally emptying into the North Sea, the Mediterranean Sea, the

Adriatic Sea and the Black Sea.

The Alps are located between the temperate and subtropical latitudes. It is the dividing line between the central temperate humid continental climate and South Asia tropical dry summer climate. At the same time it has altitudinal climatic characteristics. Vegetation of the Alps changes vertically. It can be divided into the subtropical evergreen sclerophyllous forest (south slope below 800 m); forest belt (800 to 1800 meters), the lower part is mixed forest, the upper part is coniferous forest zone; meadow belt is above the forest belt; on the top of all those is bare rock and Perennially snow on the mountain peak.

Several plant belts reflect altitude and climate differences of Alps. A variety of deciduous trees grow on the bottom of the valleys and the low slopes such as oak, beech, linden, poplar, elm, chestnut, mountain ash, birch and Norway maple. Conifers are common at the higher elevations. The main plants there are spruce, larch and other kinds of pine. In most places in the Western Alps, spruce trees can be found at up to 2195 meters above sea level. Larches are able to resist cold, drought and windy condition. It can grow at an altitude of up to 2500 meters, however, spruce are usually found mixed with it in the lower places.

Below the permanent snow line and above the tree line, there is a 914 m wide area where the trace of glacial erosion has been spotted. This area is covered with lush grass, some cattle and sheep are grazing here in the short period of summer. These particular grasses are known as "alpages" (mountain summer pastures). The name of the Alps and its vegetation evolved from this word. They are located above the valley. In the south coast of the Alps and south Italy Alps, lie mainly Mediterranean plants, shore pine, palm, sparse woodland and tequila as well as many Prickly pears.

There are a few animals that have adapted well to alpine environments. Although the bear has disappeared, the ibex (like chamois, exceptional agility) was saved by Italy Royal hunting reservation. Marmot hides in underground channels during winters while mountain rabbit and Thunderbird (a grouse) become white (a kind of camouflage).

II. Tourism and Leisure

The Alps which is called "the Palace of Nature" and "the Real Geomorphology Museum" is one of the most famous scenic resorts and tourist spots. The Alps is the biggest mountain glacier in Europe. The ice covers the mountain in some areas to a thickness of 1 kilometer. Various types of glacial landforms are widely distributed, especially in glaciated landform. Only a few peaks over the ice constitute peak islands. The sharp angular mountain peak has a moraine landform which is formed by glacier erosion, glacier cliffs, horn, cirque, hanging valleys, glacial lakes and glacier accumulation. There are more than 1200 pieces of modern glaciers, a total area of about 4000 square kilometers. The Aletsch Glacier, the largest glacier which is located in southeast Switzerland is about 22.5 kilometers, an area of about 130 square kilometers.

Apline glaciers formed many lakes. Lake Geneva, the largest lake is surrounded by snow meadows and vineyards. The water does not freeze all year round. The blue lake and the sky seem to melt into one another. Henry James described the lake as An Extraordinary Blue Lake. Byron compared it to a crystal mirror, supplying the nutrients and air for reflection. Balzac called it Synonyms of Love. Besides, there are also beautiful lake resorts such as Vierwaldsstaettersee, Lake Zurich, Lake Constance, and Lake Como. Due to the good scenery, mountain glaciers make themselves popular resorts for mountaineering and skiing.

Over the past century,mountain has become a place for vacation and recuperation. In summer, the mountain will be the summer resort,while in winter it will be the paradise of sports.There are hotels, restaurants and other facilities for tourists to enjoy everything.The hotel of highest terrain in Europe lies here—Hilton Hotel.Sitting in the hotel's revolving restaurant,people can watch the mountain scenery of the Alps.There is also the Europe's highest railway station.Taking the train, people can reach the Jungfrau directly to see the extraordinary sight of the glacier.In order to let visitors enjoy the wonderful views of snow, there are cable cars to the mountaintop at many places. If the mountaineering visitors meet with a mishap, the helicopter can provide assistance, and in the mountain there is a special hospital for the treatment of fracture or hurt.

In addition to skiing,people can also take a bath in the hot springs in the Alps.Leukerbad hot springs are located in Leukerbad—the famous hot springs place for resort in Alps.It has 22 outdoor and indoor hot spring pools.Every day,about 3 million liters of hot spring water flows into the private and public spas.Leukerbad has begun to develop into a hot spring city since Roman times,predominately Burgerbad and Alpentherme with plenty of fascinating facilities.

III. Geopark

Nature Park Eisenwurzen is located in State of Styria of Austria, belonging to the north of the Alps. The rock is made up of limestone and dolomite. Up to now, it has a history of more than 250 million years and is one of late Permian Triassic carbonate distribution areas. Since Paleocene, alpine strong inner activities created colorful landscape here, such as stream, waterfall, limestone valleys, caves and other fascinating landscapes, among which Klaus Cave is an important limestone cave in Europe. Austria's largest reptile fossils and a large number of cretaceous snails and bivalve fossils are kept in Triassic strata. The great ice age glaciers flow left important glacial traces and is the name of the alpine mu glaciations. Eisenwurzen is home to smelting iron in ancient Austria, where smelting iron workshops are everywhere. Museums, practice bases, seminars, music festivals all make this place attractive. Many tourists come here to enjoy rafting and canoeing.

The Geological Tourism Association was established in 1999.The geological tourism can be traced back to 1892, when Klaus Cava, a major European gypsum cave, was installed electric lamps and open to the public. A bicycle riding tour provides you an opportunity to explore the geological features in different geological ages. In addition, under the direction of guides, you can collect fossils to make special sovenirs.

Section 2 Cozia Mountain—Ecological Homeland

The Cozia National Park,located in the central-southern part of the Southern Carpathians, in the north-east part of Valcea County, in the south-eastern Lotru Mountains and the east of Capatanii Mountains on the middle course of Olt River. It suddenly rises from the surrounding depression. Olt River washes its feet. It appears as a rock giant made of steep slopes and a large number of forts. Cozia National Park with an area of 17100 hectares was declared natural protected area on March 6, 2000.

I. Beautiful Ecological Landscapes

There are cristaline formations in the North, and in the South there are sedimentary. The area is quite abrupt, which makes the aspect of the Oltului Valley to be a spectacular one. The flora of the park is very rich, there are about 930 species. Besides its peculiar aspect of flora elements, Cozia National Park has a good number of lichen species. Also the National Park is the shelter of many species of animals, the rarest animals are: the pseudo-scorpion, the viper, the wild cat, the marten, the black goat, etc. It represents a mountainous area with flora and fauna specific Southern Carpathians.

The park has many spectacular massives, Bulzu Top (1506 meters), The Gardului Valleys, Caprariile, The Sphynx of Cozia, Pietrele Vulturilor, Pietrele Rosiei, Coltii Foarfecii, Traian's Tower, Teofil's Tower, the Stone Gates of Cozia. Surfaces are almost completely covered with vegetation, easy to hike. Tourists are accompanied by picturesque sceneries along the way there.

II. Cultural Attractions

It is a nationally valuable natural resource (landscapes, hot springs, geology, hydrology, fauna, flora etc.) and also an extraordinary anthropic resource (monasteries, monuments, traditions and local communities etc).

Cozia national park is a vast area full of history. Evidence shows that this area has been lived from the oldest times. There are many localities in the land formerly held by Seneslau, where the population continues traditions and customs immemorial. The closest communities to the National Park are the two cities Brezoi and Calimanesti and the villages Racovita, Perisani, Berislavesti and Salatrucel. Calimanesti city is known as a major tourist destination due to the mineral springs. Brezoi city was a major industrial center for woodworking, but now this activity has almost come to an end, therefore the city is facing an economic decline. With little means of subsistence, agriculture (livestock and fruit) is the main economic activity for the inhabitants. Inside the National Park, there are two monk communities: Turnu monastery and Stanisoara monastery.

Many magnificent churches and monasteries were built here. Cozia Monastery is the most famous one.It experienced the Romanian 600 years development of art, Sacred Boon, peace, dignity and religion. Built this sanctuary in this secluded spot not only for the beauty of its surroundings, but certainly also for military and strategic reasons, as the monastery was, at the beginning, fortified with tall defensive walls, like a stronghold. Ancient Mircea Reign was first mentioned by documents in 1388. Mircea's portrait can be seen in all its majesty on the wall at the right of the narthex of the big church of Cozia Monastery, clothed in Medieval costume, holding the miniature of the monastery in his hand and, standing beside him, his son whom he later associated to the throne. This portrait is painted in the northern chapel and in the monastery's hospice ("Bolnita"). Mircea died at the beginning of 1418, at the princely residence of Arges, and his remains were brought to Cozia Monastery and buried in a sarcophagus, resembling those which were, at the time, highly favored in the Occidental countries, and ornamented gravestone was set upon the tomb. This gravestone was impaired during the 1916—1918 foreign occupation and – through the care of the diocese of Ramnic—it was replaced in 1938 with a new tombstone upon which the following inscription was engraved: "Here lies Mircea, prince of Wallachia, passed away in the year 1418." After Cozia was embellished and extended by later new founders, other repairs have been made in the following centuries or in the first decades of the 20th century under the patronage of the Board of Historical Monuments. However, the buildings were seriously damaged and some were even destroyed because of the fights on the valley of the Olt during the First World War and the foreign occupation, which followed. Cozia has nevertheless regained its former aspect, but only in the years of the popular power did it acquire its seven windows, each adorned with different sculptural and floral compositions which belong to the time of Mircea the Ancient. In middle of the mountains, there are rely masterpiece of

Ortodox Romanian architecture, rich in marvellous icons and surrounded by beautiful garden and splendid plantations. From Monastery Turcu, a long road in forest is up and down , between stones, conducts us to Pausa or Stanisoara Monastery, and for brave people, up to Cozia.

III.Tourism Activities

Cozia National Park is a well-known tourist destination by Romanian and foreign tourists for its good positon. It's close to many monasteries and two Spa resorts-Calimanesti and Caciulata.You can also appreciate beautiful Cheile waterfall and Lotisorului waterfall as well as the charming, Capatanei, Doabra-Calinesti, Defileul Oltulu.The main tourist activities are as follows: hiking, doing sports, outdoor camps, competitions or visiting places of worship, historical areas and monuments, developing and acquiring knowledge in the natural sciences, Spa treatment, etc.

Section 3 Gaina Mountain—A Love Fairyland

Gaina Mountain is a part of the Apuseni Mountains, at a height of 1486 m. In the Apuseni Mountains every single village or dwelling has its own history, dating back to the Roman times and tells the story of their evolution up to the present. The inhabitants of the Apuseni Mountains established this convenient meeting place to meet and keep in touch as the Gaina Mountain peak is flat and commands a good view. Ganina Mountain is best known for the Maiden Fair held here around July 20 every year on Saint Elijah's Day.It is the largest Romanian traditional feast in the open air.

I.Curious Legend

Gaina Mountain has a breathtaking view and a long history full of myths and legends. Maiden Fair was first mentioned in documents in 1816 and was held at 1467 m high on the Gaina Peak in a superb clearing surrounded by white clouds. Though it's called the Maidens Fair, no one buys or sells young wome—even though some come here to find husbands. The purpose of the fair was and is to keep people in touch with their roots and create a sense of community among the Romanian mountain villagers.

There's also a legend about the Maidens Fair. A charmed hen that was laying golden eggs, had its shelter on Hen Peak. People used to protect her and in return, the hen used to come down, once a year, from its secret dwelling space as a beautiful goddess to bless the young married couples with a golden egg for happiness and long life. People were applauding, praying and giving thanks. In the sound of their applause the goddess raised her hands to the sky and turned back into a Hen, hiding herself from the mortals' eyes. So the seasons found them, thus starting a habit of faith and love. At that time, the mountain peaks were covered with white clouds, so the mountain was called "The Gaina Mountain"because "gaian" means hen. Afterwards, some greedy and evil people decided to hunt her and continuously searched for her valuable eggs. One day someone stole them, but the he ended up falling down a deep strait, losing the golden orbs in the process. Returning to her nest and not seeing the eggs, the hen decided to leave the place forever and settled on another mountain, at Rosia Montana. The people mourned her, begged her to go back to them but the miracle did not happened. Gaina mountain remained behind with barren peaks, haunted by rains, wild winds and snows, by tears and legends. People come to meet the mountain as often as they can, hoping they will be able to tame, to quench its patience, harmony and longing.

II. Single Party Folk

The Maidens Fair in Gaina Mountain takes place every year in July attracts people from all the regions of the country to join. They enjoy music, traditional dances and other local festivities. Traditionally during this festival, thousands of Romanian people dressed up in traditional clothes descend to Gaina Mountain hoping to meet "that special someone". It's a moment of joy for the young boys and girls to play, take part in party, sing, dance and make the aquaintance of boys and girls coming from far away and then eventually get married. Local people think that a couple can be happy only if their wedding is done on Gaina Mountain. Actually it is a large single party, well-known in Central and Eastern Europe.

The celebration starts early in the morning, when the famous band of alpenhorn women from Avram Iancu makes the announcement. The large folk festival includes traditional Transylvanian dances, folkloric costumes and crafts such as fine textiles, weaving looms,sculpted flutes and many pottery objects. People from other areas bring coats adorned with flowers, fur caps, wild fruits, medicine plants. Those from the Apuseni Mountains bring alpenhorns, wooden pails, canteens and wooden tubs. The custom of arriving one day ahead is still practiced. This is why the Saturday night celebration in Avram Iancu seems to be more impressive than the mountain fair itself. Every participant brings food from home, drinks home-made cherry palinca (strong brandy), eat "mamaliga" (polenta) with milk, lard bacon and onion.

III.Tourist Experience

A stunning landscape, clean air, tasty food and traditional dance provide the Maidens Festival with a great recipe for the maintenance of local folk traditions. If visitors want to experience the joy of the festival, going to the mountain by car is definitely the most convenient and comfortable way, as you can reach the bottom of the mountain at Vidra by car. From there you can climb up on foot. From Campeni which is close to the Gaina Mountain you can also start on the road towards Abrud and then further on to the Rosia Montana, and all of the sudden you find yourself in "The Metal Fortress" of the Apuseni Mountain, in the land of the gold. Gaina Mountain peak, the mountain climbing from Avram Iancu commune to Gaina Mountain peak is 9 km and a hotel named Craiul pension is in the midway, 5 km from the top of the mout peak.

Section 4 Covasna Mountain—The Pearl of Hot Spring

Covasna Mountain is located in Covasna, a central county of Romania. The name comes from the Slavic word "quasi", which means "sour-sour" (referring to the taste of mineral water here). Covasna county covers an area of 3710 square kilometer with a population of 220000 (2002).It is 31 km from the capital city Sfântu Gheorghe (Olt Riverside), 60 km from Brasov in southwest, adjacent to Brasov in northeast and contiguous to Buzău in southeast. Sfântu Gheorghe has a population of 67000 and it is a sympathic city of Transylvania in spite of smallness in size. There are rolling hills, lush jungles, clean rivers and lakes.

I. Fascinating Attractions

Covasna has a beautiful, untouched nature. A picturesque place is the Quay of Varghis on the Varghis Valley, in the Rarghita Mountains. The river cut in stone a narrow path which is 3 km long, and of an impressive wildness and natural beauty, with about 60 caves. The biggest one is the Meresti Cave and it is the longest cave in the Oriental Carpathians. The city center can be found "Devil's Pond", the name was given by locals, symbol of the city. Devil's Pond is an eruption of mud and gas (carbon oxides and sulfur), opened to the public in 1881 and initially used for treatment. According to tradition, in 1700 this natural phenomenon was further north, but mysteriously moved into the center, leaving his old place a little brother, "Little Mud Devil". Devil's Pond is, in the opinion of geologists, an emanation of carbon: mineral water burst forth from the ground water and gas are kept in swirling, swarming. In the 19th century there were several eruptions: in 1837, 1857, 1864 and 1885, the highest being in 1837, and the last major eruption took place in 1984. Currently

Mud Devil is completely harmless.

Anthropic attractions are mainly museums and churches. Such as Roman-Catholic Church-Ghelita (1245), valuable due to its age, architectural style (late Romanesque) and inside wall paintings; Reformed Church-Sfantu Gheorghe, Fortified Church-Biborteni (15th century), it was painted in Italian Renaissance style, preserving original fragments of the fresco, Fortified Church-Olteni, Fortified Church-Baraolt (1569), Church-Aita Mare. Ceausescu Villa is located in an isolated portion of the Valley Fairy particular beauty.

II.Unique Hot Spring Resources

Covasna County is richly endowed by nature. The relief consists mainly of mountains accounting for 60% of the total area. The post-volcanic mineralizations have given it springs (Carbon, conbonnate, iodin, bromine, iron, arsensic are 3.2-2.4 g/L), mineral mud and mofettes (emissions of carbon dioxide). The mineral water springs are the highlight of the county. There are more than 1500 springs and about 1000 spring resorts are located in the depression of Covasna at an altitude of 564 m.

The permanent springs have considerable flow, and some of them have a flow of 10000 liters per hour. Table water is very different in taste and curative effects. Mofettes are scattered on a surface of 40 hectares. Carbogaseous mofettes can increase the dilatation of blood vessels, reduce blood pressure, increase the muscular and cerebral blood flow, increase the temperature of body extremities so that it can cure cardiovascular diseases, central and peripherical neuro system diseases, locomotion system diseases, digestive tube and afferent glands diseases, Kidney, masculine genitals, urinary ways diseases, skin, endocrine, gynecological diseases and senile diseases. Mofettes are another important factors of the curative springs, unique in the Europe.

Climate is also one of the reasons of the curative springs. Covasna has subalpine climate with cool summers and chilly winters. The annual average temperature is 7°C and the humidity 75%-80%. It is 17°C in average in summer and 5°C in winter. The air is so rich in negative ions that it is helpful to soothe the central nervous system. The richness of the mineral resources as well as the natural resources and other medical treatment offer a maximal curative effect. Among the treatment facilities of the springs, we could mention: the devices for mofettes, facilities for warm mineral water baths, for internal mineral water cure, devices for aerosols and inhalations, paraffin treatments. Success of the treatment of certain diseases makes the spa one of the most famous cure springs in Europe.

III. Tourists Activities

Accommpdations in Covasna is very convenient. Over 10 hotels and numerous guesthouses cater for different tourists. Delux hotels are equipped with specialized medical personnel for treatment. Hotel Clermont is close to the forest, providing you with quiet environment, fresh air and fitness facilities, a good place for weekend.

Section 5 Bergstrasse-Odenwald Mountain—Geological Wonder

The Bergisch-Odenwald Geo-park in southwestern Germany, a UNESCO World Heritage Site since February, 2004, lies east to west between Main River and the river Rhine, north of Leica valley and south of Messel pit, covering an area of 2300 square kilometers.

I. Unique Stratum

Once depicted as "a continent floating between granite and sandstone", the unique strata in the park have documented major global historical events about 500 million years ago in central Europe.

The area among Rhine, Main Valley and Lycra not only exposed various magmatic rocks and sedimentary rocks, also left two global geological relics. The first is formed by the Variscan orogeny magmatic arc, the early canyons of continental collision. Second is formation of the Rhine graben, representing the initial stage of the European continental splitting during the period of

Alps, which is unique in the central European region. By studying the typical rock formation and the features of the formation of various stages, we can get a comprehensive understanding. Therefore, this region, with special geological significance, provides a special way to study the earth's history and to understand the process of the earth dynamics.

II. Tourism Resources

The park has explored an experience-oriented geological tourism network based on the unique geological background, which includes a variety of facilities and geological tourism products. Locals support the sustainable development concept and geo-tourism activities. They believe it's a long-term common task for Bergisch-Odenwald Geo-park's network building. The Bergisch-Odenwald Geo-park Visitor Information System ranges from the natural landscapes between granite and sandstone to the discovery of every section area. Each geological landscape represents a certain specific linkage and development of geological and cultural landscapes.

Chapter 5

World Famous Mountains in North America

Section 1 Mount Hood—The Landmark of the North America

Mount Hood, is a strato volcano in the Cascade Volcanic Arc of northern Oregon. It was formed by a subduction zone on the Pacific coast and rests in the Pacific Northwest region of the United States. It is located about 50 miles (80km) east-southeast of Portland, on the border between Clackamas and Hood River counties. In addition to being Oregon's highest mountain, it is one of the loftiest mountains in the nation based on its prominence.

I. Volcanic Activity

Mount Hood is the highest point in Oregon and the fourth highest in the Cascade Range. It is considered the Oregon volcano most likely to erupt, though based on its history, an explosive eruption is unlikely. Still, the odds of an eruption in the next 30 years are estimated at between 3 and 7 percent, so the U.S. Geological Survey (USGS) characterizes it as "potentially active", but the mountain is informally considered dormant.

The glacially eroded summit area consists of several and esitic or dacitic lava domes; Pleistocene collapses produced avalanches and lahars (rapidly moving mudflows) that traveled across the Columbia River to the north. The latest minor eruptive event occurred in August 1907. The glaciers on the mountain's upper slopes may be a source of potentially dangerous lahars when the mountain next erupts. There are vents near the summit that are known for emitting gases such as carbon dioxide and sulfur dioxide.

Since 1950, there have been several earthquake swarms each year at Mount Hood, most notably in July 1980 and June 2002. Seismic activity is monitored by the USGS Cascades Volcano Observatory in Vancouver, Washington, which issues weekly updates (and daily updates if significant eruptive activity is occurring at a Cascades volcano).

II. Glaciers

Mount Hood was first seen by European explorers in 1792 and is believed to have maintained a consistent summit elevation, varying by no more than a few feet due to mild seismic activity.

A 1993 survey by a scientific party reported a height of 11240 feet (3430 m), claimed to be accurate to within 1.25 inches (32 mm). Many modern sources likewise list 11240 feet (3430 m) as the height. However, numerous others place the peak's height one foot lower, at 11239 feet (3426 m).

Mount Hood is host to 12 named glaciers or snow fields, the most visited

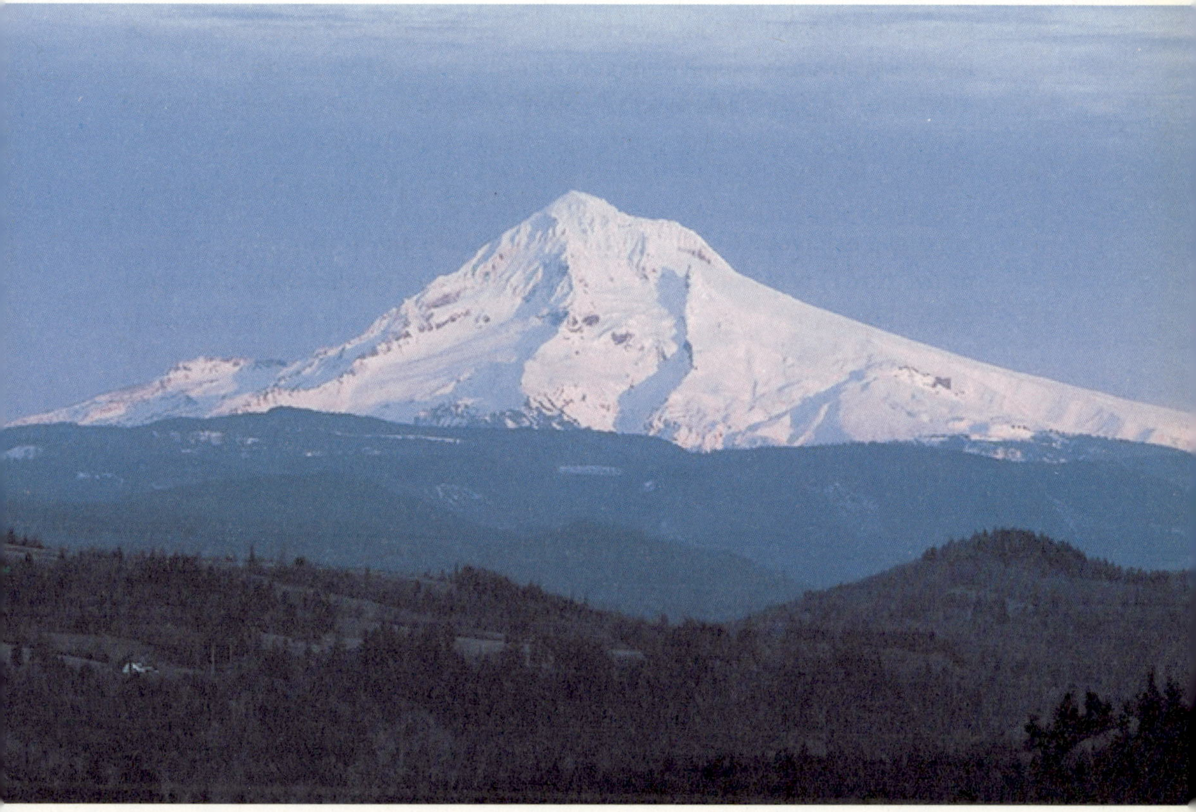

of which is Palmer Glacier, partially within the Timberline Lodge ski area and on the most popular climbing route. The glaciers are almost exclusively above the 6000 feet (1800 m) level, which also is about the average tree line elevation on Mount Hood. More than 80 percent of the glacial surface area is above 7000 feet (2100 m). The glaciers and permanent snow fields have an area of 3331 acres (13.48 km^2) and contain a volume of about 282000 acre feet (0.348 km^3). Eliot Glacier is the largest glacier by volume at 73000 acre feet (0.090 km^3), and has the thickest depth measured by ice radar at 361 feet (110 m). The largest glacier by surface area is the Coe-Ladd Glacier system at 531 acres (2.149 km^2). Glaciers and snowfields cover about 80 percent of the mountain above the 6900-feet (2100 m) level. The glaciers declined by an average of 34 percent from 1907—2004. Glaciers on Mount Hood retreated through the first half of the 20th century, advanced or at least slowed their retreat in the 1960s and 1970s, and have since returned to a pattern of retreat. The neo-glacial maximum extents formed in the early 18th century. During the last major glacial event between 29000 and 10000 years ago, glaciers reached down to the 2600-to-2300-foot (790 to 700 m) level, a distance of 9.3 miles (15 km) from the summit. The retreat released considerable outwash, some of which filled and flattened the upper Hood River Valley near Parkdale and formed Dee Flat.

III. Tourist Attractions

There are 8 wilderness, encompassing 311448 acres, located in the Mt. Hood National Forest. These areas include 124000 acres of newly designated Wilderness.

1. Government Camp

Government Camp is a small, private mountain community at 3900 feet on Mt. Hood's south side. The community is a launching point for numerous outdoor adventures including skiing, hiking, mountain biking, huckleberry picking and exploring the Barlow Road. A trail system surrounds the community for both winter and summer use. The community has a tradition of winter sports dating back to the early 1900s. Developed skiing and snowboarding opportunities are available at Timberline, Summit, and Ski Bowl Resorts.

2. Timberline Lodge

Perched above Government Camp (and accessible by paved road) is Timberline Lodge. A National Historic Landmark, Timberline Lodge was constructed during the Great Depression of the 1930s by craftspeople working under the Federal Works Projects Administration. This stately Cascadian building was constructed of stone and large timbers and has been thoughtfully maintained. Publicly owned, and privately operated, Timberline Lodge is open to the public as a hotel, restaurant, and ski resort. Nearly two million visitors from all over the globe enjoy the lodge's warm hospitality each year. Forest Service interpretive staff provide tours of the lodge. Climbers and hikers headed into the Mt. Hood Wilderness frequently begin their ascents here. Due to its high elevation (6000 feet) and proximity to the Palmer Snow Field, Timberline Ski Area is unique in its ability to offer year-round skiing and snowboarding.

3. Timothy Lake

Timothy Lake is one of the most popular family camping and fishing destinations in the Mt. Hood National Forest. The lake's south shore features four developed campgrounds and boat ramps. Two other nearby campgrounds accommodate equestrians. Three smaller, less developed campgrounds are found in the north. A trail system for hikers, mountain bikers and equestrians circles the lake. The Pacific Crest National Scenic Trail also traverses the area along the east side of Timothy Lake. The tributaries that feed Timothy Lake have outstanding wetlands habitat. Oak Grove Fork Meadow by Clackamas Lake, Timothy Lake's North Arm and Little Crater Meadow are great places to spot wildlife which depend on wetlands. Timothy Lake is an artificial lake constructed by Portland General Electric company in 1958 for hydroelectric power. The State of Oregon stocks rainbow and brook trout in this 1400 acre lake. Motorboats are allowed, and a 10 MPH speed limit is in place.

4. Clackamas Rivers

In 1988, Congress designated 47 miles of the Clackamas River, from its origins in the Olallie Lake Scenic Area to Big Cliff, as part of the Federal Wild and Scenic Rivers System. Outstanding scenery and proximity to Portland make this section of the Clackamas River one of the most popular recreation areas in Oregon. The river has carved a deep gorge with rocky cliffs and tree-laden slopes. Whitewater boating and year-round hiking and riding are among the many recreational pursuits here. Facilities are available for day-use and overnight camping beside the river. The Clackamas River contains diverse fish habitats, vital to a productive fishery. In addition, over 1664 km miles of fish-bearing streams and rivers flow into the Clackamas River. Anadromous spring Chinook Salmon, Coho Salmon, and Steelhead Trout use these waters for spawning, rearing, and migration. Resident fish include Cutthroat Trout,

Rainbow Trout, Brook Trout, and the threatened Steelhead and Chinook Salmon species.

IV. Recreations

The Mount Hood National Forest is one of the most-visited National Forests in the United States, with over four million visitors annually. The common recreational activities include fishing, boating, hiking, hunting, horseback-riding, skiing, mountain-biking, berry-picking and mushroom collecting.

There are six main routes to approach the mountain with about 30 total variations for summiting. The climbs range in difficulty from class 2 to class 5.9. The most popular route, dubbed the south route, begins at Timberline Lodge and proceeds up Palmer Glacier to Crater Rock, the large prominence at the head of the glacier. French's Dome is a popular climbing area located on the lower west side of Mt. Hood. This andesite crag offers 14 climbing routes, with heights ranging from 80 feet to 160 feet. The most popular climbing route is the Giant's Staircase, rated at 5.6 degree Most of the routes are fixed with bolts, while some require the occasional natural placement.

Section 2 Mount Rainier—Winter Resort

Mount Rainier is a massive stratovolcano located 54 miles (87 km) southeast of Seattle in the state of Washington, United States. It is the most topographically prominent mountain in the contiguous United States and the Cascade Volcanic Arc, with a summit elevation of 14411 ft (4392 m). Mt. Rainier is considered one of the most dangerous volcanoes in the world, and it is on the Decade Volcano list by IAVCEI (International Association of Volcanology and Chemistry of the Earth's Interior). Because of its large amount of glacial ice, Mt. Rainier could potentially produce massive lahars that would threaten the whole Puyallup River valley. In 1890, the United States Board on Geographic Names declared that the mountain would be known as "Rainier". Following this in 1897, the Pacific Forest Reserve became the Mount Rainier Forest Reserve, and in 1899, the United States set up Mount Rainier National Park, centered this area of about 98000 hectares in order to protect its solemn, frozen natural scenery.

I. Geographical Setting

Mount Rainier is the highest mountain in Washington and the Cascade Range. Mount Rainier has a topographic prominence of 13211 ft (4027 m), greater than K2, the world's second-tallest mountain. On clear days it dominates the southeastern horizon in most of the Seattle-Tacoma metropolitan area to such an extent that locals sometimes refer to it simply as "the Mountain". On days of exceptional clarity, it can also be seen from as far away as Portland, Oregon and Victoria, British Columbia.

There are three summits in Mount Rainier. Its highest peak is considered "Columbia Peak". The following is "Successful Point", with an altitude of 4315 meters, located in the south edge of the summit and at the top ridge of Sarkozy Cliff. The lowest is the "Liberty Cap", with an elevation 4301 meters above sea level, in the northwest edge which can overlook "Free Ridge", "Sunset Theatre", and "Willis Wall".

The summit is topped by two volcanic craters, each more than 1000 ft (305 m) in diameter, with the larger east crater overlapping the west crater. Geothermal heat from the volcano keeps areas of both crater rims free of snow and ice, and has formed the world's largest volcanic glacier cave network, with nearly 2 mi (3.2 km) of passages. A small crater lake about 130 by 30 ft

(40 by 9.1 m) in size and 16 ft (5 m) deep, the highest in North America with a surface elevation of 14203 ft (4329 m), occupies the lowest portion of the west crater below more than 100 ft (30 m) of ice and is accessible only via the caves.

The Carbon, Puyallup, Mowich, Nisqually, and Cowlitz Rivers begin at eponymous glaciers of Mount Rainier. The sources of the White River are Winthrop, Emmons, and Fryingpan Glaciers. The White, Carbon, and Mowich join the Puyallup River, which discharges into Commencement Bay at Tacoma; the Nisqually empties into Puget Sound east of Lacey; and the Cowlitz joins the Columbia River between Kelso and Longview.

There are still a lot of steaming caves and warm springs in Mount Rainier. Towering Mount Rainier is the navigational landmark east to Oregon and shipping into west coast of the Phuket Strait from the Pacific Ocean. Mount Rainier is often shrouded by clouds and fog, only visible on the sunny days in summer. Emmons Glacier, located in its eastern slope, is the largest glacier in America, and the rests, such as Eritrea Glacier, Cowlitz Glacier, and England Hamm Glacier, etc. are all very famous. Widely distributed glaciers melt in summer, thus forming a variety of fast-flowing streams and cascades of waterfalls. And the sound of flowing water echoes in the valley. Here is the most famous tourist resort in the state of Washington, including glaciers, waterfalls, forests, lakes, and abundant wildlife and other natural landscape.

II. Volcanic Activity

Mount Rainier is a stratovolcano in the Cascade Volcanic Arc. Its early lava deposits are estimated at more than 840000 years old. The early deposits formed a "proto-Rainier" or an ancestral cone prior to the present-day cone. The present cone is more than 500000 years old.

Mount Rainier is highly eroded, with glaciers on its slopes, and appears to be made mostly of andesite. Rainier probably once stood even higher than today at about 16000 ft (4900 m) before a major debris avalanche and the resulting Osceola Mudflow approximately 5000 years ago. In the past, Rainier had large debris avalanches, and has also produced enormous lahars (volcanic mudflows) due to the large amount of glacial ice present. Its lahars have reached all the way to the site of present-day Tacoma and south Seattle. This massive avalanche of rock and ice removed the top 1600 ft (500 m) of Rainier, bringing its height down to around 14100 ft (4300 m). About 530 to 550 years ago, the Electron Mudflow occurred, although this was not as large-scale as the Osceola Mudflow.

After the major collapse approximately 5000 years ago, subsequent eruptions of lava and tephra built up the modern summit cone until about as recently as 1000 years ago. As many as 11 Holocene tephra layers have been found in Rainier.

III. Glaciers

Glacier is the most remarkable and dynamic geologic feature of Mount Rainier. Together with everlasting snow areas, the 26 major glaciers cover about 93 square km of the mountain, and the volume of the ice and snow is about 4.2 cubic km.

Glaciers move under the influence of gravity. During May 1970, Nisqually Glacier was measured moving as fast as 29 inches (74 cm) per day. Due to the large quantities of melt water under glacier, flow rates are generally greater in summer than in winter. The volume of glaciers on Mount Rainier has changed significantly in the past. For example, during the last ice age, from about 25000 to 15000 years ago, glaciers covered most of the area which is now the Mount Rainier National Park and extended to the present Puget Sound Basin.

Between the 14th century and 1850, many of the glaciers on Mount Rainier descended along valleys to the farthest extent since the last ice age. Many of the glacier movements occurred worldwide during this time which is known to geologists as the Little Ice Age. During the Little Ice Age, the Nisqually Glacier advanced to a position 650 to 800 ft (200 to 240 m) down valley from the site of the Glacier Bridge, Tahoma and South Tahoma Glaciers merged at the base of Glacier Island, and the terminus of Emmons Glacier reached within 1.2 mi (1.9 km) of the White River Campground.

Retreat of the Little Ice Age glaciers was slow until about 1920 when it became faster. Mount Rainier's glaciers fall to it's third-quarter of height between the Little Ice Age and 1950. From 1950 to the early 1980s, however, many of the major glaciers developed for the relatively cooler temperatures of the mid-century. The development of Carbon, Cowlitz, Emmons, and Nisqually Glaciers during the late 1970s and early 1980s is the result of high snowfalls. Since the early-1980s, however, many glaciers have been thinning and melting and some development have slowed.

IV. Recreations

Mount Rainier is a Yearning place for climbers because of the largest glaciers in the south of Alaska in the USA. It needs two to three days to reach the top for most of the climbers. Climbing teams needs experience in glacier travel, self-rescue, and wilderness travel. About 8000 to 13000 people attempt to climb it each year, and about 90% of them via routes from Camp Muir on the southeast flank, the rest ascend Emmons Glacier via Camp Schurman on the northeast.

Mount Rainier National Park is a good place for skiing and traveling in winter. Hiking, backcountry skiing, photography, and camping in the park is very popular. From 1971 to 1972 the winter snowfall had set a world record in the paradise valley, it provided excellent conditions for skiing, and improved the charming of winter mount Rainier. In mount Rainier, you can stroll along the 145 km mountain road, and it has a poetic name - for a trail. The scenery on both sides of the trails changes with different altitude. The lower is the dense forest, and silver ice world is in the higher places.

The two scenery spots "Heaven" and "Sunrise" are particularly cherished and protected. The "Heaven" located in the north of mount Rainier in southern RON Meyer Mountain, is about 1402 meters high. It is also one of the most popular scenery spots in Mount Rainier National Park. And it has beautiful mountain scenery, the flowing water, beautiful waterfalls and lakes. The "sunrise" located in north of Mount Rainier is the highest scenery spot in National Park, and also the best place for watching the mountain scenery. You can not only enjoy the magnificent spectacle of glaciers, and also overlook another beautiful mount: Mont Baker and the Pacific Ocean.

Section 3 The Shasta Mount—Wonderland of Oz

The Shasta-Trinity National Forest is a federally designated forest in northern California, USA. It is the largest national forest in California and is managed by the U.S. Forest Service. The 2210485-acre (894552 ha.) forest encompasses five wilderness areas, hundreds of mountain lakes and 6278 miles (10103 km) of streams and rivers. Major features include Shasta Lake, the largest man-made lake in California and Mount Shasta.

The Shasta National Forest and the Trinity National Forest were administratively combined in 1954 and officially became the Shasta–Trinity National Forest. The west part (formerly the Trinity National Forest) is mainly located in eastern California Coast Ranges, primarily in Trinity County, and stretches into parts of Tehama, Shasta, and Humboldt counties. It has an area of 1043677 acres (422361 ha.). The east part (formerly the Shasta National Forest) is located between the Central Valley in California and the north part of the Shasta Valley. It covers parts of Siskiyou, Shasta, Trinity, and Modoc counties and has an area of 1166155 acres (471926 ha.).

I. Natural Ecology

The Shasta–Trinity National Forest lies at the intersection of the Eastern Klamath Mountains and the Southern Cascades (Miles & Goudy, 1997), and is largely forested, though at a low elevation. There are areas of chaparral, woodland, and grassland. At high elevations in the Trinity Alps, Eddys, and Mt. Shasta, the forest gives way to montane chaparral, subalpine woodlands, and ultimately to alpine rock and scree.

Starting with lower elevations in the foothills around Shasta Lake, north of Redding, the forests and woodlands are covered by gray pine, knobcone pine, ponderosa pine, blue oak, black oak, quercetin tree and Douglas-fir. Shrubs are quite diversified, including whiteleaf manzanita, wedgeleaf ceanothus, California buckeye, California coffeeberry and western redbud, which are commonly found at lower elevations .

In moist stream canyons, other trees and shrubs prevail—bigleaf maple, western spicebush (Calycanthus Occidentalis), dogwood, white alder and willows. At mid-elevations, sugar pine, incense-cedar, white fir and Jeffrey pine join Douglas-fir, ponderosa pine, and canyon live oak, while the other pines and oaks drop out of the mix. Huckleberry oak, shrub tanoak, manzanita, and bush chinquapin are important understory components. In the east Cascades and north Mt. Shasta, bitterbrushes and Dahurian buckthorns are very common. On the serpentines of Klamath Mountains at middle elevation, incense-cedar and Jeffrey pine woodlands are inhabited by Garrya elliptica, cork tree, and hoary manzanita. Farther west, there are mainly tanoaks, Douglas-firs and golden chinquapins on the long ridge of South Fork Mountain which divides the Shasta–Trinity and Six Rivers National Forests. Upper subalpine forests are full of red firs, mountain hemlocks, western white pines and lodgepole pines; at the highest elevations, foxtails and white bark pines are common. Montane meadows and stream sides in the Klamath Ranges are marked by an abundance of California pitcher plants and western azalea and occasional Orford de cedar.

II. Lakes and Rivers

Shasta, Lewiston and Trinity Lakes are part of the Whiskey–Shasta–Trinity National Recreation Area. Shasta Lake has 365 miles (587 km) of shoreline made up of many arms and inlets. The four major arms of the lake are: Sacramento, McCloud, Squaw Creek and Pit where there are abundant sceneries with unusual geologic and historic flavors.

Lewiston Lake, near the town of Weaverville, lying just downstream from Trinity Dam and Lake and just north of the town of Lewiston, is a constant level lake.

Iron Canyon (northeast of Shasta Lake, near the town of Big Bend), Lewiston, Lake McCloud (south of the town of McCloud), Shasta and Trinity Lakes are large reservoirs extensively used for fishing, boating and camping. Houseboats can also be rented at Shasta Lake.

There are several alpine lakes in the Trinity Divide area (west and southwest of the town of Mt. Shasta City), where people go fishing. The Trinity River, near the town of Weaverville, is very popular for salmon and steelhead angling. The same is true with the Stuart Fork of the Trinity River and such streams as Canyon Creek (closed to fishing below Canyon Creek Falls), Coffee, Grizzly, Rush and Swift Creeks, all of which drain the Trinity Alps Wilderness.

III. Recreations

The Shasta–Trinity National Forest offers a wide range of recreational activities including hiking, backpacking, mountain climbing, horseback riding, camping, boating, fishing, sightseeing, downhill skiing and riding, snowboarding, cross-country skiing, and snowmobiling.

Shasta–Trinity National Forest has over 460 miles (736km) of walk ways including a 154-mile (248 km) section of the Pacific Crest Trail in both the east and west sides.

The 500-mile Volcanic Legacy Scenic Byway, beginning at Lassen Volcanic National Park, stretching to Mount Shasta and ending at Crater Lake National Park, offers a view of northern California's volcanic sceneries.

Beginning in McCloud, the Modoc Volcanic Scenic Byway travels through some unique volcanic sceneries in the eastern forest on its way to Medicine Lake, Lava Beds National Monument, and Tule Lake.

In the lavaflow area of Medicine Lake Volcano, is the Little Mt. Hoffman fire lookout. It now provides lodging and recreation overnight, with its original architecture style properly kept. From a height of 7309 feet (2228 m), Little Mt. Hoffman offers a view of Mt. Shasta, Lassen Peak, Mt. McLoughlin and a variety of other landforms. From the Tule Lake basin in the north to the Fall River valley in the south, the lookout offers a full view of some of northern California's most notable sceneries. There is also Hirz lookout near Lake Shasta and the Post Creek lookout (somewhat near the town of Platina, on the southern end of the forest). The Post Creek lookout was built in 1934 by the Civilian Conservation Corps. With its complete installation, this comfortable cabin accommodates up to eight people. It can be rented, too. In its back room, people can get a great view of the landscape.

Section 4 Blue Ridge Mount & Shenandoah National Park
—Blue Ridge Lizard

Shenandoah National Park encompasses part of the Blue Ridge Mountains in the U.S. state of Virginia, covers an area of nearly 800 km^2. This national park is long and narrow, with the broad Shenandoah River and Valley on the west side, and the rolling hills of the Virginia Piedmont on the east. Although the scenic Skyline Drive is likely the most prominent feature of the Park, almost 40% of the land area 79579 acres (322.04 km^2) has been designated as wilderness and is protected as part of the National Wilderness Preservation System. The highest peak Hawksbill Mountain is 4051 feet (1235 m).

I. Geological Landcapes

Shenandoah National Park lies along the Blue Ridge Mountains in north-central Virginia. These mountains form a distinct highland rising to elevations above 4000 feet (1200 m). Local topographic relief between the Blue Ridge Mountains and Shenandoah Valley exceeds 3000 feet (910 m) at some locations. The crest of the range divides the Shenandoah River drainage basin, part of the Potomac River drainage, on the west side, from the James and Rappahannock River drainage basins on the east side.

Some of the rocks exposed in the park date back to over one billion years in age, making them among the oldest in Virginia. Bedrock in the park includes Grenville-age granitic basement rocks (1.2-1.0 billion years old) and a cover sequence of metamorphosed Neoproterozoic (570-550 million years old) sedimentary and volcanic rocks of the Swift Run and Catoctin formations and early Cambrian (542-520 million years old) clastic rocks of the Chilhowee Group. Quaternary surficial deposits are common and mantle much of the bedrock throughout the park.

The park is located along the western part of the Blue Ridge anticlinorium, a regional-scale Paleozoic structure at the eastern margin of the Appalachian fold and thrust belt. Rocks within the park were folded, faulted, distorted and metamorphosed during the late Paleozoic Alleghanian orogeny (325 to 260million years ago). The rugged topography of Blue Ridge Mountains is a result of differential erosion during the Cenozoic, although some post-Paleozoic tectonic activity occurred in the region.

II. Formation of the Park

Shenandoah was authorized in 1926 and fully established on December 26, 1935. Prior to being a park, much of the area was farmland and there are still remnants of old farms in several places. The Commonwealth of Virginia slowly acquired the land through eminent domain and then gave it to the U.S. Federal Government provided it would be designated a National Park.

In the creation of the park, a number of families and entire communities were required to vacate portions of the Blue Ridge Mountains. Many residents in the 500 homes in eight affected counties of Virginia were vehemently opposed to losing their homes and communities. Most of the families removed came from Madison County, Page County and Rappahannock County.

Nearly 90% of the inhabitants worked on the land for a living. Many worked in the apple orchards in the valley and in areas near the eastern slopes. The work to create the National Park and Skyline Drive began following a terrible drought in 1930 which destroyed the crops of many families in the area who farmed in the mountainous terrain, as well as many of the apple orchards where they worked picking crops. Nevertheless, it remains a fact that they were displaced, often against their will, and even for a very few who managed to stay, their communities were lost. A little-known fact is that, while some families were removed by force, a few others (who mostly had also become difficult to deal with) were allowed to stay after their properties were acquired, living in the park until nature took its course and they gradually died. The policy allowed the elderly and disabled who so wished to remain with life tenancy. The lost communities and homes were a price paid for one of the country's most beautiful National Parks and scenic roadways.

III. Attractions

1. The Corbin Cabin

The Corbin Cabin is a log structure built by George T. Corbin in 1910 in the Nicholson Hollow area of what is now Shenandoah National Park. Corbin was forced to vacate the land on which the cabin sat in 1938, when the land was added to Shenandoah National Park. The cabin is unique and it is one of a small number of buildings located in Nicholson Hollow spared during the creation of the park, and still remains standing despite recent forest fires. The cabin is maintained by the Potomac Appalachian Trail Club and is accessible within the park by means of Nicholson.

2. Camp Hoover

Rapidan Camp (also known at times as Camp Hoover) in Shenandoah National Park in Madison County, Virginia, was built by U.S. President Herbert Hoover and his wife Lou Henry Hoover, and served as their rustic retreat throughout Hoover's administration from 1929 to 1933.

3. Skyline Drive

The park is best known for Skyline Drive, a 105-mile (169 km) road that runs the entire length of the park along the ridge of the mountains. The drive is particularly popular in the fall when the leaves are changing colors. 101 miles (162 km) of the Appalachian Trail are also in the park. Of the trails, one of the most popular is Old Rag Mountain, which offers a thrilling rock scramble and some of the most breathtaking views in Virginia. There is also horseback riding, camping, bicycling, and many waterfalls. The Skyline Drive is the first National Park Service road east of the Mississippi River listed as a National Historic Landmark on the National Register of Historic Places. It is also designated as a National Scenic Byway.

4. The Shenandoah Valley

The Shenandoah Valley is both a geographic valley and cultural region of western Virginia and the Eastern Panhandle of West Virginia in the United States. The valley is bounded to the east by the Blue Ridge Mountains, to the west by the eastern front of the Ridge-and-Valley Appalachians (excluding Massanutten Mountain), to the north by the Potomac River and to the south by the James River. The cultural region covers a larger area that includes all of the valley plus the Virginia highlands to the west, and the Roanoke Valley to the south. It is physiographically located within the Ridge and Valley province and is a portion of the Great Appalachian Valley.

Named for the river that stretches much of its length, the Shenandoah Valley encompasses nine counties in Virginia and two counties in West Virginia. The central section of the Shenandoah Valley is split in half by the Massanutten Mountain range, with the smaller associated Page Valley lying to its east and the Fort Valley within the mountain range.

Chapter 6

World Famous Mountains in South America

Section 1 Araripe Mountain—Plateau Fossil

The Geopark Araripe is located in the Southern Brazilian state of Ceara sedimentary area, belonging to Ceara Araripe sedimentary basins. Located near the equator and the Atlantic Ocean, it has an area of 5000 square kilometers being nearest point from Brazil to Europe and North America. The park was established by Technology and Higher Education Secretariat in Ceara with the cooperation of local university of Cariri. In December 2005, it was included in the Global Geopark Network , and the parks here are mainly known for ancient fossils.

I. Tourism Facilities

Araripe Geopark is located in south Ceara, standing on 750-meter-high Santa Cruz. It is located near the city of Santana Cariri, which can overlook the panoramic view of part of the basin area of Araripe.

Yucca Paleontology Museum is located in the city of Santana Do Caririshi, which is the base for research projects, including local fossil finding. It has become the main channel to publicize the importance of paleontology to visitors. From Santa Cruz, visitors can only reach this research base through several trails. People are interested in combining science with local religions and huge cross which show the local mystery together. This cross shows the past two centuries.

Riacho Meio Park is the best position to observe the rich landscapes of Araripe basin. This area is rich in bushes and there also is a typical local flora and fauna. Representatives of local attractions are the three uncontaminated springs that are still spewing. This area provides food, watchtowers, information station and natural pools along the way. This park is restricted to use and subjected to the supervision of visitors and research community from local school. Its maintaining status of natural environment and amenities are satisfactory. The visitors' reception infrastructure of the park is perfect and it has a Ring Road to reach the most important sights. These attractions can be for people to enjoy and study the flora and fauna and natural water features here.

The countryside of Santana Do Cariri will build Pterosaus park, with an area of 23 hectares, belonging to the local university in Cariri and it will become a major part of the Geopark Araripe and the only park of this type in Brazil. The main purpose of this project is to reconstruct the environment in Chapada Araripe of the Cretaceous period. The initial purpose was to protect and maintain the mining of this region. From the outside layers of sedimentary rocks can be seen in this area, which contains important precious fossil. From this point of view, this area requires a simple construction that is similar to shade sheltered platform. It is to enhance the protection of the building and provide support for the excavation and the paleontological research. By digging, professors, researchers, scholars and visitors will be able to study and understand the local sedimentary layers of fossil storage conditions. Later, we can reshape the earth's life history environment through copies of animals and plant fossils of the Cretaceous period. Cretaceous period is the period of the flower appearing on earth. Plant fossils can often be found in sedimentary rocks and these rocks are used in paving the house ground and outside wall decoration of municipal building. Pterosaurs Park as another center of local tour will be further consolidated. Although this remote village has no auxiliary facilities, it receives annually about 18 thousand visitors every year, including researchers and academics, who are interested in studying the 7000 fossils collected in the Yucca Paleontology Museum.

II. Typical Landscapes

The historic Chavez mine is a part of "Chavez Mining and Industry" mining company. It explores several mines located in Santana Do Cariri and the city of new Olinda, providing raw materials for the cement production enterprises and plants acid and some special additives for cast and wash mining. Choosing this place as a major part of the Araripe Geopark is to reveal the potentially instructive importance of the geological gypsum layers. This terrain renders its two unconnected stratum whose upper layer is firmer. On the other hand, since this is a mine no longer in use, so this area was converted into useful gypsum. Protection of the natural environment and the surrounding topography can be perfect embodiment. At present, due to the exploitation of the hole formed by the mine opening, surrounding environment suffers strong impact, but due to the re-arrangement of the outside cover, the impact is thus eased. The establishment of Geopark Araripe and its system has an educational effect on raising the awareness of local people to protect and maintain these paleontological heritages. At the same time, it offers a variety of options for local tourism development, creates job opportunities, generates income for all people and brings another useful way for this uncontrolled exploitation of important fossil storage.

Cariri Quarry, three kilometers from the town of new Olinda, you can get there through CE-166 expressway between Olinda and Santana Do Cariri. It consist of invertebrates, vertebrates and plant fossils, whose rocks are yellow to cream-colored horizontal parallel limestone flakes. Mining activities in Cariri alters the natural landscape and forms a new landscape. Some of these large number of fossils can be collected with restriction, because many of them are the scrap produced after exploitation. Since the 19th century, there is a tradition in the local building to use Cariri stones, which is unlike the rest places in this state who use bricks.

A series of small waterfalls are distributed in the source of Batateira River, whose scenery is very beautiful, covered with a large number of dense vegetation that has not been exploited by human beings. The region of Batateura river is divided into regions for different purposes, such as recreation, services and supplies. At the source of the river, near a spring there is lush vegetation, some trails, some private estates and clubs in the middle of roadsides and the farm. Despite having a public club, people also use the river water to develop a artificial swimming pool, a small waterfall and some other entertainment facilities. People also use the water to supply the entire building. Most of the regional distributions are large farms and residentials. Around the Crato city, a series of springs provide a water source to the creeks and rivers in this region and some traditional leisure activities and eco-tourism have been developed in this resorts. Visitors can walk through some trails to reach the area to explore its rich natural landscape.

Colina Do Horto area has completely become the city area of Juazeiro Do Norte, so it is occupied by a large number of buildings, but there are still very few natural features. Tourism-related activities, especially religious tourism, from pilgrimage events to the Padre Cicero have been strengthened. It is regarded as one of the most important religious event of whole Brazil. In the 5 main activities here every year, more than 2.5 million pilgrims from northeastern area and other places of Brazil gather here. During the pilgrimage, Colina Do Horto not only becomes the pilgrimage center with a large crowd, holly articles, the prayer place of nine consecutive days and the visiting places of religious believers, but also the shopping mall of religious handmade products.

III. Development Strategy

Government of Ceara state successfully held the "Geopark and Geological Tourism International Symposium" in the Nordeste Bank, Passare, Fortaleza through the city secretariat. The main purpose of this symposium was to introduce the "UNESCO World Geopark Plan" to the participants, emphasizing the importance of Araripe geopark for the development of Cariri, contributing to creating the new geopark in Brazil and America. Although Araripe geopark and Ceara government have made a lot of efforts, it is still a great challenge for them to portray Araripe to be a successful example of the global geopark network. For this reason, Araripe geopark and Ceara government have decided to learn the successful example—Portugal Natuteqiao Geopark, formulating "City Program" strategy, led by the city secretariat, tourism, environment, culture and science secretariat, regional university of Cariri and other entities including local company and culture, social enterprises. Moreover, this strategy is also possible for young people to join in it through the university, local groups and a combination of geology, biology, anthropology, history, archaeology, museology, economics, architecture, environmental science, management, marketing, design, information science, tourism and many other subject's international and domestic cooperation. What is most important is to establish a management agency for this strategy to ensure the Ararip geopark stability and running outside the political cycle. An important goal of the "city program" is to make use of the geological heritage which has not been explored now to promote tourism.

Section 2 Guaramiranga Mountain Chain—Ecological Forest

Guaramiranga Mountain Chain, covering an area of 3822 km^2, stands in Northeastern state of Ceará in Brazil. It includes 12 autonomous regions and it is located at an altitude of 865 m. Its mountains and valleys present a beautiful picture.

I. Natural Features

Guaramiranga is known locally for its temperate climate and lush green scenery. The temperature in Guaramiranga varies between 15 and 23 degrees Celsius through the year. Its average annual rainfall is about 1560 mm and its average annual temperature is 20.9°C. September is the driest season of a year, with a rainfall of only 28 mm. November is the warmest seasaon, with an average temperature of 21.6°C. It is a tropical forest with colorful flowers. The majotity of the tropical forest is located at high altitude, and sub-tropical rain forest is at medium altitude. In the area of low altitude, there are lots of thick shrubberies.

II. Leisure and Tourism

The tropical rain forest and the traditional, unique villages there give tourists a feeling of primitive ecology, where they can enjoy music, operas, art and some original ecology experiences. In local language, Guaramiran refers to "red bird". For those who are fond of outdoor sports and ecological tour, it is a good place to go climbing, hiking, bicycle-riding, walking and having a bird's-eye view of the scenery. Of course, you can also experience local culture, music, opera and arts festivals.

There is only an hour's driving from Mt. Guaramiranga to the capital, Fortaleza, which is in a Northeastern state of Brazil. Seeing from the highest point of the mountain, you can enjoy two different spectacular views: one is a semiarid zone, also called "steppe"; the other is mountains with thick and green plants. Many comfortable hotels, restaurants are available all year round. Guaramiranga hosts a number of events throughout the year including a Festival of Jazz&Blues which is held every Carnival.Besides its culture, its natural scenery, exquisite handicrafts and cooking are also appeal to tourists.

Section 3 Mt. Quixadá—Paradise of Paragliding

Mt. Quixadá, Brazil, is located in the oldest mountain which came into being at Precambrian, about 600 million years ago. The mountain area is characterized by weathering, which carves countless cliffs and steep rock peaks. The stone forests make the mountains not only a unique landscape, but also a paradise for climbing and other extreme sports.

I. Natural Landscapes

The predominant climate type in Quixadá is tropical semiarid, and the rainfall there in winter is heavier than that in summer. The annual average temperature is 27.1°C, and the rainfall average is 765 mm a year. The driest month there is October with the rainfall of only 2 mm. Quixadá covers a hyperarid area, planted with mainly caatinga-cactus and dense spiny shrubs, while at the higher area, there is a forest of spiny plants.

II. Tourism Development

There's a natural memorial hall of the stone forest in Quixada, which is about 160 kilometers away from Fortaleza. It's a conservation area aiming at protecting the rare, unique and beautiful stone forest.

For those who have a passion for outdoor sports and ecotourism, this is an ideal place for them to experience various activities, such as hiking, speed skating, mountain-climbing, cross-country tours, horse riding, cycling, walking, eye views, gliding, parachuting, etc. Quixadá and Ibiapaba mountains are hailed as the "Paradise for Paragliding" (covering over 300km).

Though not fully developed yet, Quixadá has the greatest potential for tourism, particularly eco-tourism and extreme sports tourism. In addition to the boulders in the area, extreme sports are also available on "Acude do Cedro", the oldest dam in Brazil with a history of over a hundred years. Two nature reserves in this area are the Natural Stone Forest Memorial built in October 31, 2002, and a conservation area of private heritage-Texas Blues Manor founded in November 5,1998.

Section 4 Mt. Ibipaba—Paradise of Skydiving

Mt. Ibipaba stretches over 110 km to the northeast part of Ceara, with more than 40 km of seashore and many peaks over 1000 m. There are many cliffs in northeast Ceara while it slopes gently in the west, with an average height of 750 m.

I. Climate and Vegetation

In the tropical Mt. Ibipaba, the rainfall in winter is heavier than that in summer. Its average annual temperature is 26.1°C and average annual rainfall is 725 mm. November is the hottest time of a year, with an average temperature of 27.1°C. The average temperature in June is 25°C but the recorded temperature of some cities there can be as low as 13°C. Mt. Ibipaba has a moderate climate all year round and the rain mainly falls in Ceara. But the rainfall in the area about several kilometers west of Ceara decreases sharply, where semiarid vegetation can be found. The southern part of Mt. Ibipaba is mainly tropical grassland, but the northeastern part is covered with thick forests known as "Atlantic forests". It is abundant for vegetables and flowers, which are exported to Europe, and also sugarcanes.

II. Leisure and Tourism

Natives of different ethnic groups live together in this famous tourist resort, such as the Tapuias and the Tabajaras. Before the invasion of Portuguese, these aborigines introduced many kinds of crops to Europeans.

Mt. Ibipaba is a paradise for those who love ecological tour, where they can enjoy hiking, rock fall, mountain biking, bird watching, gliding. With a flight distance of over 300 km, the resort is hailed as the "paradise of skydiving". Besides, you can enjoy multi-culture, music, films and arts festivals.

Section 5 Kamaqua Highland—Ecological Highland

I. Ecological Tourism

Kamaqua Highlands is located in Rio Grande do Sul, south of Brazil. It is the headstream of Kamaqua River, and the vegetation along the hills and streams—sparse woods, grassland and shrubs—are reserved properly.

Inhabitants in its southeast part mainly work on family husbandry. Due to the characteristics of its social economy and ecological environment with the absence of traditional science, modern agriculture is yet to be developed in the region.

The economy there mainly depends on livestock like cattle and sheep. Local specialties include bread, cake, cheese, wine, honey and jam. Tourism for original ecology and sightseeing is also springing up.

II. Tourism Development

Kamaqua Highlands Project puts forward the regional development strategies and action plans to encourage the integrated sustainable development. The project initiated in 2006 is intended to promote and encourage animal husbandry as it's regarded as an ecological mode of production taking advantage of local grassland and other natural resources. With its development in the past 6 years, the project has now started to create the collective brand of Kamaqua. The brand is applied to some local products, such as mutton, homemade cakes, arts and crafts, leather, wool, tourism activities. The project also considers common history of the region as well as its social, environmental, cultural and economic characteristic. Kamaqua Project is considered to be a success in developing the differential agriculture in about half of the southern region of Rio Grande do Sul. The participation of Brazilian Agricultural Research Corporation (Embrapa) in the project aims at developing an economic practice based on the agrarian structure of household ownership.

Chapter 7

World Famous Mountains in Oceania

Section 1 Mount Gambier—Geological Volcano

The city of Gambier is located on the flanks of an extinct volcano. With a population of about 27000 people. it is the largest regional city in Southern Australia. As the regional city, it draws people from the southeast and Victoria Harbor to come here for shopping, sporting, pub-going and fine food. The location of the city is indirectly related to the volcano, but the local water resources are directly related to it. The relatively shallow groundwater was attractive to the early settlers, but eventually the water inside the crater known as the Blue Lake became the water source to supply a slowly growing population. The region supports a large tourism industry of national and international guests who flock to view the spectacular volcanics and the unique blue Lake which changes colour twice a year. Mount Gambier is the largest city of southern Australia. With 436 km from Adelaide and 441 km from Melbourne, and it is an easy drive from either city. Mount Gambier's location between Adelaide and Melbourne makes it an ideal stopover for travellers to and from Kangaroo Island, and also a perfect destination for longer stays to enjoy the sea city's natural and cultural beauty of the surrounding region, the caves and sinkholes, coastline, rivers, lakes and wineries.

I. Ecological Environment

Mount Gambier got its first name on December 3, 1800, when Lieutenant James Grant with Lady Nelson inspected here and sighted two prominent peaks, of which he named one as Gambier's Mountain after Lord Gambier. It was not until 1839 that Stephen Henty from Portland became the first white man to actually gaze on the beauty of the Blue Lake. He returned with cattles in 1841. Huts were built for his stockman near The Valley Lake and the cave in the centre of the city was used as a water supply. Stockyards were erected in the then dry bed of Browns Lake showing that water levels have been known to fall then rise in variable rainfalls. As far back as 1859 water levels of the Leg of Mutton Lake were recorded as being too low to quench the thirst of a bullock team. By 1875 levels had risen to form the Leg of Mutton shape. The later part of this century was notable for very high rainfall totals and also land clearing had been so significant that government authorities were beginning to encourage landowners to replanting trees.

The lushness of the Mount Gambier area is not only due to its annual rainfall. Its life blood is the abundance of underground water which lies in the wedge shaped block of limestone beneath the earth's surface. Moving slowly southwards towards the ocean through the limestone and its arterial system of caves and crevices, water is plentiful and contributes to the beauty of the city's parks and gardens and to the rural sector when pumped to the surface. Limestone is formed in a marine environment and made up of fossils and corals, extends from the coast to the Murray River. At Port MacDonnell located on the coast, the limestone is more than 320 metres thick. Rainfall soaks down through the surface into the limestone which acts like a huge sponge and is stored in the pore spaces. Known as an unconfined aquifer due to the groundwater being stored at atmospheric pressure, a gradient exists where the inland water is located higher than sea-level and slowly moves southwards underground, finally discharging to the ocean all along the southern coast. This abundance of extractable "groundwater" contributes greatly to the beauty of the city's parks and gardens and to the rural sector. Mount Gambier's famous Blue Lake, Little Blue Lake, Ewens Ponds and Piccaninnie Ponds are just a few of the locations which provide a "window" into this underground water system.

II. Geomorphologic Landscapes

Located in Southern Australia on the plains of Victoria's Western district and South Australia's South East (Limestone Coast) is Australia's most extensive volcanic province. The Mount Gambier sub-province is the westernmost part of the Newer Volcanics Province and is located in the South East region of South Australia. It hosts 17 eruptive centres (Sheard, 1990) including the youngest volcanic centres of the entire province. These centres being Mount Gambier and Mount Schank show a great complexity in eruption styles and also composition (Van Otterloo et al. 2010). A maximum volcanic thickness of 80 cm has been established for Mount Gambier. Coverage area is 65 km^2 were estimated.

Mount Gambier is located within what is known as the Otway Basin. It was formed about 70 million years ago when Australia separated from the super continent known as Gondwanaland. The plate is still moving towards Asia at around 5 to7 centimetres per year, eventually becoming part of that landmass. 30 million years ago, the land was covered with a warm shallow ocean. The remains of fish bones, shells and fossils fell to the ocean floor, forming a huge wedge of limestone which now underlies the entire region - thus the name "The Limestone Coast" and Mount Gambier - Heart of the Limestone Coast.The sea had transgressed and regressed across this part of Australia about three times. When travelling through the lower part of the south east, each of the hills that are driven over are sand dunes and represent points where the sea stopped for a period of time. It is now also known that the sand dunes overlay geological faults.

Creeks from both Ewens Ponds and Piccaninnie Ponds carry millions of litres of water an hour to the ocean. Just down the beach from Piccaninnie Ponds, discharging groundwater can be seen bubbling up through the sandy beach.

Rural industries draw underground water from bores sunk at various depths into the limestone creating not only a richness of colour but also significant wealth generation to the region. Limestone is an important product to industry. It is a major building stone for domestic and industrial buildings and is used extensively for road construction. Other significant uses include agricultural lime, glass and fibre-glass, sculpture and calcium based products such as tablets, toothpaste and talcum powder. As the underground water slowly extends towards the coast, thus causing the solution of the limestone structure, there are many cave formation near this district.

III. The Blue Lake

There are many famous Blue Lakes in the world with two well-known examples—Crater Lake and Lake Tahoe in USA. Mount Gambier's Blue Lake is unique being the only example to change colour each year. Each year in response to a warming of the air temperature which is transferred to the lake's surface water, it gradually changes from the winter sombre blue to brilliant turquoise blue, before returning to its winter hue in March.

Colour Change Theory—Why is the Blue Lake blue?

A range of explanations have been proposed over the last century for the lakes colour change. It was also proposed that the blue colour should be caused by fluorescence of dissolved organic matter which builds up seasonally in the upper layers of the lake. Another theory was that the blue colour was caused by absorption of all incident visible radiation except blue by finely crystalline calcite in the surface of the lake. However, the natural colour of water is blue, for the same reason the sky is blue. Therefore, the Blue Lake (and all lakes) should be blue. The question to answer therefore: Why does the Blue Lake become less blue in winter?

Winter—August

In winter the lake is green-grey. It is thoroughly stirred up with dead algae which are mixed into the top of the lake at its lowest. The lake appears less blue due to absorption of blue light by humic substances in the near-surface water. Low rates of calcite precipitation are insufficient to remove the humic substances from the water column hence the water clarity is poor.

Autumn—March

As the top layer of water cools in autumn the calcite production slows dramatically but the mass flux of organic material continues. The concentrations of algae in the near surface water increases and the colour returns to aqua. New and old humic substances are mixed into the surface water from below, which is the probable cause of the colour change. The addition of humic substances to the water increases the absorbency of light in the blue end of the spectrum.

Summer—February

In summer, the calcite continues to form. The calcite continues to strip the humic substances (which come mostly from dead algae in the lake) from the water (through a chemical reaction) in the top of the lake, and the calcite and humic substances settle to the bottom of the lake. As more and more humic substances are removed through the summer, the lake becomes deeper and deeper blue. The humis substances being produced by algae deeper in the lake do not get into the water near the top of the lake because the lake stratification in summer prevents mixing of the two water layers.

Spring—November

The lake commences stratification in spring forming a thin layer of warm water which cuts off deep circulation in the lake. Degassing of CO_2 modifies the PH of the surface water promoting precipitation of calcite. An abundance of white calcite forms near the surface of the lake, making the water appear brighter blue. The calcite comes from the groundwater inflow from the adjacent limestone and dolomite aquifer. The high rates of calcite production remove the humic acids from the water column. The spring colour change results principally from the introduction of significant quantities of fine crystalline calcite.

IV. Travel and Leisure

Tourism generates around $100 million for the Mount Gambier economy. The city is a major accommodation gateway for the region. Major tourism attractions include the Blue Lake and Valley Lake Wildlife Park and caves such as Umpherston Sinkhole, Cave Gardens and Engelbrecht Cave. The region around Mount Gambier also has many water-filled caves and sinkholes which attract cave divers from around the globe. Popular sites include Ewens Ponds and Piccaninnie Ponds.

The City Council has put a large amount of money into developing a site at the main traffic artery known as the Main Corner. Inside the building many of the region stories are shown by films of which there are two most attractive for public enjoyment. One film details the indigenous story of the regional volcanic history which starts in the mount burr area, and by travelling then to Mount Schank before finally stopping at Mount Gambier, the following part of this film is the story of what is described around the location of the new volcano, describing in graphic details the volcanic history of western Victoria before migration of South Australia.

Section 2 Southern Alps—Mountain for Leisure

New Zealand is located in the South Pacific Ocean, between Antarctica and the Equator. New Zealand consists of the north island and south island, Stewart Island and some islands nearby. It covers an area of 27.0534 square kilometers. The coastline is 6900 kilometers long. The territory of mountains, plains, mountains and hills accounts for about 75% of its total area. The four seasons is not obvious, the temperature difference is small. New Zealand has a temperate climate with moderately high rainfall and many hours of sunshine. While the far north has subtropical weather during summer, and inland alpine areas of the South Island can be as cold as-10°C (14°F) in winter, most of the country lies close to the coast, which means mild temperatures. Among the total population, 78.8% are the immigrants of Europe, 14.5% are Maoris and 6.7% are Asian people. Southern Alps is the mountain range on South Island, New Zealand. It is the highest range in Australasia. Making up the loftiest portion of the mountains that extend the length of the island, the Alps extend from Haast Pass, at the head of Wanaka Lake, northeastward to Arthur's Pass. They vary in elevation from 3000 feet (900 meters) to 16 peaks above 10000 feet (3050 meters) and culminate in Mount Cook (12316 feet [3754 meters]). Glaciers descend from the permanently snow-clad top of the range, and major

rivers. Therefore there are abundant earthquakes in this area.

New Zealand's Southern Alps have a number of glaciers, the largest being Tasman glacier, which you can view by taking a short walk from Mount Cook village. New Zealand's most famous glaciers are the Franz Josef and Fox on the South Island's West Coast. Gouged out by moving ice over thousands of years, these spectacular glaciers are easily accessible to mountaineers and hikers. You can walk up to the glaciers or do a heli-hike. The sunlight here can quickly burn skin from September to April, especially between 10am and 4pm, even on cloudy days. New Zealand's average rainfall is high and evenly spread throughout the year. Over the northern and central areas of New Zealand more rain falls in winter than in summer, whereas for much of the southern part of New Zealand, winter is the season of least rainfall. As well as producing areas of stunning native forest, the high rainfall makes New Zealand an ideal place for farming and horticulture. Snow typically appears during the months of June through October, though cold snaps can occur outside these months. Most snow in New Zealand falls in the mountainous areas, like the Central Plateau in the north, and the Southern Alps in the south. It also falls heavily in inland Canterbury and Otago. The North Island of New Zealand has a "spine" of mountain ranges running through the middle, with gentle rolling farmland on both sides. The central North Island is dominated by the Volcanic Plateau, an active volcanic and thermal area. The massive Southern Alps form the backbone of the South Island. To the east of the Southern Alps is the rolling farmland of Otago and Southland, and the vast, flat Canterbury Plains. New Zealand's oldest rocks are over 500 million years old, and were once part of Gondwanaland. This massive super-continent started to split up about 160 million years ago, and New Zealand separated from it about 85 million years ago. New Zealand sits on two tectonic plates —the Pacific and the Australian. Fifteen of these gigantic moving chunks of crust make up the Earth's surface. The North Island and some parts of the South Island sit on the Australian Plate, while the rest of the South Island sits on the Pacific. Because these plates are constantly shifting and grinding into each other, New Zealand gets a lot of geological action.

I. The Misty Cloud

Mount Cook National Park is in the South Island in New Zealand. The region is renowned for its incredibly clear starry nights, brilliant sunny days, remarkable turquoise blue lakes, valleys of emerald green and snow-capped mountains. The park covers a little over 700 km^2. Glaciers cover 40% of the park area. There are 15 peaks over 3000 metres and about 140 peaks over 2000 metres. Among them the highest mountain is Mt. Cook, at 3753 metres, which is also the second highest mountain in Oceania. In a Maoris legend, the Mother of the Earth and the Father of the Sky combined and gave birth to a lot of children. After they arrived at New Zealand, they changed the huge into South Mountain and the children into Mount Cook, one of which is called "Aorangi", that is "the misty cloud", referring to the glaciers they saw.

Glaciers, steep, mountain forests, springs, and wild animals make up the national park. About two thirds of the park is covered by beech trees and podocarpus macrophyllus, some of which are 800 years old. Parrots in the park include the kea, the only alpine parrot and the well-camouflaged pipit. Most of the park is above the tree line so that the plant life consists mainly of alpine plants such as the Mount Cook lily.

Before the erosion of glaciers, there are two beautiful lakes, Lake Pukaki and Lake Tekapo. Behind them are Mt. Cook and all the peaks. The alpine village of Mount Cook provides a host of accommodation and is a stepping stone to numerous activities from thrilling scenic flights to leisurely hikes, glacier boat tours, superb fly fishing and 4WD adventures. The alpine village of Mount Cook, located in Mount Cook National Park, provides a range of accommodation from an international style hotel to motels, backpackers and camping.

During the winter guided ski experiences onto New Zealand's longest glacier, the Tasman, is a popular activity and a unique Mount Cook wedding location. The springboard for any holiday with easy access to the awe-inspiring beauty of Mount Cook, Twizel is just 20 minutes from 5 boating and leisure lakes, including a world class rowing course and Formula One speedboat area. Twizel's extensive outdoor options include helibiking, skydiving, kayaking, golf, Lord of the Rings tours, flyfishing, Kaki breeding hide tours and more. Central to all the attractions of the Mount Cook Mackenzie region, with the Southern Alps as a backdrop, the alpine retreat of Twizel is close to five picturesque lakes, including a world-standard rowing course and Formula One class boating area at Lake Ruataniwha.If fishing is your love and catching salmon, brown or 17kg (37.4lb) rainbow trout is what you dream of then don't go past any of Twizel's rivers, lakes or canals.

II. The City of Adventure

Located on the northern shore of Lake Wakatipu, Queenstown is a beautiful town with an altitude of 310 meters, surrounded by Southern Alps boasting of picturesque mountain and lake sceneries. Its population is only 18000, of whom 80% are of European and American descent, 10% Asian and 10% other races. According to some geographical research, in the Ice Age about 15000 years ago, Queenstown was covered by glaciers. Because of its varied geographical landscape, New Zealand has been hailed as a "living geography classroom". Meanwhile, Queenstown is a region of the most breathtaking landscape in the country, hence known as "the most famous paradise for outdoor activities".

Queenstown has the world's first commercial bungee site—Kawarau

Bridge, whose operation could be dated back to 1988. Inspired by the vine bungee jumping in Vanuatu, Henry van Asch and AJ Hackett from New Zealand created this unique tourism program—bungee jumping for their motherland. Since then, this activity has swept the globe with its fascination.

In addition, Queenstown is also the birthplace of commercial jet boating. Visitors can enjoy the magnificent scenery of the canyon on the famous Shotover River and take the Kawarau Jet in Queenstown Pier to experience the excitement provided by Shotover River Canyons. Rafting is available on Shotover River and Kawarau River all year round. Even in the winter, you can also take a helicopter to Shotover River to enjoy the fun of rafting there. Among all the rivers that provide rafting services, Kawarau River has the largest flow. Therefore, it is an ideal choice for beginners. If you seek much more thrill, Skippers Canyon on Shotover River will be a real challenge for you. As a winter resort, Queenstown has several ski fields. Among them, Coronet Peak is the oldest and most renowned skifield in the Southern Lakes region. Whether it is snowboarding or freestyle skiing, or come alone or with the whole family, the varied landforms and terrains in the Coronet Peak could meet the requirements of any person. Typically, the skiing season is from early June to October. When winter is over, the ski runs will become biking downhill trails.

III. The Blue Treasure—Lake Tekapo

Located at the eastern foot of the Southern Alps, Lake Tekapo is a glacier damming lake in the middle of the South Island of New Zealand. It covers an area of 96 square km with its length of about 24 km, width 6 km and depth 190 meters. Lake Tekapo is just like a crystal clear sapphire, hiding in the Southern Alps between Christchurch and Queenstown. New Zealand's highest peak Mount Cook standing majestically in the distance with the gentle Lake Tekapo's quiet accompany by its side, like a mirror reflecting Mount Cook's stalwart figure. The lake's original outflow was at its southern end, into the Tekapo River. Later, water from the lake is diverted through a tunnel under the town to the power stations, with a height of 8 meters. Through 20000 years, Lake Tekapo is formed by the erosion of the glaciers of the Southern Alps and surrounded by the piles of rockfill. The water comes from the melting of the snow in the Mount Cook and other mountains, so the water temperature has been maintained at 7-10 degrees Celsius, not suitable for swimming, but suitable for trouts' survival. Because the regulation of dams, the water is maintained at an altitude between 704-710 meters. The exit of the dam is the lake port, and the water flows eastward into the South Pacific. The charming

Lake Tekapo is surrounded by trees shrouded in brilliant sunshine and endless snow-capped mountains. Originally, it is just an untapped glacier. The fine rock powder and dust caused by ice movement was first suspended in the water. Through years of accumulation, they become special turquoise rocks in the bottom of the lake. In the sunlight, the surface of the lake will appear to be milk blue magically, just like a fascinating dream.

On the lakeshore, there grows a very special type of flower, which will turn lavender-like purple when fully muture.This beautiful wildflower is lupine, so outstanding and unforgetable against backdrop of blue water and green grasslands.Whether you come in passionate summer or freezing winter, Lake Tekapo will let you enjoy endless tourism activities, such as, a flight viewing the whole picture of the Lake, biking in nearby mountains, horseback riding, sea kayaking and trout fishing. In summer, you can go water-skiing on the Lake; in winter, you can go skiing in Mount Cook. You can even look through the telescope to count the stars under the romantic night sky.

Church of the Good Shepherd was built in 1935 and named to honor a bravery shepherd dog for its contribution in the development of the mountain areas. This simple and unsophisticated stone-made church has become a symbol of Lake Tekapo. Through its windows, the green grass, purple lupine, blue water and white snow-capped mountains are so artistically arranged in the frame, just like a fine painting. It is an absolutely dreamlike feeling for tourists.

IV. Paradise of the Wild Life

Kaikoura is a small town between Christchurch and Picton. It takes 2.5 hours' drive to the North of Christchurch, which is the largest city of the South Island. It is the gateway to the Southern Ocean's Marine Mammal Sanctuary and one of the very few places where people can see through the whales, dolphins, seals, albatross, penguins and other seabirds in one day. Warm tropical Bay and rich nutrient cold from the South Pole intersect here. The nutrition is mixed into Canyon and then pushed on to the ocean surface, bringing lots of plankton. The formation of the phytoplankton provides food for zooplankton and krill which are the food of squid and small fish. As the food chain, the squid and small fish become the food of big fish, birds, seals, dolphins, sharks and whales. However, this small peninsular is located on the east coast of the Southern Island and forms a paradise of all kinds of the marine lifes.

You can take a cruise trip on the sea. During the trip, you will get the valuable opportunities to appreciate the lagenorhynchus obscurus, hector's Dolphin, New Zealand fur seals, etc. The lovely seals seem stupid on the continent but rather cute in the water. The most surprising one must be sperm whale. You will find their elegant streamline body dancing near and far in the blue ocean occasionally just like a slim beauty. Dusky dolphin is the special animal in rich marine biota on Kaikoura coast and one of cheerful and lively elves in the Southern Ocean. There are various kinds of sea birds in the Kaikoura town where is famous of Seals, penguins and a whole host of fish and shellfish. Kaikoura is the largest inhabitant of albatross. More than 14 kinds of species of albatross come to this small town every year. It brings you an unforgetable diving experience when various kinds of marine animals live along the coastline of Kaikoura. Being escorted, you will explore the sea forests and the lime coral reefs, in which live the lobsters, octopus, long shell sponge and invertebrate animals.

Bibliography

[1] Chen Shasha, Sun Keqin. Study on Sustainable Development of World Cultural and Natural Heritage——A Case of Mount Emei and Leshan Giant Buddha[J]. Resource Development & Market. 2010(12).
[2] Ge Xiaoyin. Literati and Scenic Spots[M]. Beijing: Democracy & Science,1992.
[3] Han Sangil[Korea]. Korea Soraksan National Park[J]. Journal of Chinese Landscape Architecture,2005(11).
[4] Han Xin. Well-known Mountains of the World[M]. Beijing: Orient Press,2007.
[5] Hu Shanfeng. Development and Sustainable Utlization of Huangshan Mountain[J]. Scientia Geographica Sinica, 2002(3).
[6] Hu Shanfeng, Zhu Hongbing. On the Tourism Sustainable Development of Heritage Site with Mountains—a Case Study of Huangshan Mountain Scenic Area[J]. Journal of Hefei University of Technology(Social Sciences),2013(1).
[7] Hu Wenwen, Zhangyin. Evaluation of Bi-type tourist destinations to the structure of the recreational value – a Case Study of Beijing Fragrant Hill Park[J]. Tourism Forum, 2012(1).
[8] Jin Lijuan. Research on Forest Recreational Resource Evaluation and Management Countermeasure of the Fragrant Hill Park[D]. Thesis of Forestry University of Beijing, 2005.
[9] Kirkpatrick, R. (1999) Bateman Contemporary Atlas of New Zealand. Auckland: David Bateman.
[10] Lambert, M. (ed) (1989) Air New Zealand Almanack Wellington: New Zealand Press Association.
[11] Li Qunxiao. On Tourism Economy of Fragrance Hill[D]. Thesis of Minzu University of China, 2012.

[12] Li Tiesong, Hu Dapeng. Study on the Types and Exploitation of Tourist Resources in Mount Emei[J]. Journal of Sichuan Teachers College(Philosophy & Social Sciences), 2000(4).

[13] Li Xuefei. Study on the Tourism Environment Bearing Capacity of Mount Emei Scenic Area[J]. Academic Trends, 2007(2).

[14] Liu Qiang. Research on the Value of Chinese Famous Mountainous Scenic Spots from the Perspective of Cultural Landscape. An Hui Agriculture Science[J], 2012,40(15).

[15] Liu Shuzhen, Li Yougen. SWOT Analysis of the Tourism Development of Huangshan City[J]. Value Engineering, 2009(1).

[16] Lu Jingshan, Dong Shubao. Famous Mountains of the World (4th Edition)[M]. Changchun: Changchun Press, 2004.

[17] Lu yunting. On Characteristics, Categories and Tourism Functions of Famous Mountains[J]. Resource Guide Journal, 2009(6).

[18] Luo Hui. Probe of Protection Planning of World Heritage Sites— a Case Study of Mount E'mei Scenic Spot[J]. Planners, 2007(3).

[19] Ma Aiyun, Jia Suhong, Jiang Hong. Advantages of Moun Tai's Tourism Resources and Protection of Ecology Environment[J]. Journal of Tai'an Institute of Education, 2008(3).

[20] Huangshan Mountain. Baidu Encyclopedia.

[21] Orsman, H. and Moore, J. (eds) (1988) Heinemann Dictionary of New Zealand Quotations. Auckland: Heinemann.

[22] QIN Chengxun, Wang Jie. On the Development of Mountain Economy of China's Western Regions on the Basis of Ecological Civilization[J]. Ecological Economy, 2012(10).

[23] Qiu Jianping. Geological Landscape of South Africa's Table Mountain[J]. Zhejiang Land & Resources, 2010(1).

[24] Reed, A. W. (1975) Place Names of New Zealand. Wellington: A.H. & A.W. Reed.

[25] Tang Qianyou. On Mount Fuji's Image in Chinese Poetry of Japan. Journal of Anhui University(Philosophy & Social Sciences), 2012(6).

[26] Wang Haozheng. Record of Actual Dangerous Events in Chinese Climbers' Climbing the World's Top Seven Mountains. China Social Sciences Press, 2002.

[27] Wang Juan, Wen Fei. The Spatial and Temporal Characteristics of the International Tourism Market in Huangshan Mountain Scenic Spot[J]. Tourism Forum, 2007(8).

[28] Wu Yanzhao. Research on the Integration of Tourism Resources in Huangshan City[D]. Thesis of Minzu University of China, 2011.

[29] Xie Ninggao. Famous Mountains and Long Rivers of China[M]. Beijing: China International Broadcasting Publishing House, 2010.

[30] Xie Ninggao. Famous Mountains, Scenery and Legacy[M]. Beijing: Zhonghua Publishing House, 2011.

[31] Xu Bin. Famous Mountains of the World[M]. Changchun: Changchun Press, 2007.

[32] Yang Jiong, Meng Hua, Wang Leiting, Niu Jian. Protection and Development of Geological Heritage Based on Public Cognition——A Case of Mount Tai Geopark[J]. Resource Development & Market, 2010(1).

[33] Yang Kun. Competitiveness Research on Taishan Scenic Spots[D]. Thesis of Ocean University of China, 2012.

[34] Yang Naiyun, Lei Falin. Chocolate Hills & Tarsier[J]. Tourism, 2007(1).

[35] Zangmin. Study on Management Mode to Tourism Resource and Sustainable Development Strategy of Eco-tourism in Mount Tai[D]. Thesis of Shandong Agriculture University, 2010.

[36] Zhang Hui, Zhou Chunmei. Research on Further Development of Tourism Product of Mountain Tourisn Destination – A Case of Emei[J]. Resource Development & Market, 2007(8).

[37] Zhang Jiangxun[Japan]. Exploitation and Protection of Mount Fuji- a Famous Mountain in Japan[R]. Statements to the Research Association of World Famous Mountains, 2013.

[38] Zheng Deliang, Yuan Jianhua. SWOT Analysis and Development Suggestions of Tourism Industry in Mount Tai[J]. Journal of Shandong Institute of Business and Technology, 2009(1).

[39] Zheng Xiang. Study on Mountain Tourism Strategy Innovation on the Basis of Industrial Cluster Theory[J]. China Market, 2008(48).

[40] Zhu BO, Liang Zhenmin, Guo Zhuanying. On the Development Tendency of Tourism of Mount Tai in Tai'an City[J]. Guangdong Agricultural Sciences, 2010,(5).

Participants

Place	Name	Position
Jiangxi, China	Huang Yuejin	Chairman of the Jiangxi Provincial CPPCC, China
	Yin Meigen	Mayor of the Jiujiang Municipal Government, China
	Wei Hongbin	Chairman of the Jiujiang Municipal CPPCC, China
	Liao Qizhi	Deputy Mayor of the Jiujiang Municipal Government, China
	Zhang Zhiming	Deputy Director of the Foreign Affairs Office of Jiangxi Province, China
	Lv Yuqi	Vice Director of the Education Department of Jiangxi Provincial Government, China
	Yang Jian	Chairman of the Board of Lushan Administration Bureau, Secretary General, World Famous Mountain Association, China
	Lu Ye	Representative of UNESCO Beijing Office, China
	Chen Min	Director of the International Office, Education Department of Jiangxi Provincial Government, China
	Wang Fengpeng	Secretary General of the Jiujiang Municipal Government, China
	Hong Hua	Secretary General of the Jiujiang Municipal CPPCC, China
	Shu Ruipeng	Director of the Foreign Affairs Office of Jiujiang Municipal Government
	Xiong Wei	Member of the Board, Director of the Propaganda Department of Lushan Administration Bureau, China
Australia	Joane McKnight	Board Member responsible for Sustainable Tourism & Deputy Secretary General for Oceania, World Famous Mountains Association
	Amanda Bell	Travel Executive, Ashurst Internationa

Place	Name	Position
USA	James N. Anderson	Ph.D, Assistant to the Vice President, Director of International Education, Armstrong Atlantic State University
	Dr. Laura Barrett	Assistant to the Vice President-International Education, Dean of the College of Liberal Arts, professor of literature, Armstrong Atlantic State University
	Richard McGrath	Ph.D., Professor of Economics, Armstrong Atlantic State University
	GARY L. LARSEN	Ph.D. in Public Administration and Policy, Executive MBA, B.S in Watershed Sciences, Adjunct Professor of Public Administration, Board member of and Deputy Secretary General in charge of strategic planning, World Famous Mountains Association (WFMA) Portland State University
	Roy W. Koch	Senior Fellow, Institute for Sustainable Solutions, Professor Emeritus of Civil Engineering and Environmental Science, Provost and Vice President Emeritus for Academic Affairs, Portland State University
	Rex Ziak	Famous Mountain, geological park and World Heritage Studies Specialist
Brazil	Monica Alves Amorim	Deputy Director for Brazilian Society of Study, Research and Technology; Deputy Secretary General for South America, World Famous Mountains Association; Professor of Federal University of Ceara-UFC
	Tito Lívio Cruz Romão	Head (coordinator) of the department of international affairs, Federal University of Ceara-UFC
South Africa	Dr. Wendy Annecke	Acting General Manager, SANParks: Cape Research Centre
	Michael Dyssel	Lecturer, Faculty of Arts, University of Western Cape
Germany	Ute Ritschel	Organizer of European Forest Art Association
	Walter Frenz	Full Professor/ Prof. Dr. jur., RWTH Aachen University
Taiwan, China	Chen Lung-shebg	Honary Chairman of the board of the International Exchange of Mt. Jade, Taiwan
Philippines	Fr. Ruel "Dudz" F. Lero	Ph.D., Vice President for Academic Affairs, Holy Name University
	Maria Paz J. Espiritu	Research Coordinatoe, Holy Name University, Corner Lesage and Gallares Sts. Tagbilaran City

Place	Name	Position
Thailand	Niwes Nantachit	Assoc. Prof., President, Chiang Mai University
	Rien Loveemongkol	Assit. Prof., Dean, Language Institute Chiang Mai University
France	Philippe DORBAIRE	Le Président de l'Université de Jiujiang,à,Professeur Philippe DORBAIRE,Directeur de IPAG,Université de Poitiers,Poitiers, France
	Dr. Guo Yugan	Confucius Institute at Université de Poitiers
Hongkong, China	Dr. Young Chun Yeon	Chairman of the Association for Geoconservation, Hong Kong
	Tsao King Kwun	Professor, department of Government & Public Admin, Chinese Univeristy of Hong Kong
Canada	John Potts	Acting Executive Director, UFV-International, University of the Fraser Valley
UK	Xavier Jacques	Deputy Dean Education, School Design, Engineering & Computing, Bournemouth University, School of DEC
	Fintan Donohue	Chief Executive, Gazelle College Group; Principal and Chief Executive of North Hertfordshire College
	Corrienne Peasgood	Principal, City College Norwich
Russia	Ebzeeva Yulia	Professor and Dr., Dean of the Literature School
Italy	Maurizio Davolio	President of AITR (Italian Association of Responsible Tourism) and President of EARTH (European Alliance of Responsible Tourism and Hospitality)
Japan	Yokoyama Norio	Director, Takada-Jiiujiang Friendship Association
	Harimoto Norihiro	Professor of University of Graduate School of Economic, Josai University
Yunnan, China	Ding Wenli	Vice President of Yunnan Normal University,Normal University
	Ming Qingzhong	Director of Research Administration Office,Yunnan
Guangdong, China	Tang Xiaochun	Faculty of Resourse and Environment, Guangdong University of Business Studies
Beijing, China	Sun Zhongquan	Vice president of North China Electric Power University
Shandong, China	Wang Qinggong	Chancellor, Taishan University, China
	Yin Min	Director of the Chancellor's Office, Taishan University, China
	Peng Shuzhen	Dean of the Faculty of Tourism, Taishan University, China

Place	Name	Position
Guest for the Forum on Public Diplomacy, China	Zhao Qizheng	Former Vice Mayor of Shanghai, Director-general of the Management Committee of Shanghai Pudong New Area, Minister of the State Council Information Office of China and Vice Chairman of the Foreign Affairs Committee of the Chinese People's Political Consultative Conference, the dean of the School of Journalism and Communication, Renmin University of China
	Hua Liming	Former Chinese Ambassador to Iran, the United Arab Emirates and the Netherlands, and the Chinese Permanent Representative to the Organization for Prohibition of Chemical Weapons, Distinguished Research Fellow at CIIS and Executive director of United Nations Association of China
	Wu Zhenglong	Vice Chairman of the China National Committee for Pacific Economic Cooperation, Former Ambassador of China to Croatia
	Lv Fengding	Former Chinese ambassador of Sweden and Nigeria, Member of Chinese People's Political Consultative Conference(CPPCC)
Experts in the Field of Public Diplomacy, China	Jiang Fei	Director for the Center of World Media Studies, Institute of Journalism and Communication, Chinese Academy of Social Sciences
	Zhang Yuqiang	Deputy Director of International Strategy and Development Research Center and Deputy curator of the Museum of media of Communication University of China Professor of journalism at the Communication University of China, Deputy Director of International Strategy and Development Research Center and Deputy curator of the Museum of media of Communication University of China
	Zhang Hongzhong	Assistant Dean of Art and Communication School, Beijing Normal University, Director of Communication results Research
	Liu Tao	Associate Dean of College of Communication, Northwest Normal University
	Chen Guan	Professor, School of Business, Renmin University of China
	Liu Rong	Office of School Alumni, Beijing Foreign Studies University

Place	Name	Position
Jiujiang University, China	Zheng Xiang	Chancellor, Jiujiang University
	Gan Xiaoqing	President, Jiujiang University
	Wu Taoe	Member of the Board, Vice President, Jiujiang University
	Ouyang Chun	Member of the Board, Vice President, Jiujiang University
	Ji Gangchang	Vice President, Jiujiang University
	Tao Chunyuan	Vice President, Jiujiang University
	Yang Yanlin	Member of the Board, Vice President, Jiujiang University
	Yang Yaofang	Assistant to the President, Director the Jiujiang University Hospital
	Lei Weizhen	Assistant to the President, Jiujiang University
	Li Ningning	Executive Deputy Director & Professor at Lushan Cultural Research Center, Jiujiang University
	Li Songzhi	Vice-dean of College of Tourism and Territorial Resources, Jiujiang University
	Liao Liang	Den of the Faculty of Life Science, Jiujiang University

Postscript

World famous mountains are the common wealth of the whole world and the spiritual home of humanities. They not only reflect the power and elegance of the nature, but also embody the culture, knowledge, history and wisdom of human beings. How to conserve and utilize the world famous mountains on a sustainable basis is a daunting task in front of mankind.

The 1st World Famous Mountains Conference was held in Lushan, China in October, 2009. More than 200 guests and delegates from 26 countries across 5 continents gathered together to conduct in-depth discussions, covering a wide range of topics related to world famous mountains, such as, conservation and management, resource development, exchanges and cooperation. The delegates signed the Constitution of World Famous Mountain Association and issued the "Lushan Declaration", which was indeed a milestone in the history of exchanges, cooperation and research among world famous mountains.

In May of 2013, the 1st International Conference on World Famous Mountains Research and Public Diplomacy was convened at Jiujiang University at the foot of Lushan. The theme—"Friendship, Cooperation and Development" is highly relevant, which serves as a bridge among different mountains and cultures. In addition, this event provided a new channel of communication and cooperation for different countries and nations. At the conference, the World Famous Mountains Research Institute was also inaugurated, which was another significant milestone in the history of world famous mountains research, conservation and utilization.

No matter how old you are, who you are or where you are, you should be given the opportunity to learn about and appreciate the world famous mountains—the common treasure of mankind. Meanwhile, as unique integrated resources, famous mountains in the world should exert their social functions to promote the exchanges, cooperation and development among peoples. These are the reasons the book *An Overview of the World Famous Mountains* came into being.

In particular, the compilation of the book *An Overview of the World Famous Mountains* has been valued greatly by the Chancellor of Jiujiang University, Dr. Zheng Xiang, who also wrote its preface. Here, heartfelt gratitude goes to other university leaders, relevant departments and many faculty members as well, for their care, support and coordination.

The editors of *An Overview of the World Famous Mountains* are Han Kun and Li Songzhi, the subeditors are Sang Longyang, Gong Wei, Wei Weixin, Xiong Yunming. This book is mainly written by teachers of College of Tourism and Territorial Resources, includes Li Xiangyu, Jia Chao, Yao Lina, Wang Yanhua, Zhang Xinhua, Guo Ying, Wang Lixia; translated into English by teachers of the Translation Institute for Guoxue (National Chinese Classics) of Jiujiang University. In the compilation of this book, all the editors and translators had done a great deal of work, consulting many materials and processing massive amounts of data. In the hope of presenting the essence of world famous mountains to the readers as much as possible, they revised several drafts and corrected translations accordingly. However, due to the limited space, only part of the world famous mountains are covered in this book. Part of photos of this book are provided by vice propaganda minister of Jiujiang University Party committee Chen Xiaosong who is also the bureau chief of Jiangxi People's Publishing House Jiujiang University branch. The rest photos are quoted from Internet, to whom we also owe many thanks. For any possible mistakes or inadequacies, your suggestions and comments are highly appreciated.